"Two leading thinkers who produced seminal texts on digital democracy and the network society when these were nebulous possibilities for most of us have teamed up. The result is a prescient and engaging book that invites all to rethink the future of networked media and democracy."

– *Zizi Papacharissi, Professor and Head of Communication, Professor of Political Science, University of Illinois*

"This book is a timely, thoughtful and thought-provoking volume on the state of politics and democracy in an increasingly networked society, dealing with a plethora of hot-button issues such as filter bubbles and fake news. The fact that this book bears almost no resemblance to *Digital Democracy* (2000) makes one realize the seismic shift in internet-based politics just in the last 18 years, and how profoundly it has affected democracies as well as autocracies."

– *S. Shyam Sundar, Distinguished Professor, The Pennsylvania State University*

Internet and Democracy in the Network Society

A seminal shift has taken place in the relationship between Internet usage and politics. At the turn of the 21st century, it was presumed that digital communication would produce many positive political effects such as improvements to political information retrieval, support for public debate and community formation or even enhancements in citizen participation in political decision making. While there have been positive effects, negative effects have also occurred including fake news and other political disinformation, social media appropriation by terrorists and extremists, 'echo chambers' and 'filter bubbles', elections influenced by hostile hackers and campaign manipulation by micro-targeting marketing. It is time for a critical re-evaluation.

Designed to encourage critical thinking on the part of the student, internationally recognized experts Jan A.G.M. van Dijk and Kenneth L. Hacker chronicle the political significance of new communication technologies for the promotion of democracy over the last two decades. Drawing upon structuration theory and network theory and real-world case studies from across the globe, the book is logically structured around the following topics:

- Political Participation and Inclusion
- Habermas and the Reconstruction of Public Space
- Media and Democracy in Authoritarian States
- Democracy and the Internet in China
- E-government and Democracy
- Views of Democracy and Internet Use

Underpinned by up-to-date literature, this important textbook is aimed at students and scholars of communication studies, political science, sociology, political communication, and international relations.

Jan A.G.M. van Dijk is an internationally recognized expert in the field of communication, his specific interest being new media studies. Van Dijk is the author of *The Network Society* (1999, 2006, 2012), *The Deepening Divide* (2005) and *Digital Skills* (2014). As Professor of Communication Science at the University of Twente, van Dijk teaches and develops the sociology of the information society, in particular the social-cultural, political, and organizational aspects.

Kenneth L. Hacker is Professor and Department Head of Communication Studies at New Mexico State University. He researches communication science in the areas of a) political communication, b) new communication technologies, c) communication and national security, and d) military family interactions. He has edited two books on presidential campaign communication and one (with Jan van Dijk) on digital democracy.

Routledge Studies in Global Information, Politics and Society

Edited by Kenneth Rogerson and Laura Roselle

Duke University and Elon University

International communication encompasses everything from one-to-one cross-cultural interactions to the global reach of a broad range of information and communications technologies and processes. *Routledge Studies in Global Information, Politics and Society* celebrates – and embraces – this depth and breadth. To completely understand communication, it must be studied in concert with many factors, since, most often, it is the foundational principle on which other subjects rest. This series provides a publishing space for scholarship in the expansive, yet intersecting, categories of communication and information processes and other disciplines.

12. Political Communication in Real Time
Theoretical and Applied Research Approaches
Edited by Dan Schill, Rita Kirk, and Amy Jasperson

13. Disability Rights Advocacy Online
Voice, Empowerment and Global Connectivity
Filippo Trevisan

14. Media Relations of the Anti-War Movement
The Battle for Hearts and Minds
Ian Taylor

15. The Politics of Data Transfer
Transatlantic Conflict and Cooperation over Data Privacy
Yuko Suda

16. The Media and the Public Sphere
A Deliberative Model of Democracy
Thomas Häussler

17. Internet and Democracy in the Network Society
Jan A.G.M. van Dijk and Kenneth L. Hacker

Internet and Democracy in the Network Society

Jan A.G.M. van Dijk
and Kenneth L. Hacker

Routledge
Taylor & Francis Group
NEW YORK AND LONDON

First published 2018
by Routledge
711 Third Avenue, New York, NY 10017

and by Routledge
2 Park Square, Milton Park, Abingdon, Oxon, OX14 4RN

Routledge is an imprint of the Taylor & Francis Group, an informa business

Library of Congress Cataloging-in-Publication Data
Names: Dijk, Jan van, 1952– editor. | Hacker, Kenneth L., editor.
Title: Internet and democracy in the network society / edited by
Jan A.G.M. van Dijk and Kenneth L. Hacker.
Description: New York : Routledge, 2018. |
Series: Routledge studies in global information, politics and society ; 17 |
Includes bibliographical references and index.
Identifiers: LCCN 2018001308 | ISBN 9780815363019 (hbk) |
ISBN 9780815363026 (pbk) | ISBN 9781351110693 (epk) |
ISBN 9781351110686 (mobipocket/kindle) | ISBN 9781351110716 (Master) |
ISBN 9781351110709 (WebPDF) | ISBN 9781351110693 (ePub)
Subjects: LCSH: Political participation–Technological innovations. |
Communication in politics–Technological innovations. | Information
society–Political aspects. | Internet–Political aspects. | Democracy.
Classification: LCC JF799.5 .I67 2018 | DDC 320.0285/4678–dc23
LC record available at https://lccn.loc.gov/2018001308

ISBN: 978-0-815-36301-9 (hbk)
ISBN: 978-0-815-36302-6 (pbk)
ISBN: 978-1-351-11071-6 (ebk)

Typeset in Bembo
by Out of House Publishing

Contents

Figures

Tables

Series Editor's Foreword

Digital Democracy was published in the year 2000, and was one of the first academic works to substantively examine democracy within a changing communicative and networked society. We are proud to publish the sequel to this seminal work in this series. In *Internet and Democracy in the Network Society*, Jan A.G.M. van Dijk and Kenneth L. Hacker re-assess political action, digital media, networks, and political systems of democracies. They address contemporary events such as the Arab Spring, the rapid increase of Chinese economic and political power, and e-government initiatives. Overall, the work attempts to look at the opportunities for and challenges to democracy posed by changes in technologies and communication.

Laura Roselle

Preface

Eighteen years after our edited book *Digital Democracy* (2000) was published, we thought it was important to examine how democracy, Internet usage and other digital communication are related in the context of the network society. Part of our task was to assemble the results of studies conducted by many renowned international experts about issues of digital public communication, as we did for our 2000 book. This time we did not edit a book but wrote it ourselves. Professor Ben Mollov from Bar-Ilan University in Israel was asked to support us in writing about the topic of using online communication for the purpose of depolarizing political discourse at a time when everybody is talking about polarizing discussions on social and other digital media. Mollov has conducted research on this topic regarding peaceful Israeli-Palestinian interactions.

While we aimed to release the book about five years ago, we are actually pleased that we took longer since the delay allowed us to address the important events of the Arab Spring, the impact of the Internet in China, the presidential election of 2016 in the United States, and the current controversies about online political deception and sabotage. In the last two years in particular, relatively new phenomena of political communication on the Internet have emerged that are often seen as drawbacks for democracy: fake news and other disinformation on the Web, so-called 'echo chambers' where only the like-minded are communicating, elections influenced by hostile hackers, 'trolls' or Twitterbots on social media and manipulation of voters via big data analysis and micro-targeting political marketing. All of these phenomena can now be critically discussed in this book. While our book published at the turn of the millennium was suffused with an optimistic spirit, this book is more realistic about using digital media and networks for democracy.

It would be a mistake to view us as skeptics or detractors when it comes to digital democracy since we are actually advocates – realistic ones. In writing this book, we did not take a particular view of democracy as a point of departure for the analysis in this book. Instead, we describe a dozen views of democracy, both substantial and procedural, and show that all of them can use digital media for their cause differently, even so-called authoritarian democracy. Let the readers choose their favorite view of democracy.

Another advantage of spending some years on the book was the chance to think more about strong theory explaining why the use of digital media supports or opposes democracy. In this book, we try to explain what is currently happening in Internet democracy by systematically elaborating structuration theory and network theory. We hope that by learning about these theories, readers will better understand the importance of digital media and networks for democracy. If we are able to help readers think about the complexities of democracy and networked communication in a network society, the book will have been a success.

Jan A.G.M. van Dijk, University of Twente, The Netherlands
Kenneth L. Hacker, New Mexico State University, United States
November 2017

1 Introduction

Origin and Mission of This Book

This book builds on the work done for our former book that we edited, *Digital Democracy: Issues of Theory and Practice* (Sage Publications, 2000). The book addressed certain theoretical and practical issues about the use of digital media in political communication. Our 2000 book was well received and praised for its shelf life. We believe that the success of that book was due to its provision of in-depth political and communication theory in a field that is so sensitive to technological and political change. However, theoretical development and empirical research have continued since that time and many new uses of digital media in politics have emerged in the last 17 years.

What has occurred since the turn of the millennium? First of all, the diffusion of the Internet and digital media has accelerated, reaching the majority of the populations of developing countries with between 70% and 95% penetration (ITU, 2017). In this period new digital media emerged such as social media. Just like the new media before them, they were assumed to provide a number of opportunities for democracy. Simultaneously, a whole new ecology of cross-media relations of traditional and digital media emerged that is able to substantially change political communication (Chadwick, 2013; Jenkins, Ford, & Green, 2013). This new cross-media ecology used everywhere might have a bigger potential impact on democracy than the new media that emerged before the year 2000.

Second, in this period the practice of using digital media in politics and democracy has matured. This practice can be for or against democracy. The expression 'against' is used because digital media can also worsen the condition of democracy. For example, they help to create 'filter bubbles' and micro-targeting political marketing for citizens who follow the same views; to distribute 'fake news'; to wipe away any editorial control and moderation; to harm privacy; to allow censorship; to undermine the democratic national state in globalization, and other potential effects to be discussed in this book. Less insidiously, the expansion of digital communication has empowered those who have more offline political power than those who have less. Despite noble efforts, researchers have not found any significant exceptions to this pattern. It is true that anyone can create a blog or social media post, but gaining an audience for them is another matter.

The importance of the Internet for politics has increased, and the era of broadcast and cable television political communication is gradually yielding to an era of Internet democracy or cross-media democracy combining broadcasting and interactive media. So, simply by replacing older media, the digital media create an ecology of media and offer all kinds of innovations in political communication.

In this book, we link the views and theories of democracy to concepts of communication in networks and the network society at large. This is a conceptual and theoretical mission. After the 2000 *Digital Democracy* book, we do not see sufficient theoretical advance in this domain. After nearly two decades of speculation and empirical analysis, it is abundantly clear that the concept of digital democracy needs a more expansive definition and theoretical underpinning. It is also clear that an explanation of networking with connection technologies requires more than empirical observations. It is important to first specify what type of democracy is under examination. To date, writing in 2017, there are no useful theories of digital media or political new media usage to explain the relation between the network society and democracy.

Of course, we do not have the pretension to offer a fully fledged theory of both democracy and digital communication. We only want to attain conceptual clarification and to offer a promising starting point for theories and empirical studies to build on in the literature.

In our *Digital Democracy* book we summarized three main issues for further research that serve as the most important questions for the current book (Hacker & van Dijk, 2000, pp. 220–222). First, we called for further conceptual clarification. A concept to be elaborated is the network concept. What is the relation between concepts of politics and democracy on the one hand and the conceptual distinctions of network theory on the other hand? How does increased digital communication and networking affect democracy? In these networks we also include cell phone and satellite networks, in fact all connection technologies. The answer to these questions can be aided by further clarification of concepts we addressed in our former book. The concepts of interactivity, the public sphere, public debate, community building, political participation, universal access and information or communication freedom might change in the context of myriads of new devices that are interlinking with the Internet.

A further call was to test the basic assumptions in most perspectives of digital democracy. One of the assumptions is that the new forms of communication offered by the Internet can change communication content and encourage more political communication. We were rather skeptical, but not pessimistic, about this assumption in the former book. New instruments of communication do not necessarily bring about new politics, more political motivation or more participation. "No technology is able to 'fix' a lack of political motivation, lack of time, effort and skills required for full participation in democratic activities" (Hacker & van Dijk, 2000, p. 210). Yet this claim is made again and again. After the year 2000, blogging was assumed to have some revolutionary impact. In the year 2004, the claim reappeared alongside the rise of participatory media in the so-called Web 2.0. Shortly afterwards, social media were adopted on a massive scale over a short period of time and are also used for political communication. Indeed, we know that after the year 2000 Internet users have become ever more active and creative, instead of just consuming website content. But does this mean that they have also become more politically engaged? The literature regarding political participation and uses of digital media continues to be marked by a conflation between correlation and causation in relation to digital media use and political engagement. In the United States, for example, digital communication has risen dramatically across all age groups while political engagement has remained fairly flat across time, as has political knowledge and faith in the government.

A final call we made in our 2000 book was for careful empirical observations to be made in evaluation research of the effects of digital democracy applications. Most often, precise goals or expected effects are not formulated in advance. The beneficial contribution of these applications to democracy is simply assumed; it is a matter of belief. With this handicap in mind, we still want to carefully balance the achievements and shortcomings of particular practices of digital democracy, comparing them with particular goals and norms.

The Claims of Digital Democracy Made in the Year 2000 and 17 Years After

Around the year 2000, fairly strong claims were made by advocates of digital democracy, as summarized by Tsagarousianou (1999):

1. Digital democracy improves political information retrieval and exchange between governments, public administrations, representatives, political and community organizations and individual citizens.
2. Digital democracy supports public debate, deliberation and community formation.
3. Digital democracy enhances participation in political decision making by citizens.

In the year 2000 we concluded that *more and better information access* were among the most important accomplishments of digital democracy at that time. However, we found that its value for democracy was quite another affair. Accessible, reliable and valid information is a necessary condition of democracy, but is it sufficient? We thought not. There are numerous steps between retrieving information and it having any impact on decision making. First, is the information reliable and valid or is it disinformation? Second, is the information not abundant and perceived as information overload by many people? The crucial question that follows is what one actually does with the information. Is it transformed into political action? We cited authors arguing that decisions are not necessarily improved by the simple expedience of acquiring information. Decisions are ultimately matters of judgement. The art of judgement may be hampered by an abundance of information (Hacker & van Dijk, 2000, p. 215). Since the year 2000, political information sources have multiplied. However, have the benefits in terms of political knowledge and action also grown?

A second claim made about digital democracy was its *support of public debate, deliberation and community formation*. In the year 2000, we concluded that the first attempts to launch debates, deliberation and communities lacked an adequate level and quality of interactivity. We observed little interactivity between contributors. Most people only read the contributions of others and did not contribute themselves. When they did, the most frequent people addressed were political representatives who did not respond or only returned automatic messages. Frequently, the debate was dominated by a few people. Finally, we observed a lack of pressure to come to a consensus or even to form conclusions as compared to face-to-face discussion groups (Hacker & van Dijk, 2000, p. 216). After the year 2000, the number of blogs, online communities and debates increased dramatically. In one decade, an important new platform used on a massive scale for the purpose of debate was born: social media. Social media platforms are used by ordinary members of the population rather than being limited to the elite that dominated online political debates in the 1990s. Have these new media of public-opinion-making facilitated public debate on a greater scale and in a better way than before?

The third claim was the enhancement of *participation in political decision making* by citizens using digital media. We found that there was no perceivable effect of the use of digital media on decision making by institutional politics at that time. This was in spite of the fact that a considerable amount of horizontal communication about what to do or who to vote for was initiated at that time. However, it did not have any effect on political decision making at that time. Any potential effect seemed to be blocked by the system of representative democracy (Hacker & van Dijk, 2000, pp. 216–217). It is striking that terms such as tele-democracy, tele-polls and tele-referenda that started the discussions about digital democracy in the 1980s (Arterton, 1987; Becker, 1981) have become extinct or have been exchanged with more vague terms not referring to direct democracy.

Is the claim of direct democracy by means of digital media one to be discarded? In the last 17 years, more powerful technologies for online voting and opinion making have arrived compared to the so-called cable television box remote voting (Arterton, 1987). We now have electronic voting in some countries and perhaps even proposals to use social media or more secure

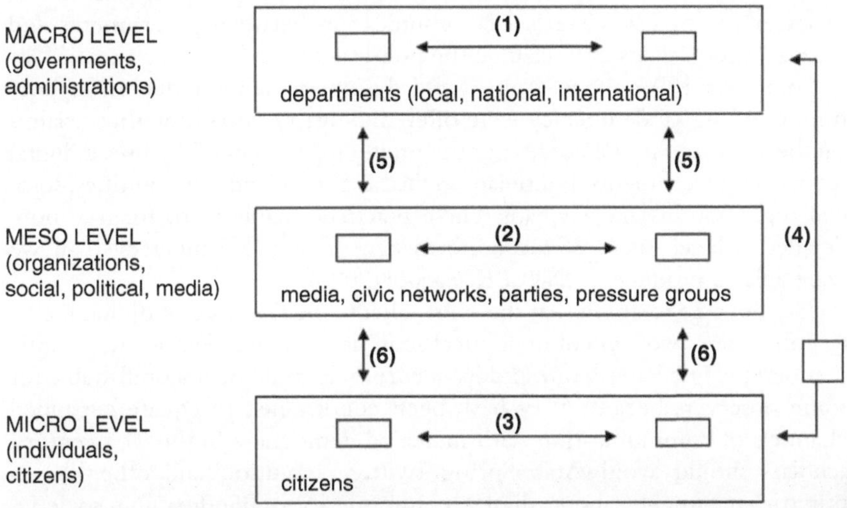

Figure 1.1 Levels and links of communication in the political system.
(*Source*: Hacker & van Dijk, 2000, p. 217)

messaging services for reliable voting. Why are these services not offered for this purpose?

One of the reasons is that direct and representative democracy are part of separate levels of political communication that perhaps do not reach each other. In our 2000 book we presented a model of political interactivity between and inside levels of the political system (Hacker & van Dijk, 2000, p. 217). See Figure 1.1. At the macro-level we observed the exchange of government departments (arrow 1), at the meso-level party, community and pressure group communication (arrow 2) and at the micro-level communication between individual citizens (arrow 3), all levels using digital media horizontally. Next, we observed two-way vertical communication between governments and political organizations such as parties and economic organizations like businesses (arrow 5). We also saw frequent two-way vertical communication between political organizations and citizens (e-campaigning) and businesses and consumers (e-commerce), depicted in arrow 6. However, crucially direct vertical two-way communication between citizens and government was buffered (arrow 4) because governments rarely responded to individual messages from citizens. They used the mass media and their own websites to reach citizens collectively and individually surveyed citizen and voter behavior to create personal data. The other way round, some citizens tried to directly address governments but in fact had to use their representatives (the meso-level) to reach them. In this way direct democracy does not come to pass at all. Now, 17 years later, we wonder whether new platforms such as social media, e-government services and explorations of e-voting or e-referenda are able to bring more real opportunities and practices for two-way vertical communication between governments and citizens, and perhaps even change the political system.

So, in the 1990s many utopian and dystopian claims about the opportunities of digital democracy were offered. Now, 17 years later, those claims can be evaluated in the context of the growing practices of the use of digital media by governments, politicians, political parties and communities, societal organizations and civilians. These practices enable us to form a more detailed balance sheet of the performance of digital democracy than we were able to produce in *Digital Democracy* (2000).

It is possible to argue that the most salient contributions of digital media to politics are involvement in political activities, whether democratic or anti-democratic. The latter word, and its occurrence, could be uncomfortable for some observers because they have been conditioned to equate expanded channels of communication with increased democracy. In the 21st century, scholars should avoid 'Arab Spring Twitter revolution' and other deterministic statements about digital communication transforming societies or giving birth to democracies. Currently, a more cautious and data-based approach to the connections between Internet usage and political participation is needed. Actual findings tend to be more modest and less radical than the breathless praise of online technologies for democratization suggests. Data showed, for example, early in the 21st century, that both television and the Internet were prominent sources for political information and that the Internet never replaced TV as was anticipated.

Major changes in the world have occurred with movements toward both democratization and globalization. Globalization and the expansion of network societies are obviously related, but the politics of both remain unclear. China's blend of authoritarianism with expanded networking and capitalism offers new opportunities of communication and democracy. Slowly but surely, certain forms of public opinion formation and expression are emerging among online Chinese citizens. Messaging systems such as Weibo offer this opportunity. However, while connectivity and democracy are statistically correlated, the direction of causality is unexplained. Web applications are not a magic wand to conjure up democratic systems. Although there is much excitement about closed societies like China expanding Internet usage, we have to remind ourselves that just half of the Chinese population are Internet users. In the meantime, the Chinese government continues to increase its proficiency at filtering and manipulating regular Internet use. This leaves the new public spaces completely under the control of the Chinese government.

Pitfalls in Views of Technology for Politics

In this book we will often come across doubtful reasoning about the assumed effects of digital technology on political practices. There are four questionable ideas or types of reasoning behind estimations of the consequences of new technologies. They were listed a long time ago by Joseph Corn (1986) and we think they are still valid.

The first pitfall is *the idea of a total revolution*, assuming that new technologies will radically change our lives. In this context it means that digital media will revolutionize the political system. This is a conspicuous refrain in many thoughts about the present and the future of technology. However, this refrain has resounded many times in history. A first example is the invention of electricity, which was estimated to lead to a radical decentralization of society in the 19th century, notably just before the rise of massive bureaucracies. Another example is the advent of radio that spurred expectations that people themselves could become broadcasters and direct democracy would lie ahead. What actually happened was the rise of communism and fascism shortly afterwards and people had to listen to radio speeches by Hitler and Stalin. In the 1970s and 1980s, people thought that new Cable TV with home boxes and remote controls to vote would support direct or tele-democracy (Arterton, 1987). The result was a system of 500 plus channels 'with nothing on' but commercials and scarcely offering interactivity

Currently, the same refrain can be heard. It is argued that the participative and decentralized nature of the contemporary Internet will cause the traditional mass media and institutional politics to fade away. The first mistake of these deterministic arguments is that technological opportunities are converted into social realities much too quickly. Technological innovations rarely lead to societal revolutions straightaway. They only find their way into fertile soil when they appear alongside social, economic and cultural innovations, and are subsequently perhaps accelerated and amplified by these technologies. The pitfall described here is often wishful thinking. The hope that tomorrow will be better than today is the driving force behind the idea of a total revolution.

The second pitfall is the exact opposite of the former. This is the *assumption of social continuity*. Here, new technologies are seen as mere continuous improvements of existing technology. In the early 20th century the motor car was viewed as an improved coach. The Internet is deemed to be faster: it is an electronic highway. Potential societal effects are not the subject of much news. When television political marketing turned into social media marketing with the same objectives, this did not seem to have any basic effect on contemporary election campaigns. What is wrong with this pragmatic and sober argument? In the first place, this type of reasoning underestimates the transforming potential of using digital media. Not all changes brought forward with the aid of digital media are merely incremental. Technologies that are disruptive for political affairs might appear, such as the rise of 'big data' and micro-targeting technologies of political marketing, to be discussed in this book. The diffusion of the Internet in China transformed its totalitarian-controlled public sphere within the space of a few years. For the first time, Chinese citizens could exchange messages to each other on a massive scale. But transformation is not yet a revolution. This would require structural changes in society. The Chinese Communist

Party is still the only party in power and the Chinese do not have freedom of speech on the Internet.

The technology itself can be revolutionary or sometimes disruptive. The most important revolutionary characteristic of present-day digital technology is the creation of an all-embracing, digitally enhanced infrastructure for our (network) society, the theme of this book. This might lead to a number of substantial social changes in democracies. Some of these changes will never be discovered by following the argument of social continuity. They are called second-order effects of new technology: social side-effects that are not foreseen.

A third pitfall is the idea that new technology can solve most, if not all, social problems. This is the voluntarist idea of a *technological fix*. This is also called 'solutionism' (Morozov, 2013). The new technology such as new media is seen as a solution to a large number of societal problems. In politics, Internet democracy is supposed to be the solution. It is assumed to support political participation, knowledge and efficacy, and to increase voter turnout. The obvious mistake in this simple reasoning is that it is much too superficial. The problems mentioned have much deeper causes. They are not to be solved solely by digital media as a set of instruments when no organizational and political measures are taken simultaneously. Moreover, in this argument a certain type of technology is often related to one particular effect only. Online elections are supposed to result in higher turnout. One ignores side-effects such as the secrecy of the vote when security fails and the loss of confidentiality of the vote in a separate room of a polling station.

The fourth pitfall will be discussed very often in this book. This is *instrumentalism*. Often, technology is seen as some kind of lever. This is understandable because information and communication technology is a general-purpose technology. It can be used for any purpose, good or bad. They can be liberating and and can control us. However, the instrumentalist view behind this is *much too simple*. First, the political context of the use of technology and the political theory explaining the context and use are often ignored. The characteristics of the availing political system are disregarded. This also means that other mediators such as political views and norms, to be discussed below, are neglected. Second, the relation between a particular use of these tools and political goals is often neglected. To give two examples: The use of social media for democracy can be good or bad, but the bad use of these media by ISIS makes them into a quite different tool. Social media can be used for interaction or dialogue and for information, but for ISIS they are *only* a tool for propaganda and recruiting. Twitter can be used for political expression and dialogue, but President Trump is *only* using it for expression in the shape of a rhetorical megaphone.

Instrumentalism easily leads to the idea of a technological fix. However, the difference between the two is that the idea of a technological fix is always framed in a positive manner while instrumentalism can also be linked to negative uses and consequences. However, most arguments in the literature have a positive tenor. Social, political and communication research about the political effects of digital media is infected by the fever of instrumentalism. Thousands of articles and papers in the last 20 years have been written about the assumed effect of the Internet as an instrument for democracy toppling dictators, supporting political engagement and community building. The smartest authors carefully admit that it is actually *the use* of digital or social media that might have these effects. In fact, they hope that their favorite tool is doing the work they wish it to do. So, the background idea still is instrumentalism. It does not have to be positive. Those who emphasize the supposed negative effects of digital and social media, such as dictators using the same tools to survey and censor these media and to manipulate their content, fall into the same pitfall.

The best argument against this use of digital media for both good and bad purposes is the fact that often completely different goals are reached than were previously expected. For example, one expects to save time using digital media, but in fact our calendars or schedules are filled immediately with more appointments and tasks because it allows us to accept and schedule them. In this book we will observe that the Internet offers free knowledge and information for everybody. Unfortunately, we also have to notice that bigger (digital) divides of usage and skills appear than before. These unforeseen effects are so-called *second-order* effects. They usually have much deeper social causes than the *first-order* effects expected by people with an instrumentalist view of technology.

The confusion is amplified by another well-known idea of technology effects: the mutual shaping of technology and its social use. Here, both the instrument (the means) and the goals are continually reshaped. This idea is not a pitfall in itself, but it can lead to confusion. Some people mix up improvements in social media for political use (a means) with mending democracy (a goal). A related problem is that a means is able to corrupt a particular goal. It can cause new problems. Sometimes the cure is worse than the problem to be solved. When governments offer e-participation applications consulting the citizenry about particular policy plans and do not give an adequate response to the input of citizens, a reaction often observed: they make things worse. Then citizens have less faith in democracy. In the presidential race between Clinton and Trump in 2016, people suddenly realized that the use of social media in campaigns (the means) not only has the goal of providing more information and participation outlets for voters, but also is open to manipulation via distributing disinformation, 'fake news', and micro-targeting messages enhancing 'filter bubbles'. They caused new problems.

The Social and Material Basis of Democracy

In this book, the views of a total revolution, and its flipside of persistent continuity, a technological fix and instrumentalism, are countered by views on technology that are primarily determined by the social and political context and the actual use of digital media. Technology is not only defining but also enabling for users. The context should be framed in a historical perspective. Contemporary democracy, as we currently know it, is only 100 to 250 years old. It was first created in the Western nation states of Europe and the Americas as the aftermath of modernization, industrialization, economic growth and education for everybody. Other parts of the world followed with increasing development and decolonization, sometimes with other views of democracy than Western ones (see below). Lutz and du Toit (2014) distinguish waves of democratic upturns and downturns in the 20th century. However, it is not certain that democracy will survive in the centuries that follow. Democracy, in every view, needs a solid and material base to flourish.

The first base is a particular level of economic performance and literacy. Otherwise, citizens will not have the time and material or mental resources for democratic activities. The fact that democracy is currently on the rise in several developing countries is supported by economic growth, rising literacy and the spread of global and local media. It is possible to maintain the view that there is political progress in the world today in terms of the percentage of nations that are moving toward democratic systems. From 1974, the percentage of states considered democratic increased from about 25% to approximately 60% in 1994 (Diamond, 2005). Notably, this increase predates the World Wide Web and large-scale use of digital communication. Other sources, such as the annual Democracy Index of 165 countries and two territories by the journalists of *The Economist*, are less optimististic about the evolution of democracy in the world after the advent of the Web. In 2016 they categorized 19 countries as 'Full democracies', 57 countries as 'Flawed democracies' (including the U.S. after the campaign of Trump and Clinton), 40 countries as 'Hybrid regimes' and 51 countries as 'Authoritarian regimes'. Some 72 countries experienced a decline in their total score compared with 2015. Now a majority of the global population lives in countries of the last two categories (Economist Intelligence Unit, 2017).

Second, a number of institutional foundations of democracy are needed. Primarily, a moderately strong nation state is needed, the context of all current democratic systems. So-called failed states prevent any democracy. Overly strong nation states are also not a solid base for democracy; they lean to authoritarianism. The rise of international terrorism is also likely to lead to authoritarian states that will opt for security curtailing freedom. When states are preoccupied with war, internal strife or terrorism, citizen and democratic rights are almost certain to be restricted. The same might happen when waves of migration put a nation under pressure. Imagine that in the future tens of millions of inhabitants of Africa and Asia migrate to the Northern, Western and other affluent European and American countries fleeing severe drought or flooding after climate change. We wonder why the democracies of these countries would survive. The nation states concerned are likely to step up extreme oppressive measures, and authoritarian anti-migration parties will prevail.

The nation state is also under pressure from growing globalization. International institutions such as the UN, the World Trade Organization, the International Criminal Court and federations or unions of nation states like the EU infringe on certain competencies of nation states. Loss of these competencies might not only mean a loss of sovereignty but also of democracy when these institutions are less democratic. Additionally, nation states are also losing control of international trade, financial markets and powerful transnational companies. The rise of the Internet and its global networking could undermine the power of nation states even further and perhaps make them less instead of more democratic.

Currently, in a number of Western countries there is a growing trend or movement against globalization. This theme is catered for by populist parties, both from the right and the left. Populism can be seen as a corrective or a threat to democracy (Mudde & Kaltwasser, 2012). As many anti-migration and national populist parties and candidates in Europe and the U.S. have an authoritarian leadership, democracy might indeed be under pressure.

Mueller (2010) argues that for democracy new Internet governance institutions should be created, not based on states but on individual networkers. However, van Dijk (2012) responds that this is not (yet) a realistic position. The power of networking should be accepted but has to be controlled by nation states networking themselves, effecting influence and creating trans-governmental agreements or treaties to manage Internet problems.

Another required institutional base of democracy is a working civil society between the state and the market. This means social and cultural associations in which citizens can organize themselves. It also means informal groups in which individuals with shared interests coalesce and pursue these interests within public space (Lutz & du Toit, 2014). Many developing countries do not have a strong civil society. Others have a civil society which is ripped apart by religious and regional strife. The coming of the Internet and digital media with their organizing and opinion-making capacities will not necessarily support or nurture civil societies; these digital media may just as easily enforce fragmentation and conflict in these societies.

A third base of democracy is not only sufficient material resources for the society as a whole but also their distribution. With high social and economic inequality, democracy in practice fails because citizens do not have equal opportunities to participate in the democratic process. Many observers have emphasized that in the last decades social and economic inequality has increased substantially, both globally and nationally (e.g. Milanovic, 2016; Piketty, 2014; Stiglitz, 2013). Stiglitz shows that inequality in the United States has grown so much that democracy is in peril. Unfortunately, the advent of computers and the Internet has only increased inequality, instead of decreasing it (van Dijk, 2005). It created the phenomenon of the digital divide. While potential resources of information and communication have become freely available on the Web, in reality some social categories are benefiting significantly more from these opportunities than others. Inequalities of skills and use of digital media are increasing (van Dijk & van Deursen, 2014).

A last material and social base of democracy consists of the political efficacy of particular formal procedures of political and election systems of representation. More and more democracies are becoming *formal* democracies, consisting of elections and the rules of election systems. Many citizens and voters are disappointed about the results and the choices they have made at the ballot box. Many systems of elections and representation are immovable, with voters having insufficient influence over change. While the American political tradition upholds a desire for a two-party system, the results now seem to lead to more polarization and something called a gridlock. The district and majority representative electoral system of the UK gives few opportunities for small and new parties or individual citizens. It is not certain that the alternatives and digital procedures and systems discussed in this book will fare better.

All these parts of the social and material basis of democracy might be more important for the future and fate of democracy than for the theme of this book: the opportunities and risks of digital democracy. When we are discussing these opportunities and risks, we will always relate to them.

The (Digital) Media Basis of Democracy

Democracy also requires a number of public media that are carriers of political information and communication. These media have properties that are both defining and enabling for practices of democracy. Some properties are equal in both old and new media. All public media should be open and free for both senders and receivers. They should be accessible to everybody in terms of cost and competencies of use and they should be different in terms of their perspectives and social support.

General Digital Media Properties

Other properties are different in old and new media. The traditional media of broadcasting and the press are produced and inhabited by professional journalists. The new interactive media of narrowcasting are created by both professional and civic journalists or receivers. These digital media also offer affordances for new types of social interaction that did not exist in the far or near past. Online receivers can comment on anything that appears in the old and new media. Whether anyone pays attention to them is another matter, of course. The key point is that passive audience members watching movies or TV are matched by active users who also watch movies and TV but interact with each other in ways that previous audience members did not.

These properties that enable people to speak back look like new forms of participation. So, the temptation arises to consider them as forms of democratic participation and evidence of growing democracy. Clearly, users of new communication technologies enjoy the affordances that the technologies offer to them. These feel like progress to being made toward greater personal empowerment. However, what any of this means for politics and political communication is yet to be explained in any convincing manner. Faster information, easier conversations, lower entry costs into discussions, websites, and texting, more sources of political information than ever before, and thousands of political resources available in seconds, all sounds like better information and potential participation. Yet without communication and political theory to evaluate these changes, we are only left with a bewildering amount of possible changes that can move both toward and away from democracy. Participation in content creation, interacting with others, composing e-mails, designing websites, writing blogs, and publishing online documents looks like creating or generating more digital democracy or political activism in general. However, participation, involvement and engagement will not necessarily produce more democratic politics at the level of a nation or a political system.

These changes in political communication ecology cannot only be understood by a list of technology attributes, a survey of user patterns, or cultural changes that accompany the sociotechnical changes. Rather, an analysis of how all three of these work together in relation to political goals is required. It is certainly time to cease assuming any automatic political effect of Internet or new media adoption and usage. In the time that the Internet has become a mass phenomenon, there has been no accompanying surge in political participation in established democratic systems, as we try to show in Chapter 3. It was never valid to assume that increasing network connectivity and digital media activity in society produces democracy without changes in political systems. It is all the more invalid to hope that the media technologies of the Internet or digital communication will fix deep problems of political motivation among citizens and crises of the political system at large.

Since our book of 2000, we have seen the collapse of two main assumptions about digital democracy. The first was automatic democratization following the establishment of networks and the second was that new media are simply extensions of offline communication. Soon it became apparent that revolutions and democratization in societies require more than Facebook and Twitter. The idea that new media are simply more of what we do offline fell apart because people are doing things with digital media today that they are unable to do offline. Their online political communication is increasing over time because the Internet of 2017 is quite different from that of 2000.

New Trends in Digital Media

Since the year 2000, two important trends have appeared in the media system carrying political communication. The first is the rise of *spreadable media* (Jenkins et al., 2013). These are social (and other digital) media that spread or share content between people such as citizens. This is different from the traditional 'sticky' media of broadcasting and other centralized media serving steady content to a relatively isolated and passive audience. In this way, "the public is not simply consumers of pre-constructed messages but people who are shaping, sharing, reframing and remixing media in ways which might not have been previously imagined" (Jenkins et al., 2013, p. 2).

The phrase 'remixing' refers to the second trend: the rise of a *hybrid media system* of cross-media that are linked and referring to each other (Chadwick, 2013). By means of cross-media, political communication circulates between broadcasting or print media (offline and online), telephony and e-mail, messaging, websites or social media. In this way, people such as citizens and political institutions "pursue their values and interests both with and within different but interrelated media" (Chadwick, 2013, p. 18)

Network Properties

Network properties are one of the most important characteristics of the current digital media base of democracy. This is because digital media are increasingly networked. This book primarily focuses on the relation between social and digital media networks in the context of the network society. By following network theory, we are able to observe that all networks, whether used in social, political, economic or cultural exchange, have properties that reveal particular effects.

The first effect of networks is that they become ever more powerful after a particular tipping point of connectedness has been reached. This is the point when they reach *critical mass.* It does not make very much sense to adopt a network connection, for instance for e-mail, when you can reach only 2% of your personal network with it. But when you can reach 30% to 35% this makes a difference and you are likely to think about getting connected. Then concerns with *network externality* appear: the network gets bigger and bigger, as if it grows automatically. This effect is also important for democracy. When only a small minority is connected to a network such as the Internet, this channel simply cannot have much political influence. At least, it has a low democratic potential. When the network connects the vast majority of a population it might become ever more important. In the 1990s only a minority of the populations of developed countries was connected to the Internet. These were the days of 'television democracy'. It is only fairly recently that 50% to 90% or more of the people in these countries have gone online, and only now that the era of 'Internet democracy' appears on the horizon.

The second effect of networks is *network exchange*, which works on the basis of the so-called peer-to-peer principle. In networks things are collectively produced by independent people who work at a distance but can nevertheless have a common goal as they are connected. This goal might be the exchange of music and video files, but it can also be the creation of an encyclopedia or a knowledge network. Therefore, the principle is also called the Wikipedia effect. Benkler (2006) has shown that this is a new way to create wealth in society that appears alongside the classical production of individuals (such as authors) and organizations (such as media companies). It has become a new principle for the creation of political opinion and action too. The collective production of political opinion and action in networks diverges from their traditional production by individual citizens, offline communities, political parties and broadcast or press media companies.

Third, networks have a large number of *global properties*. These are the size, inclusiveness, connectivity, connectedness, density, centralization, and other properties of a network. They will be discussed in Chapter 2. We argue that when using networks these properties have considerable political significance.

Strategic Characteristics of Networks for Democracy

Computer networks also have a number of characteristics which are strategically important in defining the opportunities and limits of democracy. They are also part of the media base of democracy. We will describe five characteristics: access, design, control, legality or security, and communication content. See van Dijk (2012, pp. 253–263) for a more general discussion.

When networks are becoming the nervous system of society, *access to networks* must be the most vital characteristic. Lack of access, or marginal access, simply means social exclusion. In a democracy it means political exclusion. Even before e-voting arrives, this means that high-quality political and voting information will be limited to citizens with access to information and communication networks, primarily the Internet. Those not able to use them will only keep the formal right to vote. For non-Internet users, when only traditional broadcast or press media are left, they have fewer sources to inform themselves.

Who *designs the network infrastructure* for democracy and in what way? Contrary to nervous systems, social and media networks are more or less constructed according to a plan. This plan for the information and communication infrastructure of political democracy can be designed following the model of a market (e-commerce), a forum (online deliberation) or a supposedly neutral technical information exchange. The choice very much depends on the view of democracy advocated (see below). Some take the view that they want to use the Web mainly for web-campaigning for elections. Here the same web techniques are designed as the marketing techniques used in e-commerce, selling candidates, parties and referendum choices or trying to convince voters. Other people take the view that they want to use the Web for participation and deliberation in communities and discussion groups. In this case, the design focuses on interaction instead of sending targeting messages with the purpose of persuasion. Furthermore, other views construct a Web designed by users themselves with their own websites, weblogs, social media profiles and messages.

Who *controls the network infrastructure* such as the Internet? Is it the government on behalf of citizens, is it the self-organization of the Internet (the Internet Society, ICANN and other bodies organizing the Internet), is it the web community and the users themselves? Or perhaps the market (Microsoft, Google, Apple, Facebook, Amazon and others)? American commercial platforms control the majority of Internet exchange. It is not surprising that they also have increasing power over the network infrastructure of political communication worldwide.

There might even be a fifth candidate for control, which Lawrence Lessig (1999) calls 'code'. This is comprised of the technical characteristics of the Web that can have a decisive influence on usage opportunities, among them democratic opportunities. The most important one is TCP/IP, which defines the Internet as a public medium. Without this technical protocol, the Internet would not be a decentralized network as we know it, enabling for instance peer-to-peer networking. Other characteristics are the algorithms used by the providers of social media. As the Internet has become a society by itself, struggles for control dominate this medium just like they dominate the society as a whole. These struggles for control most likely have effects on the opportunities for democracy, both online and offline.

In the 1980s and early 1990s the Internet was largely controlled by the web community and the Internet regulating bodies. After the breakthrough of the World Wide Web, the Internet was commercialized and governments made their first attempts to control the network. Business corporations and national governments now try to control the Internet. The most important corporations are the American companies Microsoft, Google, Apple and Facebook, which are engaged in fierce platform competition (Parker, Van Alstyne, & Choudary, 2016; van Dijk, 2012). All of them try to offer their own standards, applications and hardware such as operating systems, browsers, search engines, social networking sites, mobile phones and tablets.

Networks not only possess (infra)structures but they also carry *content*, among others, of a political kind. The nature of communication might change politics online. A transformation of political practice can be expected, where politics as an oral and written medium changes into an activity where people type on keyboards and view screens. Traditionally, politics involves verbal skills, management capacities and the art of negotiation. It has always been a collective routine of speakers and organizers. When the use of computer networks and other digital media comes to dominate politics and democracy, this routine will transform into people working primarily as individuals in networking and using terminals, screens and interfaces. Or they could meet as before while continually using smartphones, other mobile computers and screens in meeting rooms. This might substantially change communication content, as well-known digital media research shows.

Mental Effects and Media Routines Using Digital Media

There is more to consider than the technological properties of old and new media for democracy. Obviously their use is also very important. Digital media might have mental effects and be associated with media routines not seen before in the traditional media. In using contemporary digital media, the technical properties of enhanced visual information, the use of hypertext, and practices of briefly perceiving or scanning messages, preferably in abstracts or fragments, must have an influence on human perception and cognition. It might also have effects on political information retrieval and communication. Reception might also include quicker responses to messages and more simultaneous monitoring of multiple sources of information. Attention paid to single sources of messages might be lower than that associated with previous kinds of messages. It might be that the brain and mind are reorganized for processing digital media stimuli. This calls for an extensive neuroscience research program on the retrieval of digital political information and communication. Very little empirical research has been conducted in this field related to political communication.

Structuration of Political Systems and Democracy

How are the social and the media bases of democracy related? This question can be answered by structuration theory, the other basic theory alongside network theory used to explain digital democracy in this book. Structuration theory was developed by Antony Giddens in the 1980s. Versions of this theory have since been created that focus on the role of technology and organization, such as Adaptive Structuration Theory (DeSanctis & Poole, 2004). Structuration means that social structures instantiated by rules and resources are continually transformed by human action. The core of structuration theory is that the structures of social systems are continually (re) shaped by the action of people according to their views, norms and facilities. Technology such as digital media offer a kind of facility. An important question in this book is whether and how the use of these facilities are (re)shaping a particular social system by changing its structures: a political system. Some of these changes are shaping democratic structures (rules and resources). A system can be a society, an organization or a particular life-sphere, respectively working at a macro-, meso- or micro level. In a political system, structuration can change the macro level of this system, for instance making it more or less democratic. At the meso level, political organizations such as political parties, communities and movements can be transformed by facilities such as the use of digital media. The same can happen with political (inter)action and communication at the micro level between individual citizens.

To apply structuration theory to the use of digital media in political systems, the original model of structuration designed by Giddens (1984)

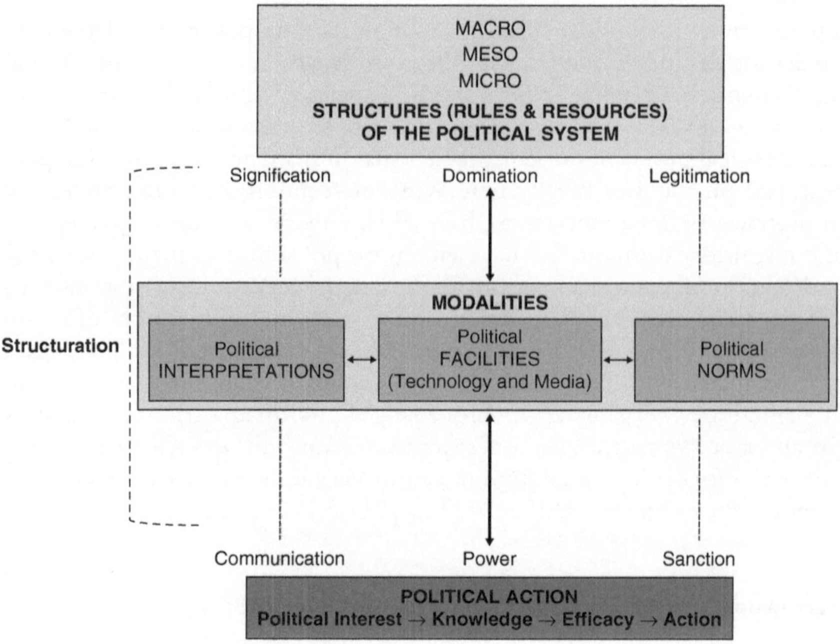

Figure 1.2 A structuration model of political action and systems.
(Inspired by Giddens, 1984, p. 29)

is our point of departure. Completing the original model for the political domain, we have filled in three modalities between political action and political systems (see Figure 1.2). The core of this model is the axis of the exchange between action and systems via the modality of technology such as digital media. This is the problematic of the majority of books, articles and papers about the effect of digital media on democracy. Unfortunately, there are two deficiencies in these publications.

The first is that the political context is often missing. The characteristics of the political systems and ongoing political action in which digital media are used are neglected. The focus is very much on the use of digital media by citizens for democracy increasing their political involvement and efficacy. This is the pitfall of instrumentalism, as discussed above. In this context, the other modalities drawn in the model are also ignored. These are the political interpretations (such as views of democracy) and political norms (such as the political culture in particular countries). In this book, particular views of digital democracy and typical digital practices comprising a particular digital political culture are very important. The viewpoint is not only one of power and domination but also the viewpoint of communication and signification and the viewpoint of sanction and legitimation of action and systems. In Figure 1.2 we have added a modality of communication and signification on the left-hand side, which is discussed in this book using communication theory, and a modality of legitimation and sanction on the right-hand side, discussed using political theory.

The second deficiency in these publications is that the problematic of digital media as a tool for democracy is one-sided. Instead of focusing on the interplay between political systems and action, a bottom-up perspective of democratization of political systems via digital media involving people in political action is created. The top-down perspective of institutions of political systems controlling and manipulating political action using digital media for surveillance, election marketing and the transmission of persuasive government information is largely ignored. One of the reasons for this is that most (survey) research takes an individualist view of political action, explaining it via individual characteristics such as political attitudes, knowledge or involvement and media use (Boulianne, 2009). A relational view of collective political action in networks, organizations and communities is rarely put forward (Anderson & Paskeviciute, 2005; Campbell, 2013). The same goes for the system view of comparing political systems internationally in their use of digital media (Anduiza, Jensen, & Jorba, 2012; Wolfsfeld, Segev, & Sheafer, 2013).

A fundamental assumption of structuration theory in political communication is the presence of a continual interplay of politics and media, with the result of a particular structuration (a change) of existing political systems. The pivotal question to be answered here is whether the use of digital technology really changes the structures (rules and resources, as listed in Figure 1.2 in the top box) of political systems and democracy. The principle here is politics first and media second. The double-faceted statement is that changes in the political context lead to changes in media performance, which in turn lead to further changes in the political context. This *politics-media-politics cycle* (Wolfsfeld, 2011) is in fact an example of structuration theory because media use changes politics and politics changes media use. This means that in this book we first depart from politics and political theory and second from (digital) media and media theory. The other modalities (communication-signification and sanction-legitimation) are just as important as the axis of power and domination via digital media. They are continually mediated by contagion and discourse in networks. The two most important theories used to explore the network society in this book, structuration and network theory, are both social or political theories and media or communication theories.

Basic Views and Definitions

Digital Democracy Definition

In this section we will define two basic terms in the title of the book: democracy and network society. However, we start with a term that we have already used several times above. In 2000 we defined *digital democracy* as a "collection of attempts to practice democracy without the limits of time, space and other physical conditions, using ICT and computer-mediated communication 'CMC' instead, as an addition, not a replacement for traditional 'analogue' political practices" (Hacker and van Dijk, 2000, p. 1). This is a rather formal and instrumental definition that does not provide a complete picture of what democracy means. We coined this definition after having observed that several very different classical views of democracy are related to particular applications of digital media in politics, which we will discuss below.

First we have to clarify what we want to change in this instrumental definition. The terms ICT and CMC have lost some popularity. Second, digital media and online communication are not mere additions to traditional media and offline communication. These types of media and communication are increasingly integrated. For example, political meetings today are continuously supported by smartphones, wireless computer access and the screens of broadcasting and networking, including social media. Today we talk about digital media, networks and the Internet. At this time, we seek to define digital democracy as *the collective use of information and communication technology for practices of politics and democracy in both online and offline environments.*

Our focus is how this technology *use* and these *practices* affect changes in democracy as a system, specifically in the context of network societies. They are not simply instruments, as discussed above. This technology also means more than using the Internet. This public medium all too often is equated with digital media, just like Internet politics is used as a synonym for digital democracy. In this book, we also discuss the influence of private and closed computer networks on politics and government. Both the private networks of (trans)national corporations, political organizations (for marketing) and the internal networks of public administrations can have a big effect on politics and democracy. It is not justified to equate politics with 'informational politics' in the public media, as Castells does: "outside the media there is only political marginality" (Castells, 1997, p. 312). Besides the Internet, though often connected to it, private media such as mobile telephony (including instant messaging and WhatsApp) are also increasingly used for politics and for democratic experiments.

Views of Democracy

In this book we always relate the concept of democracy with particular views of it. As scholars we examine the most important current views of democracy held by others. We will try to avoid the inclination to suggest our own views of democracy. Two typologies of contemporary democracy views are examined in this book. The first is *basic and substantial* (ideological), while the other is *strategic or procedural and formal.* We will start with the basic and substantial typology. Here, a distinction is often made between liberal democracy, populism and authoritarian democracy (Welzel, 2013). Liberal democracy has social, market and conservative versions. The substantial items of interest here are free elections, equal rights and civil liberties with some additional items such as economic distribution and a welfare state in the social version of liberal democracy. The second basic view is populism with its basic ideological scheme of the people versus the elite. In left-wing populism the most important items are bread-and-butter and in right-wing populism it is law-and-order (Welzel, 2013). The third basic view is authoritarian democracy. Here the authority might be a particular religion, the military or a single party. This authority might dominate the government of a state, so that authoritarian democracy always leans to autocracy and risks being undemocratic. In an international comparison of surveys of world views about democracy and human rights, Welzel (2013) has shown that this typology works. In this book we adopt a very broad conception of democracy. We accept that populism and even authoritarian democracy can be democratic. We do not want to lean on Western liberal views of democracy only. All the views mentioned have an affinity with a particular use of digital technology, from complete Internet freedom to so-called networked authoritarianism (see the following chapters).

The second typology lists procedural views of democracy, which are strategic and formal. It is inspired by the models of democracy of David Held (1987). In this typology the strategic goal of democracy could be opinion or decision making and the means of representative or direct democracy. Van Dijk (van Dijk, 1996; Hacker & van Dijk, 2000) has linked these models with particular uses of digital media in politics such as online voting, web-campaigning, online discussions and government web-services. Most of them are classical (Western) views of democracy that are much older than digital media.

The classical Western view of democracy is *legalist democracy* – a fully procedural view of democracy regarding the constitution and other laws and rules as the foundations of democracy. The three basic principles are: separation of powers (legislative and executive power, the judiciary); a system of checks and balances between the government, the public administration and the judiciary; and representation. In this view, the lack of information gathered and provided by the state and searched for by citizens is the most important democratic problem to be solved with the aid of digital media. Thus, they have to bring about an effective administration of government, a strong state and more security, such as through electronic surveillance systems. Furthermore, it can help to improve public support for the government. The means are electronic information and transaction services of the national and local government.

The second conception of democracy is called *competitive democracy*. It is mainly supported in countries with a two-party or a presidential system. According to this view, parties and leaders compete for the support of the electorate. This rather elitist view of democracy emphasizes representation and efficient decision making by leaders. Digital media are first and foremost used for information campaigns and election campaigns. In the United States, a lot of experience has been gained via this use of digital media (Bimber & Davis, 2003; Newman, 1994; Rash, 1997; Selnow, 1994; Sunstein, 2002). Public information systems, electronic voting guides and tele-polling can help voters in their choice of the best leaders and policies.

Four other views of democracy have a completely different strategic orientation. Supporters of these views fight for a socialization of politics. This implies a less prominent role for governments and politicians and a greater role for social organizations and individual citizens. The assumption is that computer networks such as the Internet will enable them to have a direct influence on politics, and even to bypass institutional politics or replace it with their own political relations. While views intending to strengthen institutional politics are mainly supported by politicians and administrators, these alternative views are defended by various social organizations and politically engaged citizens.

The most radical view of these four compared to existing political practice is *plebiscitary democracy*. According to this view, political decisions have to be made through referenda or plebiscites. This implies a preference for direct democracy instead of representative democracy. The opportunities offered by computer networks to hold tele-polls or tele-referenda and to have online discussions had an immediate appeal to the supporters of this view in the 1980s under the label of 'tele-democracy'. They are said to revive direct democracy as practiced in the Athenian agora.

Another alternative view is *pluralist democracy*. In this view, opinion formation within and between social organizations is emphasized. Democracy is not the will of the majority but that of a constantly changing coalition of minorities. Its most important value is pluralism in social and political discussion and in the media. It is a combination of direct and representative democracy, since representation is exercised not only by politicians but also by societal organizations. Digital media offer numerous opportunities for pluralism in public debates, among them Internet debates, and for discussions within political organizations. So-called 'deliberative democracy' is a version of this view

The fifth view discussed here is *participatory democracy*. Its supporters promote a socialization of politics, encouraging active citizenship. The emphasis lies on the broadest possible opinion formation about political affairs and on a particular combination of direct and representative democracy. Its most important instruments are public debates, public education and citizen participation in general. If the digital media are to play a positive role in enabling these instruments, access for all is vital.

The last view of democracy has appeared as a dominant model among the pioneers of the Internet community. This does not mean that the political views behind it are entirely new. Many observers have noticed the affinity of the Internet pioneers with the radical social movements of the 1960s and 1970s in most Western countries. These views range from classical anarchism and left-wing socialism to all kinds of libertarianism. The latter have been

Table 1.1 Six models in two dimensions of political democracy.

Primary means	*Primary goal*		
	Decision making		*Opinion formation*
REPRESENTATIVE DEMOCRACY	LEGALIST COMPETITIVE		
			PLURALIST
		LIBERTARIAN	PARTICIPATORY
DIRECT DEMOCRACY	PLEBISCITARY		

Source: van Dijk in Hacker & van Dijk (2000, p. 39)

the most important in the 1990s and afterwards. The *libertarian view* is close to the pluralist and plebiscitary views in several respects, as the opportunities for (virtual) community building, tele-polling and online debates are proclaimed. Specific to libertarianism is the wish for a small role of government and the emphasis on autonomous politics by citizens in their own associations using the horizontal communication capabilities of computer networks in general and the Internet in particular. In its most extreme form, institutional politics is held to be obsolete, to be superseded by a new political reality collectively created in networks.

These views are summarized in Table 1.1. Of course, these views of democracy are ideal types. In practice, particular political actions and systems are characterized by particular combinations of these views. However, they clarify that the uses of digital technology in politics are not neutral. They often hide particular political preferences.

Shin (2015) argues that procedural definitions are most popular among scholars, while substantive definitions are more important among populations in the world. He has combined surveys, barometers and the like worldwide and found that that the policy outcomes of governments are more important in evaluating a government to be democratic than democratic procedures. He also found that most people in the world have a poorly informed conception of democracy. They can mention no or only one characteristic of what democracy means for them. Moreover, a majority is not able to make a distinction between a democracy and an autocracy. Even in the so-called democratic West, 40% of the population reveal a poorly informed view of democracy in surveys (Shin, 2015, p. 26).

Network Society Definition

The second most important concept in the title of this book describes the social context of digital democracy: the network society that is built on networks. This means that a network society uses communication networks as a primary means of social, political, economic, and cultural organization. In a network society, political communication is likely to depend heavily on online networking. While some scholars might still prefer the concept of information society, we think that the network society concept draws more attention to the structures, systems and types of communication that characterize politics and democracy. The information society concept is a *substantial* characterization of societies in which information increasingly is the primary means and product of all processes.

The concept of the network society is a *formal* characterization emphasizing a particular social (infra)structure and organization of contemporary societies. Van Dijk (1991, 2012) has defined the network society as "a modern type of society with an infrastructure of social and media networks that characterizes its mode of organization at every level: individual, group/organizational and societal" (2012, p. 24). He compares this classification of society with the mass society that is built on an infrastructure of groups, organizations and communities ('masses'). According to van Dijk, networks are becoming the nervous system of society, politics and democracy.

At this point, the reader might wonder which societies actually qualify as network societies and which ones do not. This is a very important issue, because a Euro-American centric perspective might assume that the rest of the world's nearly 200 nations are operating with communication technologies in the same way as in Europe and North America. The advanced-technological countries of North America, Europe, Oceania and East Asia and some others clearly are network societies. However, all developing countries largely are mass societies with only urban parts evolving into a network society.

Manuel Castells defines the network society in terms of "a new social morphology of our societies"; he claims that the diffusion of a networking logic substantially modifies the operation and outcomes in processes of production, experience, power and culture (Castells, 1996, p. 469). There are two basic differences between Castells' and van Dijk's definitions. First, for Castells (p. 410), networks already are the basic units of contemporary society while van Dijk argues that modern society is in the process of becoming a network society, but still consists of individuals, pairs, groups and organizations, albeit increasingly linked by networks. The second difference is that for Castells, the social morphology of networks is pre-eminent (dominant) over social action (Castells, 1996, p. 469). However, for van Dijk networks are shaped in a dialectical interplay between structure and social action, which means that human beings are continually shaping and changing network structures and technologies. (Also see van Dijk, 2012.)

Following Castells, Barney, another author of a book called *Network Society*, defines networks "as the basic form of human organization and relationship across a wide range of social, political and economic figurations and associations" (Barney, 2004, pp. 25–26). Among them are political figurations, together shaping something that Barney calls 'network politics'.

Chapter Overview of the Book

Chapter 2 analyzes the technological characteristics of the networks shaping the network society alongside its social structures. It lists the enabling and defining properties of networks and their relevance for democracy. For instance, it is shown here that networks are not simply flat and democratic by nature, a common popular view. Networks for political communication also have powerful centers and structural constraints. They can also lead to undemocratic or even anti-democratic politics. Here, for example the concept of networked authoritarianism is discussed.

Chapter 3 is about participation and inclusion. It discusses the relation between digital media use and political participation or involvement, and whether or not both political and digital participation change democracy and political systems. Furthermore, access, skills and use of digital media and networks for all citizens and inclusion or exclusion to the network society are primary questions addressed here.

Chapter 4 describes the reconstruction of public space by means of networks and digital media, reframing the classical concept of the public sphere by Habermas inspired by the communication channels of the mass society. Habermas's normative concept of the public sphere is outdated. In this chapter we try to replace it with a neutral concept of a mosaic of public spaces in the network society. These spaces are a hybrid system of cross-media networks with online and offline communication combined. The properties of this system are examined.

Chapter 5, co-authored with Ben Mollov, observes that online discussion in the public sphere often is very polarizing but that this is not the only outcome. Online discussion can also be used for conciliatory and depolarizing discourse in situations of collaboration and for the prevention or resolution of conflicts.

After these theoretical chapters we have added three chapters about practices of democracy in particular countries and on government practices called e-government. Two chapters are about countries with governing autocracies which, according to some observers, might become more democratic when citizens start to use digital media.

Chapter 6 is about the so-called Arab Spring. Talk about Facebook and Twitter revolutions has been silenced as Arab countries moved the other way to even more authoritarian regimes, or even war and anarchy. Chapter 7 is about the public and political use of the Internet in the People's Republic of China. Some observers argue that in China a public sphere has been born, created by the use of the Internet and other digital media, and that this sphere is tearing up the totalitarian system. Is this really true?

Chapter 8 is about e-government. E-democracy and e-government are related. Digital democracy cannot work when elected governments do not inform citizens and citizens do not inform governments about their needs. Services of information, communication and transaction for citizens can be offered in the same manner of supply known by the business world. But they can also be innovated by means of co-creation or participation with citizens.

The final Chapter 9 contains a summary of the statements and observations of this book and suggests steps forward to advance theory in digital democracy research. Here the pivotal question will be answered as to in which contexts and conditions the use of digital media and networks leads to more or less democracy.

References

Anderson, C., & Paskeviciute, A. (2005). Macro-politics and micro-behavior: Mainstream politics and the frequency of political discussion in contemporary democracies. In A. Zuckerman (Ed.), *The social logic of politics: Personal networks as contexts for political behavior* (pp. 228–248). Philadelphia, PA: Temple University Press.

Anduiza, E., Jensen, M. J., & Jorba, L. (2012). *Digital media and political engagement worldwide*. New York: Cambridge University Press.

Arterton, C. F. (1987). *Teledemocracy: Can technology protect democracy?* Newbury Park, CA: Sage.

Barney, D. (2004). *The network society*. Malden, MA: Polity Press.

Becker, T. L. (1981). Teledemocracy: Bringing power back to the people. *Futurist, 15*(6), 6–9.

Benkler, Y. (2006). *The wealth of networks: How social production transforms markets and freedom*. New Haven, CT; London: Yale University Press.

Bimber, B., & Davis, R. (2003). *Campaigning online: The Internet in US elections*. Oxford, UK: Oxford University Press.

Boulianne, S. (2009). Does internet use affect engagement? A meta-analysis of research. *Political Communication, 26*(2), 193–211.

Campbell, D. E. (2013). Social networks and political participation. *Annual Review of Political Science, 16*, 33–48.

Castells, M. (1996). *The information age: Economy, society and culture. Vol. I: The rise of the network society*. Oxford, UK: Blackwell.

Castells, M. (1997). *The information age: Economy, society and culture. Vol. II: The power of identity*. Oxford, UK: Blackwell.

Chadwick, A. (2013). *The hybrid media system: Politics and power*. Oxford, UK; New York: Oxford University Press.

Corn, J. (Ed.) (1986). *Imaging tomorrow: History, technology and the American future*. Cambridge, MA: The MIT Press.

DeSanctis G., & Poole, M. S. (1994). Capturing the complexity in advanced technology use: Adaptive structuration theory. *Organization Science, 5*(2), 121–147.

Diamond, L. (2005). The state of democratization at the beginning of the 21st century. Retrieved from http://heinonline.org/HOL/LandingPage?handle=hein.journals/whith6&div=6&id=&page=

Economist Intelligence Unit (2017). Democracy Index 2016: Revenge of the "deplorables". Retrieved from www.eiu.com/public/topical_report.aspx?campaignid=DemocracyIndex2016

Giddens, A. (1984). *The constitution of society*. Cambridge, UK: Polity Press.

Hacker, K. L., & van Dijk, J. (2000). *Digital democracy: Issues of theory and practice*. London; Thousand Oaks, CA; New Delhi: Sage.

Held, D. (1987). *Models of democracy*. Cambridge, UK: Polity Press.
ITU. (2017). *Measuring the information society report* (Vol. 1). Geneva: ITU; International Telecommunication Union.
Jenkins, H., Ford, S., & Green, J. (2013). *Spreadable media: Creating value and meaning in a networked culture*. New York; London: New York University Press.
Lessig, L. (1999). *Code and other laws of cyberspace*. New York: Basic Books.
Lutz, B., & duToit, P. (2014). *Defining democracy in a digital age: Political support of social media*. New York; Basingstoke, UK: Palgrave Macmillan.
Milanovic, B. (2016). *Global inequality: A new approach for the age of globalization*. Cambridge, MA; London: Belknap Press of Harvard University Press.
Morozov, E. (2013). *To save everything, click here: The folly of technological solutionism*. New York: PublicAffairs.
Mudde, C., & Rovira Kaltwasser, C. (2012). *Populism in Europe and the Americas: Threat or corrective for democracy?* New York: Cambridge University Press.
Mueller, M. L. (2010). *Networks and states: The global politics of internet governance*. Cambridge, MA; London: The MIT Press.
Newman, B. I. (1994). *The marketing of the president: Political marketing as campaign strategy*. Thousand Oaks, CA: Sage.
Parker, G. G., Van Alstyne, M. W., & Choudary, S. P. (2016). *Platform revolution: How networked markets are transforming the economy—and how to make them work for you*. New York; London: WW Norton & Company.
Piketty, T. (2014). *Capital in the twenty-first century*. Cambridge, MA; London: The Belknap Press of Harvard University Press.
Rash, W. (1997). *Politics on the nets: Wiring the political process*. New York: Freeman.
Selnow, G. W. (1994). *High-tech campaigns: Computer technology in political communication*. Westport, CT: Praeger.
Shin, D. C. (2015). *Assessing citizen responses to democracy: A review and synthesis of recent public opinion research*. CSD working paper. Irvine, CA: Center for the Study of Democracy, University of California-Irvine.
Stiglitz, J. E. (2013). *The price of inequality: How today's divided society endangers our future*. New York; London: W.W. Norton & Company.
Sunstein, C. R. (2002). *Republic.com*. Princeton, NJ: Princeton University Press.
Tsagarousianou, R. (1999). Electronic democracy: Rhetoric and reality. *Communications: The European Journal of Communication Research, 24*(2), 189–208.
van Dijk, J. A. G. M. (1991). *De Netwerkmaatschappij: Sociale aspecten van de nieuwe media*. First Dutch edition of *The Network Society* (1999, 2006, 2012). Houten; Zaventem: Bohn Stafleu van Loghum.
van Dijk, J. A. G. M. (1996). Models of democracy. *Javnost/The Public*, 3(1), 43–56.
van Dijk, J. A. G. M. (2005). *The deepening divide: Inequality in the information society*. Thousand Oaks, CA; London; New Delhi: Sage.
van Dijk, J. A. G. M. (2012). *The network society* (3rd ed.). London; New Delhi; Thousand Oaks, CA; Singapore: Sage.
van Dijk, J. A. G. M., & van Deursen, A. J. A. M. (2014). *Digital skills: Unlocking the information society*. New York: Palgrave Macmillan.
Welzel, C. (2013). *Freedom rising: Human empowerment and the quest for emancipation* (*World Values Surveys*). New York: Cambridge University Press.
Wolfsfeld, G. (2011). *Making sense of media and politics*. New York; Abingdon, UK: Routledge.
Wolfsfeld, G., Segev, E., & Sheafer, T. (2013). Social media and the Arab Spring: Politics comes first. *The International Journal of Press/Politics, 18*(2), 115–137.

2 Network Properties and Democracy

Introduction

This book focuses on the relation between the use of computer networks and democracy in a network society. It tries to find out when, or in what ways, networks reinforce or weaken democracy. This use includes systems and structures that are not easy to change, and when they are, changes might be not fast. In the context of this book, use of digital media to improve or maintain democracy has to take political systems into account. What we will explore in this book is whether the use of digital media, such as social media, blogs and online forums by citizens or online marketing and surveillance by political parties and governments, changes social structures and political systems. Digital media use can be viewed as a modality, an intermediary between political action and systems or structures. Agency can change structures, according to structuration theory (Giddens, 1984). Still, many structures are persistent. For instance, there is no guarantee that even the most broad and frequent individual citizen participation in political activities using digital media will change the representation and decisions of professional politicians.

So, when surveys show that citizens are participating more in the political system by using digital media, we should be cautious in our optimism about this increasing or improving democracy. To find out what the effects of this participation are on the structures of the political system concerned, we have to go beyond the individual attitudes, opinions and efforts of citizens. This means we have to go further than adopting methodological individualism as the main approach. Particularly in the context of networks and the network society, we also have to look for relations between actors in the political system. An alternative notion of political activity and effects takes a relational or network approach (Tilly, 1998; Wellman & Berkowitz, 1988). Here, the prime units of analysis are not individuals but the positions of individuals and the relationships between them. In this approach, political activity is not primarily a matter of individual attributes. This fulfills our challenge of taking a network perspective toward political digital communication.

In this book, we will especially pay attention to positions, relations, structures and systems according to structuration and network theory. We will focus on both political systems and on social or computer networks as structures to be changed by political agents. We adopt the perspective that technology is both defining and enabling, meaning that defining technology is not to be read as a kind of technological determinism. One popular view to be contested here is the idea is that the Internet *in itself* is either more or less democratic than older media such as broadcasting and the press. Opposed to this, we argue that computer networks have a number of properties that are both defining and enabling their use in particular contexts. In this context, this means that they can be used for and against democracy, but not in the simple instrumental view also criticized in the Introduction.

Network properties are *strategic characteristics and operational effects of computer networks* that are used in social contexts. It is important to say that they combine technical and social aspects: the properties of computer *and* social networks. For example, both computer networks and social networks can be more or less centralized. An example is the use of the technical link structure of a search engine that draws information seekers to the most popular sites. Another example is where members of social networks look for the most popular people, in this way acting on preferential attachment, a prime mechanism of network theory. These examples will be explained below.

A number of general strategic characteristics of networks have already been discussed in the Introduction. These are access, design, control, legality, security and communication content. In this chapter we will specify these strategic characteristics in a number of concrete instances. We will also pay attention to the operational effects of computer networks, which are often called network effects. These are the defining effects of networks that can be reinforced or weakened by users according to their practical motivations. An example is the network effect of critical mass. When a network reaches a particular tipping point of the number of users, it becomes even more attractive for new users. This is a structural effect, with its strength dependent on the attractiveness of the medium concerned.

In the scientific literature and in public opinion the Internet is often seen as a special medium with the following characteristics; it generally described as a(n):

- interactive medium that departs from the one-sided communication of traditional mass media;
- active and creative medium enabling users to transform from viewers, listeners and readers to participants;
- direct medium in which individual users determine at a distance what happens in the center (e.g. politics and mass media supply);
- platform on which everybody is equal in principle as assumed expertise has to prove itself before being accepted;
- peer-to-peer medium enabling the collective creation of products online, not primarily by individual authors or businesses.

All these characteristics are real to a certain extent. However, they are superficially described and have a positive, pro-democratic bias. We have to dig deeper, analyzing more abstract network properties, and we also have to look for characteristics of networks that do not support democracy, in whatever view.

It is not easy to discuss the network properties that might be relevant for democracy in a clear and workable analytical framework. The first framework that comes to our mind is the constellation of the seven OSI layers[1] of computer networks. However, this distinction is fully technical and goes too much into detail. We need distinctions that are both technical and social. Nevertheless, the seven OSI layers can be summarized in a more workable distinction between hardware, software and applications of content. All three have particular features that are defining and enabling democracy. The properties to be discussed are listed in Table 2.1. In the next section we will start with the hardware infrastructure of networks, which has already shown a number of consequences for democracy. Then we will proceed with the software infrastructure that is very relevant for the democratic potential of networks. The ensuing section deals with the applications of networks. Here the superstructure with substantial activities of political communication will be scrutinized for features that support or hinder democracy.

Properties of Network Hardware and Democracy

A Central Exchange with Decentralized Terminals

When they serve as a set of communication platforms for political communication, computer networks such as the Internet have a number of features that depart from traditional media. These are summarized in the first three

Table 2.1 Network properties with effects for democracy listed in three layers.

Layers	*Network properties*
BASIS (hardware infrastructure)	- A central exchange with decentralized terminals - Physical access and inclusiveness - Connectivity, connectedness and critical mass - Size and density - Centralization, centrality and symmetry
CODE (software infrastructure)	- Standardization - Peer-to-peer principle - Datification and big data analysis - Algorithms and the power of 'Googlearchy' - A power law and concentration
CONTENT (superstructure: applications)	- User-generated content and the limits of attention - Limits of simultaneous input - Open and closed networking

bullet points of the media characteristics listed in the Introduction of this chapter. First, computer networks are interactive and enable active or creative contributions to political communication. The traditional media of broadcasting and the press had the one-sided communication pattern of senders with complete control over messages. They served as gatekeepers for all mediated political communication. The only access potential for readers, viewers and listeners was to send a letter to a newspaper or a broadcasting station or to call a radio program when this was offered. Other options for feedback to politics were to meet or call politicians or to visit political meetings.

With the advent of the Internet, the possibility of feedback was offered on a massive scale. A large number of political websites with interactive facilities were created. Many people established their own political websites, social media pages and blogs. According to most observers this removed gatekeeping monopolies in the political mass media, an observation we will critically discuss below. At first, the Internet was used in a fairly traditional way as a new type of broadcasting with websites only publishing information. However, since the end of the 1990s the Internet has changed substantially. The interactive potential has actually been realized, with lots of new facilities enabling Internet users to contribute so-called user-generated content. These facilities were called Web 2.0. After 2004, with the arrival of social media Web 3.0 evolved, which is a Web of networkers, virtual communities, collaborations and social networking. See Figure 3.3 on page 64.

It is important to understand that all (inter)active and creative facilities of the Internet are derived from the core property of a network as a central exchange with decentralized terminals. This property also is responsible for the first opportunity that came to the mind of people who thought that cable, telephone and computer networks would be able to radically transform democracy. However, all these opportunities for (inter)active, creative and direct political communication in computer networks will scarcely be realized if only a few people have access to these networks.

Physical Access and Inclusiveness

Networks include or exclude. You belong to them, or you don't. Among those who do, some are more included than others. This is the hard reality of inequality in networks. This will be discussed in the next chapter in the section Inclusion and Participation.

The decisive step for inclusion is physical access. In contemporary developed societies 50% to 95% of the population have physical access at home. This is the most important figure for the potential of digital democracy. It defines how many 'digital citizens' a country can have. Media platforms such as YouTube and social networking sites are filled with abundant televisual content and hyperlinks.

Physical access can be realized by home access, by access at work or at school or by public access (e.g. a library, a community access center or an Internet café). For political communication, home access is desirable. This is the best place for unrestrained Internet use and for free expression, provided that housemates do not interfere. Public places of access are less appropriate for political communication, or the use of it is constrained by time, money and censorship in undemocratic countries (usually more than at home). Unfortunately, home access is still a luxury in most countries of the world. Where home access is available in developing countries, it can be observed that its use for political communication is a minority phenomenon.

Connectivity, Connectedness and Critical Mass

Access is not the same as connectivity. *Connectivity* is a *technical* network property that equals reachability and refers to the number of *individual* actors inside a network that are linked to one another by direct or indirect ties. This number is very important to be able to assess the potential to use a network such as the Internet for political organizational purposes. Barack Obama wouldn't have been able to organize a massive grassroots campaign among the young, new basis of the Democratic Party in 2008 and 2012 without a large number of volunteers that could reach each other on the Internet and by mobile phone.

A familiar network property is *connectedness*. However, this is a *social* network property bonding groups of actors in a social network (van Dijck, 2013). Political communication is not only an activity of individuals but also of groups and communities. Well-connected groups in both social and media networks have better chances of political organization. They are more coherent and coordinated than dispersed or fragmented networks of individuals. Connectivity and connectedness both determine the potential of participation because they define who and to what extent individuals are able to communicate with each other via the network.

At a certain point, connectivity reaches a tipping point or threshold. This is called *critical mass* (Markus, 1990). From that point onwards it becomes ever more valuable for someone who is not connected to become part of the network because one can reach an increasing number of people. Then the number of connections accelerates and might reach a majority of the population. This is a prime condition to realize Internet democracy. This wouldn't make much sense if only a small minority is able to participate. Campaign funding with small donations from Internet users, as has become a regular occurrence in American election campaigns, only works because a big majority of American households is connected and frequently uses the Internet for financial operations.

Size and Density

A fairly simple global network property is *size*. Size matters in networks. The main reason for the organizational success of left-leaning American advocacy group MoveOn.org is that it has a million members. The sheer size of active members connected enables this organization to also receive millions of dollars in donations and to distribute them among its favorite liberal candidates. Equally, as in other media, on the Internet political value is first counted in numbers (voters, party members, followers, donators) and only second in the quality of user-generated content or online debate.

Other global network properties define the dispersion and influence of communication in the network. The *density* of a network is the number of actual links among actors as compared to the number of possible links. This determines the potential intensity of communication and enables political information exchange to reach a higher level. This could happen in online discussion with high-frequency interaction.

Density is supported by another network property: *transitivity*. A network has a high level of transitivity when it contains many groups of three or more actors that are interlinked. For example, when we have A, B and C, C is automatically linked to A when A is linked to B and B is linked to C. Many of these linkages in a network support the speed of communication and the organizational capacity of political activities.

Centralization, Centrality and Symmetry

Networks are not flat. In spite of our respect for Thomas Friedman and his book *The World is Flat*, networks really have centers. Just like the spider is the core of its web, computer and social networks have cores. The *centralization* of a network as a whole even decides the spread of influence inside the network.

In Figure 2.1 a so-called kite network is portrayed with three measures of *centrality*. Unit or node D has the highest degree of centrality, that is, the highest number of direct links with other actors. They can be divided into 'in-degree' or incoming ties that might indicate popularity, and 'out-degree', the number of outgoing ties that might signify expansiveness. However, unit or node F has the greatest degree of closeness, which means the extent to which an actor is close to, or can easily reach, all the other actors in the network. In this way, the unit is able to be fastest in accessing important or strategic information, directly or indirectly 'through the grapevine'. Finally, H has the highest between-ness, the extent to which an actor mediates or lays between any other two actors. This actor can be an intermediary or a broker or a gatekeeper and benefit from information provided by others in the network (I and J in Figure 2.1).

The meaning of all three measures of centrality for political inequality is that they enable the drawing of more social and material (scarce) resources

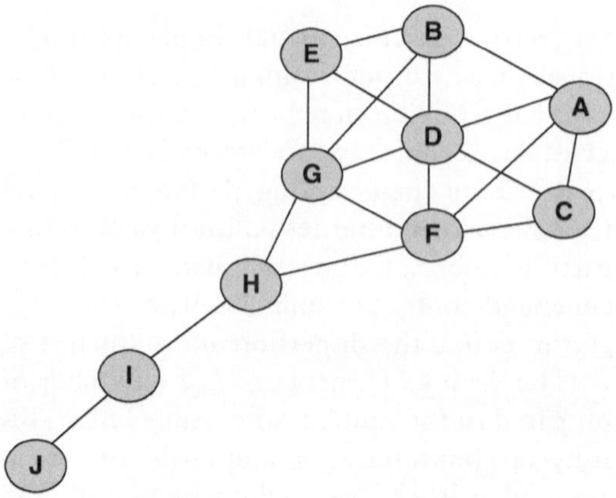

Figure 2.1 Kite network with different positions of centrality: Highest degree (D), highest closeness (F) and highest betweenness (H).

(Adapted from Krackhardt, 1990 and Bruggeman, 2008)

and more strategically important information than in the other positions. Charles Tilly (1998) has invented an appropriate name for this capacity: *opportunity hoarding*. The meaning for democracy is that individuals, or groups and organizations in a network are able to shape new political elites or reinforce existing ones. So, the distribution of positions in networks does not only have decentralizing but also centralizing effects that might result in more or less political equality. Both are enabled by the hardware properties of networks.

Additionally, the *symmetry* of communication in networks is an important aspect of (de)centralization. When content is downloaded from a political website much more frequently than facts and views are uploaded by users, network communication is asymmetric. Some citizens only retrieve information from political websites, others also produce user-generated content and interact with other citizens in discussion forums and pressure groups. The US president Donald Trump uses Twitter as a megaphone and does not respond to the reactions to his Tweets.

Properties of Network Software and Democracy

Standardization

Every media network operates with particular protocols that are standardized. Without common standards people are not able to communicate in a network. And without communication there is no democracy. The main standard of the Internet is the Internet Protocol (IP). Together with another standard, the Transmission Control Protocol (TCP), it forms the backbone of the Internet: TCP/IP. This follows the end-to-end principle: with TCP the shortest route is selected to connect the IP addresses of computers and other terminals at the ends where users are operating. The meaning of the TCP/IP protocol for network democracy will be discussed in the following section. We will first deal with standardization as such.

In his book *Network Power*, David Sing Grewal (2008) explains that a network with standards that are accepted by many people has power. This is the power to decide who is able to connect to the network and use it for communication with others. Generally, people prefer a general standard because in that case they can reach many others in the same system. In this way critical mass can be reached. This is one of the reasons for the steady popularity of Microsoft's operating systems and other software on computers and Google's operating system Android on smartphones. Next to TCP/IP operating systems such as Windows, Mac OS and Linux, browsers such as Internet Explorer, Mozilla Firefox and Chrome are important software standards. The same goes for mark-up languages such as HTML and XML and search engines such as Google, Bing and Yahoo.

Listed in this way, it seems that there is much competition. However, in fact most of the time one of the software standards is dominant and serves as a virtual standard with a lot of power to influence the potential operations of users. Examples are Windows in operating systems, Internet Explorer in browsers and Google in search engines. The struggle for power is intensified by the fierce platform competition of Microsoft, Google and Apple trying to become the dominant supplier of all these instruments: operating systems, browsers and search engines (Parker et al., 2016; van Dijk, 2012). These instruments certainly are not neutral forces. Later in the chapter we will give the example of the power of Google, called Googlearchy.

Grewal (2008, pp. 172–181) distinguishes three network properties linked to standardization:

1. *Compatibility*: when two networks are incompatible, one network can exert power over another since users must use either standard A or B and cannot use them at the same time. Windows and Mac OS are barely compatible. Compatibility increases when different standards can easily be converted and it decreases when this does not happen and standards are imposed.
2. *Availability*: this is the ease with which a network accepts entrants that want to adopt its standard. Here, network power can be attained in two opposite ways. The network can be available or accessible to a high degree and attract many new entrants, in this way building the power of numbers. However, the network can also reduce availability by offering difficult to achieve standards, in this way creating an exclusive club or other organization. Exclusivity can also be a source of power. Political

communication usually opts for high availability. However, less accessible or closed political clubs or discussion forums are also observed.

3. *Malleability*: a network standard can be more or less open to revision. Standards should actually be less malleable to serve their functions of uniformity and coordination. However, malleable standards increase the flexibility of networks to adapt to the environment. This is a dilemma. For example, there should be standards for working political discussion forums (rules and moderation), but when the nature and attendance of discussion changes, these standards should be revisable.

The discussion of these network properties of standardization might seem far-fetched in a discussion about democracy. However, it is important to realize that in contemporary society private enterprises are responsible for the complete technological design of networks and their applications, while the political activities and potentials discussed here are public and should be open, accessible and malleable to all.

Peer-to-Peer Principle

The exchange of information via a central medium by people using local terminals is considered to be the most important network property for equals that are called peers. It has a hardware basis of accessible connections as previously discussed, but it also has a software component. This is the TCP/IP protocol. *In fact, TCP/IP is the Internet.* It enables the exchange of information on an equal basis. In politics this information can be knowledge, opinions or votes. The basic, supposedly democratic, idea is that everybody can speak simultaneously and be heard by all on the network. The potential of networks to exchange information at a distance and yet come together as a group has immediately appealed to advocates of plebiscitary, pluralist, participatory and libertarian democracy. We were already talking about so-called tele-democracy in the 1980s that wanted to use this potential to propose a contemporary plebiscitary version of the Athenian agora (Arterton, 1987). From that time on, libertarian currents on the Internet saw the principle of peer-to-peer networking as the hallmark of their favorite medium enabling all kinds of self-organization.

After the year 2004, this principle was reinforced by the emergence of Web 2.0 and Web 3.0 with the rise of user-generated content and social networking. Benkler (2006) in his *Wealth of Networks* and Tapscott and Williams (2006) in *Wikinomics*, among others, appear to be strong supporters of these technologies that enable mass collaboration and social production on the Internet. However, these authors also show particular nuances. Benkler (2006, p. 247) notes that "there never has been a complex, large modern democracy in which everyone could speak and be heard by everyone else". Indeed, below we will argue that it may be easy to speak on the Internet, but difficult to be heard. Tapscott and Williams (2006, p. 25) admit that "though egalitarianism is the general rule, most peer networks have an underlying structure, where some people have more authority and influence than others". Precisely this "underlying structure" will be the subject of our focus of attention now.

The potential of peer-to-peer networking for democracy strongly depends on the role of the central exchange required for network communication. In one way or another, the network has to offer storage, processing and exchange. This can happen more at the center or more at the terminals, and has both technical and social aspects.

A technical aspect is the transformation of the decentralized TCP/IP protocol into a more centralized protocol that is supposed to be necessary to create more Internet addresses. This happens in so-called IP 6 or IP sec(urity). This new version of IP labels packages of Internet data streams with numbers that enable operators and security agencies to identify the packages, to steer them and to tap their senders and receivers. This is not a comforting idea for citizen peers in less democratic societies, societies under surveillance or for people who want to participate in online discussion forums anonymously.

The storage and processing capacity of peer-to-peer networks can be located in the center, at the terminals or in an intermediate exchange. This technical aspect also distributes power. In the first music exchange sites, such as Napster, there was a central directory of songs to distribute. Then storage capacities and directories moved to 'super nodes', as with the Gnutella service. The next step was to store them on the computers of users themselves. Finally, music and video exchange networks work with Digital Rights-management Systems to charge for downloads, and exchange is centralized again (see Benkler, 2006, pp. 419–420).

In political peer-to-peer networking, most discussion or exchange of views and information is not anonymous. In systems of electronic voting at least the authorization of voters is needed. This requires a relatively centralized system. In several online discussion forums, discussion rules and central moderation are created. Here we encounter the social rules of network exchange. See below in the section *Limits of Simultaneous and Equal Input*.

Datification and Big Data Analysis

Another software property of digital networks is the quantification it allows. Every phenomenon can be put into a quantified format so that it can be tabulated and analyzed. This transformation is called *datification* (Mayer-Schönberger & Cukier, 2013). It allows the tracing, quantifying, interpreting and predicting of people's behavior, among them citizens and voters. This can be done by screening online behavior or by filling in a database with known personal characteristics combined with online behavior. This is the fast-growing practice of digital and social media marketing in political or election campaigns. These practices are already old, using older media such as the telephone, letters and e-mail. With the arrival of 'big data' – a method of advanced data analysis extracting value from existing data – digital marketing now provides politicians with powerful tools.

> They can target micro-groups of citizens for both votes and money and appeal to each of them with a meticulously honed message, one that no one else is likely to see. It might be a banner on Facebook or a fund-raising email.
>
> (O'Neil, 2017, p.188)

Big data analysis and micro-targeting of voters has become the most important campaign tool in American elections in the last 15 years. The actual effects on voting are not yet known but scholars are concerned about political messages becoming increasingly personalized. The effectiveness of strategies for finding and persuading voters can be tested and voting behavior can be manipulated in the desired direction.

In terms of democracy, this tool has mixed and controversial effects. On the one hand, it helps politicians and citizen representatives to obtain detailed information about the needs and views of citizens or voters that could be used to meet these needs and take these views into consideration. On the other hand, the balance of power is shifting from citizens to the parties, politicians or representatives using these technologies. Particular citizens receive a greater number or different messages of election marketing than others. For example, citizens in American so-called 'swing states' get more messages and people known as Democratic or Republican get different messages. This means that informing and addressing citizens is not a public and equal approach but a commercial approach known from business marketing that targets only solvent consumers. The result of micro-targeting voters might also be an enhancement of already existing differences and more polarization in the political arena. However, we have to keep in mind that these concerns have been raised about previously introduced new political marketing techniques too.

Another problem is that premature decisions are made on the basis of big data analysis lumping people into particular categories too quickly. Big data analysis means using *more* (superfluous), *messy* (not exact) and *good enough* (only correlations) data that still could be effective (Mayer-Schönberger & Cukier, 2013). However, the results can also be superficial and simply wrong. For example, the American Democrats were not only convinced about the victory of Hillary Clinton over Donald Trump because they believed the opinion polls, but also because they thought they had a superior digital marketing campaign based on big data analysis. In fact, they had completely missed the undercurrent of the sentiment of voters in most swing states they tried to micro-target.

Programmability of Algorithms and the Power of 'Googlearchy'

Micro-targeting is not the only method that limits the information sources and views that all voters or citizens actually see. The link structure of the Web is another way. Many suggest that innumerable sites, among them political sites, are accessible to all users. The Internet is supposed to be a narrowcasting medium offering content for every imaginable preference. In this way, it is assumed that the network removes the gatekeepers controlling entry to the traditional mass media. This is supposed to give a voice to all users, marginalized or resource-poor groups included.

Practice does not meet these expectations. The number of senders and receivers and their messages and clicks on a network such as the Internet is so big that they just have to be managed by platforms. And these are programmed by software algorithms automatically processing all sources, messages, interactions, transactions, links, and likes. These also are network properties because they are essential tools for managing network traffic. Without these programs and their algorithms the Internet would be unworkable.

Unfortunately, these traffic controllers are certainly not neutral technical regulators. Their algorithms are influenced by commercial motives. The big web platforms such as Google, Microsoft, Facebook, Twitter and other social media are American corporations with business models that inform the design of these platforms by installing particular algorithms in programs to manage search engines, social networking sites with their profiles, likes, shares and in fact all user-generated content on the Internet. They steer all searches and contributions of users. They decide which political and other messages are fed into the timelines and search engine results of users. They manipulate them in order to reveal personal data and to be able to personalize advertisement. In this way, they direct user experiences, content and user relations (Beer, 2009). Of course, users are also programming their choices, searches and likes in these applications. The programs and their algorithms are constantly being adapted by evolving business models and user practices (van Dijck and Poell, 2013). However, users have to follow the rules of the programs of the platforms. The big problem is that these rules are proprietary and are protected as a business secret (Bucher, 2012; Ellison, Steinfield, & Lampe, 2011; van Dijck & Poell, 2013).

In terms of democracy this means that automatic decisions are made by programs following the rules of biased traffic controllers. They are the new gatekeepers of the network. Google's algorithms decide which source is listed and at what rank. Facebook's algorithms weigh the factors to determine whether a post is qualified to go to one's New Feeds or Timeline and they filter criminal and other unwanted messages automatically by scanning postings and chats. When these platforms are used to support democratic communication, votes and decisions, the rules are biased. It is even worse: those using them do not know the rules because they are secret. When they ask Google, Facebook or another platform supplier for an explanation, they are given an inconclusive answer full of technical details that only particular programmers partly understand.

The most known example of programmability of algorithms is the working of the Google search engine. The biased rules of this search engine has led to the term 'Googlearchy' expressing the power of Google on the Internet because it is the most popular search engine. In fact, other commercial engines have similar rules. This term refers to the rule of the most heavily linked. This rule affects both the reception and the creation of political communication on the Web. The link structure between sites is one of the most important network properties. Partly, it obeys strong statistical regularities. It is created by software of Google and other search engines designed to rank pages among the billions that are available. The most familiar software algorithm Google and others use is PageRank. This puts sites that receive lots of links from other sites at the top of the search results listing. In this way it strengthens the advance of these sites even more. Another algorithm for ranking is HITS, which uses this reinforcing structure of links at the top of the search results listing, primarily linking to the authorities such as universities, governments and long-established political parties. This also gives Google and other engines the opportunity to list commercial hits at the top of the search results listing, and in general to bring interests that pay higher up the list. In this way, the statistical procedure is biased by commercial and powerful interests.

There is no escape from these page-ranking effects when the statistical procedure is used. Only biased ranking can be removed. The basic reason is that the Internet simply is too big. Nobody is able to find and view all the information it contains alone. The inability of political information seekers on the Internet to cover all information has three basic causes. First, as a natural fact human information-seekers are unable to cognitively process the vastness of information and they need search engines and other instruments. Second, most people lack the skills to use them properly. Research indicates that users rarely look past the first page. In a 2006 study (Pass, Chowdhury, & Torgeson, 2006) observed that 90% of total clicks went to the first page and 74% to the top five search results, while the top result received 42% of all clicks. With the improvement in search engines, users are viewing even fewer hits (Jansen & Spink, 2006).

The third cause of the inability of political information seekers to find all relevant information is the preferential attachment of users. As in every network, members prefer to share links from the most popular group or network member, in this way increasing its popularity. In choosing between political information and communication sites, people tend to choose the big and familiar ones, just like television viewers have their favorite channels. Researchers have demonstrated that the biggest proportion of political information retrieval focuses on a handful of sites. For example, Hindman (2008) has tried to estimate the portions of the Internet an average user is most likely to see while searching for political information. He classified three million pages with a particular automatic program starting the selection process with 12 lists of 200 highly ranked American 'seed sites' of a variety of political categories. These were abortion, the death penalty, gun control, the U.S Presidency, U.S. Congress and general politics. He discovered a startling concentration of attention on a handful of very successful sites. The most successful sites appeared to receive between 14% and 54% of the total links pointing to a single source of information (Hindman, 2008, pp. 47–54). In the 12 lists of high-ranked American 'political sites', nine lists revealed a top ten that accounted for more than half of the total links.

The Power Law and Concentration

This concentration on particular sites when seeking information is a general pattern on the Internet (see Huberman, 2001). Advocates of the Internet as a medium for news and political communication have often claimed that Internet use is more equally distributed, with the effect of being more democratic because far more sites or channels are available and freely accessible than on television, radio or the press. Many observers even fear that the Internet leads to fragmentation of news consumption and political communication, producing in-crowds of citizens only interested in their own social and political views and cultures. In fact, both concentration and fragmentation occur. In practice, Internet use for news and political communication is more concentrated than in the traditional mass media. Hindman (2008, pp. 90–101) formulated an inventory of online and offline media audience shares using US Internet traffic data of 2006. Surprisingly, he found that the concentration of audience share is higher in online media as compared to traditional media such as broadcasting and newspapers.

How can such a combination of concentration and fragmentation be explained? Again, a particular network property or effect is responsible. It is the so-called power law in networks. This is a statistical regularity. In more common-sense language it is called the 'rich are getting richer and the poor are getting poorer effect' on the Internet. Sometimes this is also called the 'Matthew effect', referring to a similar sounding gospel of Matthew. The statistical background is that the number of links and nodes (sites or users) on a computer network such as the Internet is not divided according to a normal distribution. This would mean that most nodes have an average number of links and that few have many links or a small number of links. Instead, we have a power law distribution. This is marked by many nodes with a few links and a few nodes with a very large number of links. 'They have the power'. This distribution has a so-called 'long tail'. The middle part of this distribution is much smaller than with a normal distribution. See Figure 2.2.

The basic reason for the appearance of a power law distribution on the Internet is that it has become too big, as has been claimed before. When networks grow, their nodes tend to cluster. It is impossible that everyone has

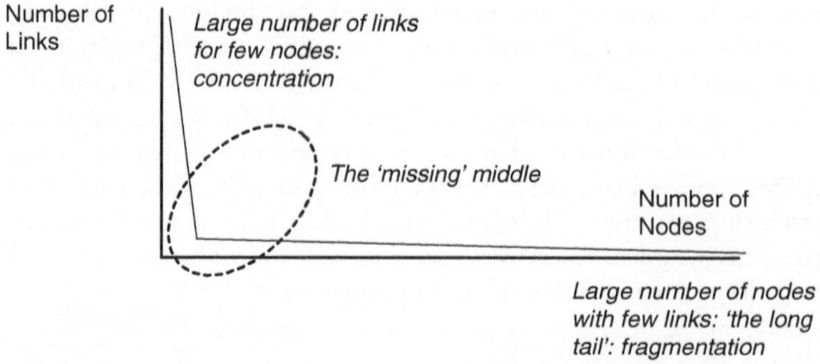

Figure 2.2 A power law distribution with number of links and nodes in a network.

a link to any other node in a large network. Clusters at a local scale link with others and create bigger clusters on a global scale. These clusters are called *small worlds* that might be linked to other small worlds, in this way creating a global world. This enables the concentration process we are discussing here. Humans realize this process, perhaps unwillingly, by making more or less free choices. First, the global network gives them more opportunities than they had before in their local world with a limited number of media and people to reach. Subsequently, they have to choose among the apparently endless possibilities. Some will make a choice by chance, browsing freely on the Internet. However, most people will link to the sites and people they know and are likely to come back too (e.g. by creating Favorites lists). This is called preferential attachment. This phenomenon can be influenced by advertisement and attractive brand names, by being accessible and easy to use, and of course by offering more information, service and other things that attract people. The crucial fact is that the bigger the attention the site attracts, the more resources it gathers to be competitive in these offerings. Finally, we have the collective phenomenon of crowd behavior. People tend to follow each other when making choices. Crowd behavior is also an important characteristic of network processes.

The choice of political websites on the Internet also is based on a relatively small number of nodes. While the choice may seem endless, in fact users are directed to a small number of choices. So, the problem of fragmentation of political communication and information on the Web might be smaller than the problem of concentration, in practice limiting pluralism and choice. This peculiar paradox can only be explained by the power law network property. Those already in power are getting ever more powerful.

The argument of concentration and less choice in practice is countered by the distribution theory of the 'long tail' first put forward by Anderson (2006). He claims that all choices can be made on the Internet because every imaginable product and idea is available there. This even goes for old products and ideas that are no longer available on regular markets. The long tail is portrayed on the right-hand-side of Figure 2.2.

In political communication, the theory of the long tail has led to claims that a vast number of small information producers and opinion givers together produce a mass of input that contributes to public life and to democratic politics (Benkler, 2006; Sunstein, 2008). This focus on small content producers is partly justified. Taken together, they do receive more of the total audience online than in traditional media (Hindman, 2008, p. 134). However, their contribution is fragmented. And they rarely aggregate or cluster to create larger, moderately read websites or blogs.

The trickling upwards of small political content producers to create bigger ones is a claim made by some observers who assert that, for instance, elite bloggers aggregate small contributions into a representative whole with a big influence on online public opinion (e.g. Benkler, 2006, p. 242). Hindman (2008) has shown that such intermediaries are rare and that it is striking that the middle ground is missing. There is a bifurcation between many small political information producers and a few large producers. Metaphorically speaking, we have a big head, a small body and a long tail. Figuratively, this small body is shown in the narrow space in the left-hand corner of the power law distribution picture in Figure 2.2.

Properties of Network Content and Democracy

User-Generated Content and the Limits of Attention

The content that can be sent and received in a medium partly depends on the properties of that medium. The main property of networks in this regard is that they enable (inter)active actors or users that do not only receive but also produce messages. The threshold for access and user input is considerably lower in the medium network of the Internet than in the traditional mass media. However, in the first 10 to 20 years of the Internet this property was scarcely realized. In that time there were only thousands of so-called peer-to- peer user groups. The Internet was primarily used as a broadcast medium because traditionally framed content was only transformed from print into electronic form. Even the advent of the World Wide Web with its hyperlinks did not substantially change the unidirectional nature of the medium. From the second half of the 1990s onwards, this started to change with new Internet applications for masses of users such as weblogs, audio-visual exchange sites, chat-boxes, social media and new forms of instant messaging such as Twitter (Web 2.0 and Web 3.0). The number of personal websites also expanded. In this way, the Internet transformed into an altogether different medium with user-generated content that started to compete with content published by established media and institutions.

The potential of user-generated content produced by average users has generated expectations of empowerment for citizens, giving a new voice to citizens who felt voiceless before. The power of elites in the established mass media and in politics to control the dissemination of information would be broken. The gatekeeping capacities of these vested interests would come to an end. These expectations show a strong dependence on the network property of interactivity and the potential of free selection because the threshold of input has become lower and because there is supposed to be access for all. The enabling property of the medium is turned into a defining property. It was assumed that users have been waiting for this opportunity but never had the chance to take advantage of it before. No attention was paid to the enabling capacities required: the motivation and the skills of users to take advantage of this opportunity.

A second and more basic problem with the overambitious interpretations of this network property is that it is not fully understood. One supposes that for every new voice there is an audience. This is a basic mistake. Suppose that every new voice on the Internet has the same time to read and to write. Then that new voice would on average find an audience of one. Fortunately, most Internet users take more time to read, listen and view than to write and to produce sounds and images. Moreover, it takes more time to produce than to consume messages on the Internet. So, the audience for a new voice is larger than one. However, it is still limited. As we intend to show, it is so much easier to speak than to be heard on the Internet. There are five basic limits to finding an audience on the Internet for new voices with user-generated political content (Hindman, 2008, pp. 131–133):

1. Political communication is only a small proportion of Web usage.
2. The link structure of the Web limits the content that citizens actually see. This is the consequence of Googlearchy, which was discussed above. Online visibility for new political voices will be extremely low on average. The general patterns of Googlearchy may be even stronger in the political field. This field is fractionally organized into subcultures and media of political communication and attention. Users with political interest first turn to the sites that reflect their own political views to inform themselves and to give their own opinions (Hindman, 2008, p. 36).
3. Much search engine use is shallow. Chances are low that citizens will find the new voices of other citizens because they lack the skills to appropriately use search engines (see next chapter). Also, those who are politically interested usually are looking for a familiar site they know (navigational query) or they ask a very simple question (content query), paying attention to the first hits only. This means that most of the indexed political content is completely irrelevant for many people as it does not find an audience.
4. The vested political media control the vast majority of Internet content. On the Internet, traditional news organizations supply most of the political news and information. User-generated content, among others

in political weblogs, frequently copies, processes and reacts to online newspapers and journals and to offline broadcasting and the press in political affairs. It is costly and requires a high level of expertise for a user to generate their own new content that is sufficiently valuable and attractive to reach an audience of some proportion. The fact that entry barriers are diminished does not remove the demands for quality and expertise. Voices of a lower quality or those usually drawing less attention can only reach large audiences under exceptional circumstances. This is the case when a political weblog, for example, touches on a scoop or scandal with information never published before.

5. Social hierarchies also emerge in alternative or new voices of the citizenry. Frequently we hear claims that the Internet is shifting power away from political elites to the voices of the citizenry, for example, on successful political blogs. These claims forget to say that a small group of A-list bloggers actually gets more political blog attention than the rest of all small blogs combined (Hindman, 2008). They also ignore the fact that successful bloggers are all but ordinary citizens. These new Internet elites are no more representative of the general public than the old political and media elites. They are completely dominated by highly educated, elite or middle-class white males (see data in Hindman, 2008).

Limits of Simultaneous and Equal Input

A network property that is often praised and used by those advancing deliberative democracy on online discussion forums is the fact that in a network with a central exchange, an unlimited number of discussants can express their voice simultaneously. The exchange processes all input and lists the result in feedback to all discussants. This is a fundamental difference with physical meetings, where less people are able to participate and take a turn. Here, some discussion leadership has to be organized. Many assume that discussion leadership is less important on online forums. When the discussants cannot see each other, many people also assume that this removes status differences as all are feel free to contribute without the influence of status, gender, ethnic origin or whatever social attribute. Unfortunately, both assumptions are wrong.

A long tradition of so-called computer-mediated communication (CMC) observations and experiments since the 1970s has shown that on online forums more discussion leadership (moderation) is required than in physical meetings, not less (see Johansen, Vallee, & Spanger, 1979; Kiesler, Siegel, & McGuire, 1984 and summaries of this research in Thurlow, Lengel, & Tomic, 2004 and van Dijk, 2012). At least this is the case when one wants to prevent disruptions like flaming, scolding, insults or group polarization and when one wants to reach some agreement or any conclusion in online discussion. In most online discussions some moderation is required simply to achieve results. This limits the complete freedom assumed.

CMC research in the 1990s has also shown that status differences do not disappear in online discussions. Some theories even claim that these differences are emphasized in CMC conditions of isolation, deindividuation and physical distance (Postmes & Spears, 1998; Spears & Lea, 1992; Walther, 1996). In these conditions people keep looking for clues of the identity of other discussants online.

A related assumption is that simultaneous input online is able to produce collective intelligence of a higher order than the intelligence that can be achieved in physical groups with limited reach. This is the assumption of the so-called wise crowd. Evidence shows that online collective intelligence can be effective when it succeeds in mobilizing the ample body of knowledge that is available in society, also in political affairs (Sunstein, 2008). However, moderation and other discussion techniques have to be adopted to correct a large number of disadvantages in group dynamics, which will be discussed in Chapter 4.

All of these social and psychological effects increase the likelihood that the potential of the network property of simultaneous and equal input will not be realized. One has to take account of these social effects when one wants to benefit from this technical network property in supporting democracy.

Open and Closed Networking

The Internet is also hailed for its supposed open character. The idea is that this is a characteristic of the Internet in itself. If this were true, it would be a network property as well. This is a property of content as the assumption is that communication on the Internet is relatively open in democratic societies. People might also consider the choice between open and proprietary sources on the Internet, but this is a network property at the level of software.

Presently, the Internet primarily is a public medium although it is also used for private communication. As a medium for political communication, the Internet seems to be more open than the traditional mass media. News spreads easily, whether it is confirmed or not. Political gossip and scandals abound on the Internet.

For evident reasons, political communication is more open than other types of communication. Politicians have a public function and they have to inform citizens and convince voters to be successful. The Internet strengthened this characteristic. Networks can easily spread all kinds of information. However, there is no additional network property that makes this into a necessity. It remains a choice enabled by technology. In previous sections, we saw that network communication can also be closed by using particular properties of network hardware and software. This also goes for political communication. In many applications, the adoption of user names and passwords is on the rise. Confidential communication can still be protected by technical means. Encryption is amply used by top government officials when they exchange views and information. Disclosers in e-mail messages from these officials and other civil servants are more the rule than exception.

The American law professor Laurence Lessig (1999, 2001) has written two books that provide many examples of the importance of so-called *technical code* for the open and closed character of the Internet as a public medium. Most of this code is about network properties. Lessig demonstrates that the open characteristic of the Internet is far from safeguarded.

Conclusions

In this chapter we have tried to show that the Internet in itself is not more democratic than older mass media. As a network, it has a number of properties that are able to both support and reduce democracy. They are defining properties and are influential. However, they are no matters of natural necessity either. They are enabling or limiting conditions that serve as opportunities and risks. To be able to take advantage of the opportunities and to reduce the risks, one has to know these properties to develop realistic politics online. So, explanation was the function of this chapter. We hope it has served to qualify both utopian and dystopian views of digital democracy.

Note

1 The seven OSI (Open System Interconnection) layers are: 1. the physical layer, 2. the data link layer, 3. the network layer, 4. the transport layer, 5. the session layer, 6. the presentation layer and 7. the application layer. In Table 2.1 the Basis (hardware) is derived from layer 1 and 2, Code (software) is derived from 3, 4 and 5, while 6 and 7 are used for Content applications.

References

Anderson, C. (2006). *The long tail*. New York: Hyperion.

Arterton, C. F. (1987). *Teledemocracy: Can technology protect democracy?* Newbury Park, CA: Sage.

Beer, D. (2009). Power to the algorithm? Participatory web cultures and the technical unconsciousness. *New Media and Society*, *11*(6), 985–1002.

Benkler, Y. (2006). *The wealth of networks: How social production transforms markets and freedom*. New Haven, CT; London: Yale University Press.

Bruggeman, J. (2008). *Social networks: An introduction*. London; New York: Routledge.

Bucher, T. (2012). Want to be on the top? Algorithmic power and the threat of invisibility on Facebook. *New Media and Society*, *14*(7), 1164–1180.

Ellison, N. B., Steinfield C., & Lampe, C. (2011). Connection strategies: Social capital implications of Facebook-enabled communication practices. *New Media and Society*, *13*(6), 873–889.

Giddens, A. (1984). The constitution of society. Cambridge, UK: Polity Press.

Grewal, D. S. (2008). *Network power: The social dynamics of globalization*. New Haven, CT; London: Yale University Press.

Hindman, M. (2008). *The myth of digital democracy*. Princeton, NJ: Princeton University Press.

Huberman, B. (2001) *The laws of the web: Patterns in the ecology of information*. Cambridge, MA; London: The MIT Press.

Jansen, B., & Spink, A. (2006). How are we searching the World Wide Web? *Information Processing and Management, 42*, 248–263.

Johansen, R., Vallee, J., & Spanger, K. (1979). *Electronic meetings: Technical alternatives and social choices*. Reading, MA: Addison-Wesley.

Kiesler, S., Siegel, J., & McGuire, T. (1984). Social-psychological aspects of computer-mediated communication. *The American Psychologist, 39*(10), 96–123.

Krackhardt, D. (1990). Assessing the political landscape: Structure, cognition and power in organizations. *Administrative Science Quarterly, 35*, 342–369.

Lessig, L. (1999). *Code and other laws of cyberspace*. New York: Basic Books.

Lessig, L. (2001). *The future of ideas: The fate of the commons in a connected world*. New York: Vintage Books.

Markus, L. (1990). Toward a 'critical mass' theory of interactive media. In J. Fulk & C. Steinfield (Eds.), *Organizations and communication technology* (pp. 194–218). Newbury Park, CA: Sage.

Mayer-Schönberger, V., & Cukier, K. (2013). *Big data: A revolution that transforms how we work, live, and think*. Boston; New York: Houghton Mifflin Harcourt.

O'Neil, C. (2017). *Weapons of math destruction: How big data increases inequality and threatens democracy*. New York: Crown Publishing Group.

Parker, G. G., Van Alstyne, M. W., & Choudary, S. P. (2016). *Platform revolution: How networked markets are transforming the economy—and how to make them work for you*. New York; London: WW Norton & Company.

Pass, G, Chowdhury, A., & Torgeson, C. (2006). A picture of search. *InfoScale, 152*, 1.

Postmes, T., & Spears, R. (1998). *Breaching or building social boundaries? Side-effects of computer-mediated communication*. Paper presented at the annual conferences of the International Communication Association, Jerusalem, 20–24 July.

Spears, R., & Lea, M. (1992). Social influence and the influence of the "social" in computer-mediated communication. In M. Lea (Ed.), *Contexts of computer-mediated communication* (pp. 30–65). Hemel Hempstead: Harvester Wheatsheaf.

Sunstein, C. (2008). *Infotopia: How many minds produce knowledge*. Oxford, UK; New York: Oxford University Press.

Tapscott, D., & Williams, A. (2006). *Wikinomics: How mass collaboration changes everything*. New York; London: Portfolio/Penguin Books.

Thurlow, C., Lengel. L., & Tomic, A. (2004). *Computer-mediated communication: Social Interaction and the Internet*. London; Thousand Oaks, CA; New Delhi: Sage.

Tilly, C. (1998). *Durable inequality*. Berkeley, CA; Los Angeles; London: University of California Press.

van Dijk, J. (2012). *The network society* (3rd ed.). London; New Delhi; Thousand Oaks, CA; Singapore: Sage.

van Dijck, J. (2013). *The culture of connectivity: A critical history of social media*. New York: Oxford University Press.

van Dijck, J., & Poell, T. (2013). Understanding social media logic. *Media and Communication, 1*(1), 2–14.

Walther, J. (1996). Computer-mediated communication: Impersonal, interpersonal and hyperpersonal interaction. *Communication Research, 2*(1), 1–43.

Wellman, B., & Berkowitz, S. D. (Eds.). (1988). *Social structures: A network approach*. Greenwich, CT; London: Jai Press.

3 Political Participation and Inclusion

Introduction

Political participation is one of the key concepts in understanding democracy in a network society. Do networking and using digital media increase the opportunities of political participation? Media and communication scholars are completely focused on the role, most often positive, of digital media on participation and democracy. Their technology perspective is instrumentalism (see the Introduction of this book). They assume that the opportunities of digital media will lead to more participation and in this way more democracy. Some skeptical scholars expect that these opportunities will lead to less participation and democracy.

Political science scholars have a completely different focus. Strikingly, from their perspective media have a fairly small role in driving political participation, while in the communication perspective it has a much greater one. Political scientists talk about political interest, knowledge and trust of citizens in terms of the government and democracy and about the characteristics of political and electoral constitutions in explaining more or less political participation. For them, media, both digital and traditional, are secondary actors in the political play.

Here we will follow the *politics-media-politics cycle* as discussed in the Introduction. We will not start with the opportunities and uses of digital media in political participation. Instead, we want to begin with the political structures of systems and political actors. Then we will focus on political participation by using media as a particular behavior that have observable relationships to political circumstances or contexts. Finally, we will discuss the effects of participation on political systems and democracies. The argument is portrayed in Figure 3.1.

There are many forms of political participation. While some scholars attempt to distinguish the concepts of political and civic participation, engagement, involvement and inclusion, others use them interchangeably. We will try to differentiate them.

The theoretical perspectives, concepts, and their operationalization in variables are all over the map at this point in time. We seek to clarify some main observations in empirical studies and how they can be theoretically

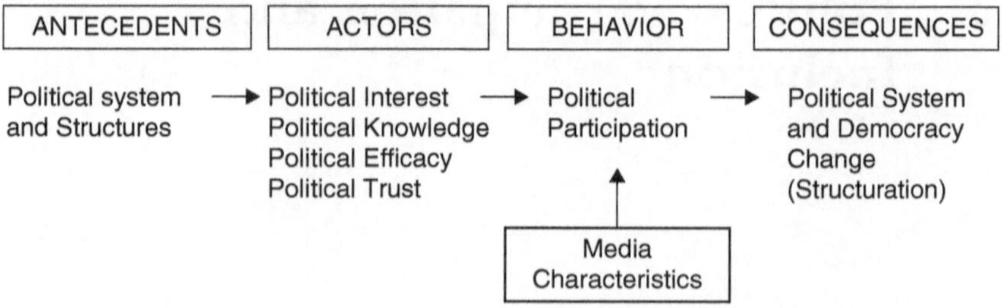

Figure 3.1 Participation with media and behavior structuring political systems.

explained. We note some attempts to organize knowledge in this area. Our own attempt is to suggest structuration and network theory as productive avenues for making sense of many levels of research in this domain.

In reviewing 20–25 years of studies on this subject, we have found no consensus on how Internet or digital media usage increases and changes political communication in relation to democracy. Moreover, we see little evidence of theoretical underpinnings or explanations for the empirical research conducted to date. We have found new affordances in the history of communication technology development and in relation to 'emerging media', but this is only to be expected as new technologies always bring about new possible activities. There appears to be a paucity of political theory in most accounts of what is most important about the role of digital media and networks in relation to citizen participation in political activities. Worse still, a popular assumption is that participation is automatically democratic.

The neglect of using political theory to establish precise goals of increasing political participation through the use of digital media has resulted in a disarray in empirical findings and conclusions regarding Internet usage and participation, engagement or democracy. This might mean that you reach conclusions about participation based on which author you have chosen to read. This, of course, is somewhat mitigated by the meta-analyses published in this area, such as those of Shelley Boulianne that we gratefully adopt in this chapter.

So, we begin this chapter by clarifying the terminology. The first is the distinction between *civic and political participation or engagement*. Civic engagement is something that provides the foundation for political participation or engagement (McDonald, 2008). Political engagement is more specific than civic engagement. It is possible to increase civic engagement without increasing political engagement. Some people are very active in building and supporting communities, usually in a local context, but they hate politics and do not even vote. We define civic participation as behavior that contributes to communities or society at large. Political participation is behavior that contributes to the governance of society and tries to affect opinion making and decision making by political representatives and governments. This includes both institutional politics such as elections and representations and non-institutional politics such as all kinds of collective action trying to influence governance. In this chapter, we also include and compare both online and offline political participation.

The second issue about terminology used is the difference between *participation, involvement and engagement*. We have no problem in interchanging these terms to the extent that they are political. For most authors they mean the same thing, and in the former paragraphs we also used them interchangeably. However, we insist on the definition of participation as behavior that can be objectively or empirically observed. We use the term *participation* with an objective flavor, talking about observable activities. The terms *involvement* and *engagement* have more a subjective feel or connotation. This is no problem except when researchers define these terms primarily as attitudes and intentions. Many surveys about political participation, engagement and involvement actually ask for attitudes, expectations and intentions and not for actual behavior in citizenship and political action. To determine whether the use of digital media and networks is likely to lead to political and democratic change, we need to establish first whether they lead to observable behavior we call participation. See the sequence of factors in Figure 3.1.

In the following section we will present a list of activities categorized under online and offline political participation. We can see which forms are more popular and what the differences are between comparable online and offline forms. Following this we will discuss the nature and levels of political participation. What is the nature of all these activities of participation? Which on the following list would you categorize as political participation?

a. wearing a campaign button
b. voting
c. liking or sharing a political message and candidate on Facebook
d. chatting with friends about politics
e. watching TV news?

Is so-called 'clicktivism' (such as liking, sharing and retweeting online posts) also a form of political participation? We will compare the forms in terms of levels of effort needed and their impact on governance. The nature of online and offline political participation is also marked by the type of activities in terms of communication and action. Traditional democracy was a practice of speaking, talking, physical action (peaceful or aggressive) and manual organization. Digital democracy seems to be a practice of typing and clicking on keyboards, uploading and downloading pictures or videos, and designing websites, web content, blogs, taking part in chats and programming software or apps. These practices are so different that they must have substantial effects or at least have effects that are not uniform across particular channels.

We will then turn to focus on individual and collective political participation. Most of the literature and research deals with individual participation, often in surveys. Most participation studies report usage patterns and usage attitudes at the individual level of analysis while most actual online participation is networked. The network perspective of this book calls us to pay attention to relational and collective characteristics of political participation. We will offer some specific models that integrate individual and collective forms or factors of political participation by actors and behavior displayed in the middle of the general model presented in Figure 3.1.

Then we will turn to the claims and achievements of online political participation research in the last 25 years. Following some meta-analyses of this research, we will discuss the achievements and pitfalls of this research. Does it show that digital media and the Internet have positive or negative effects on participation or engagement?

In the literature on online political participation two competing theses are dominant. We will compare the *reinforcement thesis*, which argues that digital media mainly work as tools to support people who are already politically interested and influential, with the *mobilization thesis* that claims that new or less formally active participants are entering the stage in online political activity. Most often, young people, low-educated persons and minorities are mentioned here.

The next section will discuss participation on social media. These media offer a new type of channel for political communication with both advantages and disadvantages for political participation. Here, two other opposing theses of digital media, in this case social media use, are discussed. The *habitual exposure thesis* argues that on social media people mainly follow news about views and discussion with other persons similar to themselves. The American presidential election of 2016 showed many signs of this behavioral pattern. The opposite *accidental exposure thesis* states that people encounter news, views and persons that they did not previously know, expect or look for. This might lead to more participation and a unifying trend of political communication because people cross their own boundaries.

In the penultimate section, one of the most important conditions of online political participation is analyzed. This is the problem of inclusion or exclusion. The digital divide, spanning from unequal physical access and different digital skills to usage of digital media, is a major problem for increasing participation for all citizens. Those without access and skills have no stake in online participation.

The last section is pivotal for the consequences of online political participation. Does this type of participation actually lead to political change and more or better democracy? This is the next question to address when research has given the assurance that digital media use leads to greater participation. Many researchers in this domain think that more online participation is equal to democratization and structural political change. There are two problems with this assumption. First, goals in online political participation can also be undemocratic. Second, online participation may have no effect on the political system of a nation.

Online and Offline Forms of Political Participation

In this book we adopt a broad conception of forms of political participation. In our view, they consist of both formal or institutional and informal or non-institutional political activities. And of course, we accept both online and offline political activities into our conception because we want to compare the nature and effects of these activities. According to a working definition by van Deth (2014, p. 351) political participation is an *activity* first of all. Second, it is done by people in their role as *citizens*. Third, it should be *voluntary* – so, obliged voting as enforced in some countries is not valid political participation, and finally, it *deals with government, politics or the state.*

Online political participation offers new opportunities for political participation of all types, which can be compared with the opportunities of traditional offline participation. Factors or attributes of digital media that facilitate participation include fast access to information and social interaction, low entry and transaction costs, and quick response times to most messages (Aichholzer & Allhutter, 2011).

In 2013 the American Pew Research Center surveyed the politically identifying online and offline political activities of Americans. We will use this survey to list and compare the most frequent online and offline political activities. See Table 3.1. This table is organized into columns of offline and online activities and into rows with individual activities that mainly use communication and collective activities that focus on political organization.

Table 3.1 shows that individual activities are practiced both offline and online. Discussion is still carried out more offline than online, although online discussion about political issues with others (such as by e-mail, text message, or on social networking sites) is the most frequent online political activity for 44% of Americans. However, only 5% of Americans say they have this discussion on a daily basis (Pew, 2013, p. 28). Commenting on online news or blogs is the second most frequent online political activity. Comments on media messages are most often done online rather than reacting to traditional media, presumably assisted by the low threshold to making online responses. The third most frequently used political activity is organizing petitions, which soon will overtake the traditional form of petitioning.

Collective and organizational political activities are still carried out more frequently offline than online. Voting in all countries of the world is done much more traditionally via the ballot box than electronically. At the time of writing, only Estonia had nationwide experience of e-voting since 2007. Other countries sometimes give only expats the opportunity to vote online. Basic problems of unequal access, security, difficulty of procedures and

Table 3.1 List of the most important political activities online and offline.

Individual and communication activities	
Offline	*Online*
Send a letter to a newspaper, magazine or broadcaster on political issue (3%)	Send e-mail or post to online newspaper, magazine, broadcaster or SNS on political issue (4%)
Call into a live radio or TV show or send a letter to express an opinion on a social or political issue (7%)	Comment or offer opinion on online news story or blog post about a political issue (18%)
Discuss political or publica affairs offline, in person, by phone or by letter (78%)	Discuss political or public affairs online, by e-mail, by text message, by SNS or on an online forum (44%)
Contact a politician or government official in person, by phone or letter (21%)	Contact a politician or government official by e-mail or text message (18%)
Endorse a political issue or candidate by mail or word of mouth (–)	Like or share a political message or candidate on SNS (23%)
Sign a political paper petition (22%)	Sign a political online petition (17%)
Collective and organizational activities	
Offline	*Online*
Donate money to political causes by cash or check (60%)	Donate money to political causes online (23%)
Attend a political rally, show or listen to a speech at a meeting (10%)	View a live political rally, show or speech on a website (–)
Attend an organized protest on the street or other public place (6%)	View an organized protest online: following & streaming online acts (–)
Work or volunteer for a political organization or candidate (7%)	Work or volunteer for an online political organization (12%)
Traditional voting in elections and referenda	E-voting in elections and referenda

(%: Percentage of American adults in 2012; Source: Pew Research Center, 2013)

infringement by housemates of individual voting at home are preventing e-voting from being implemented.

In 2016 about one-third of American social media users reported in a survey that they were exhausted by the amount of political content they encounter (Duggan & Smith, 2016). There is an interesting variation in the connections with other users on different types of social media. For example, 66% of Facebook users say that they are mainly following people they already know while 48% of Twitter users are most likely to follow people they do not know personally (Duggan & Smith, 2016).

However, only one-third of American social media users say that they often (9%) or sometimes (23%) are involved in commenting on or discussing politics in their online networks. About 70% of these users express low interest in such activity (Duggan & Smith, 2016). Less than 10% of users on Facebook and Twitter report that they post a great number of political messages themselves – 6% for Facebook and 8% for Twitter (Duggan & Smith, 2016).

Donating money to political causes is still done more frequently via traditional means than online, even in in the United States. The online medium provides more opportunities for many people to donate small amounts, as was observed in the presidential campaigns of Obama in 2008 and 2012: 45% of individual contributors in 2008 donated less than $200 and in 2012 this figure rose to 67% (Bimber, 2014).

Another online opportunity is finding more volunteers for political organizations. Here, again, the threshold is lower compared to offline volunteering. Moreover, online people can serve all kinds of political organizations alongside to traditional parties. Finally, the most important observation is that rallies, other meetings and organized protests are increasingly combined with online activity. Currently, face-to-face meetings and demonstrations are prepared, guided and evaluated online and supported by video, web-screens and mobile phones.

The Nature and Level of Political Participation

With the use of digital media and networking, the nature of political participation has changed. The most important change is the transition from offline to online participation. Table 3.1 clearly shows that similar activities are moving from offline to online contexts. As argued earlier in the chapter, the practices of speaking, talking, physical action and manual organization have changed into practices of typing and clicking on keyboards, uploading and downloading texts, pictures or videos, and designing websites, web content and apps. This offers a number of opportunities: fast access to information and social interaction, low entry and transaction costs, and quick response times. There are more opportunities for participation for people who are not traditionally involved in political participation, provided that these people have Internet access and sufficient digital skills.

However, these opportunities are also evaluated as being 'too easy' by some commentators. They are talking about 'clicktivism', simply clicking like, share and reply/retweet buttons (Koc-Michalska, Lilleker, & Vedel, 2016). Or they use the term 'slacktivism' (Morozov, 2013): actions on the Web for a particular social or political cause that need little physical effort and have little practical effect (a 'slacker' is someone who does not work hard). These two words imply that forms of political participation can be rated in terms of levels of *effort* and *effectiveness*. These ratings are both normative and factual. A norm is that a citizen has to make an effort that at least requires some physical act such as going to the ballot box. A factual rating can try to evaluate the effectiveness of participatory acts for the political system and democracy. However, effectiveness depends on the view of democracy the evaluator takes: is democracy primarily opinion making or decision making? For the first view, participation in forums and discussions is the most frequent activity in a democracy; for the second, it is voting.

In our view, so-called clicktivism and slacktivism are valid types of participation, however low they might be rated in traditional terms of effort. They are a natural part of the contemporary move from offline to online participation. The effectiveness of these types of political participation will be evaluated at the end of this chapter, when we discuss the effects of political participation on changes in political systems and democracies.

Levels of political participation can also conceived from a micro, meso and macro perspective. Micro-level effects include participation with cognitive effect, learning, attitudes or behavior at the level of individuals using the Internet for political activity. Meso-level effects concern participation in social networking, socio-cognitive change, and group effects in political discussions and actions. Macro-level changes involve participation in large media or news systems, in systems of political communication which involve institutions and organizations and the political system at large. All of these levels are part of political participation in a broad view. Such a view assumes that participants have significant motivation, skills and efficacy to expend effort on political communication. Efficacy is critical since research shows that there are highly educated and skilled citizens who become cynical and stop participating because they no longer believe that their contributions or participation matters.

Individual and Collective Participation

Thus far, we have looked at individual participation. This is common but is inadequate for describing or explaining political participation, much of which is collective action. Political mobilization usually involves a small percentage of a population but can have large-scale effects (Klandermans & Stekelenburg, 2013). Collective action is taken by citizens who have incentives for such participation. Few people are activists, in part, because many believe the goals will be accomplished by other citizens more likely to participate (Klandermans & Stekelenburg, 2013).

There are different forms of political participation. A discussion about participation must begin with the recognition that there are forms of participation at two fundamental levels: the individual and the collective. Additionally, the two levels can operate separately or together. Thus, when questions are asked about how digital media usage affects political participation, it is necessary to ask what type of participation is of concern. Individual-level participation includes activities such as making donations, signing petitions, voting, and wearing badges. Collective participation includes demonstrating, attending meetings, and forming groups with political goals (Aichholzer & Allhutter, 2011). Assess also the activities in Table 3.1.

Reviewing the literature on digital media and democracy reveals more about individual-level behaviors than collective and large-scale effects on democracy. In fact, online political communication or participation involves lots of relationships and interaction. This is the place where networking comes in. Campbell (2013) argues that individual-level correlates do a good job of predicting *who* participates but not *why* and *how* it works. "Incorporating social networks deepens our understanding of the factors that lead people to express voice in the democratic process" (Campbell, 2013, p. 33). He shows that the perspective of social networks sheds new light on those individual factors assumed to be explaining political participation such as education, religious attendance, political knowledge and political conviction. For example, social networking creates status and social sorting among people with different levels of education in participation processes and relations. Individual educational attainment on its own does not explain why political participation after the Second World War has not increased in developed and developing countries while the education levels of populations have dramatically improved. Another example is political knowledge that is not only individually acquired but is also acquired together with people with whom we interact.

Social networks in the digital era are strongly supported by computer networking or Internet use. The most important background factors of political participation, political interest, knowledge and efficacy are strongly related to network activities on the Internet (see below). This means that the dominant practice of survey research to examine individual characteristics of political participation in cross-sections of time has to be extended by research on networking followed by longitudinal research. See the model presented in Figure 3.2.

The boxes of Figure 3.2 are completions of the middle boxes of Figure 3.1. The core is a process of networking. The big question is whether the input of factors assumed to be explaining political action at Time 1 will lead to changes of these same factors producing political participation at Time 2 after a process of political Internet use.

The focus of this process of networking is observable political Internet use. This is not only caused by the demographic and political characteristics to the left of the figure, but also by technological factors emphasized in this book: network properties (see Chapter 2) and network access and skills (see a section at the end of this chapter).

Demographics such as age, gender, educational level, ethnicity, and social class also need to be investigated, as has been done by nearly all investigations. Most often, people with a high level of education (and income), middle or older age, males and majority ethnic members of a society are shown to have more political participation than their counterparts. The same occurs in online political participation, with the exception of young people who favor this type of political participation more strongly than older people.

Political interest is the main independent political factor that can best predict political action, both online and offline. When correlations between digital media use and political participation or engagement are assumed in

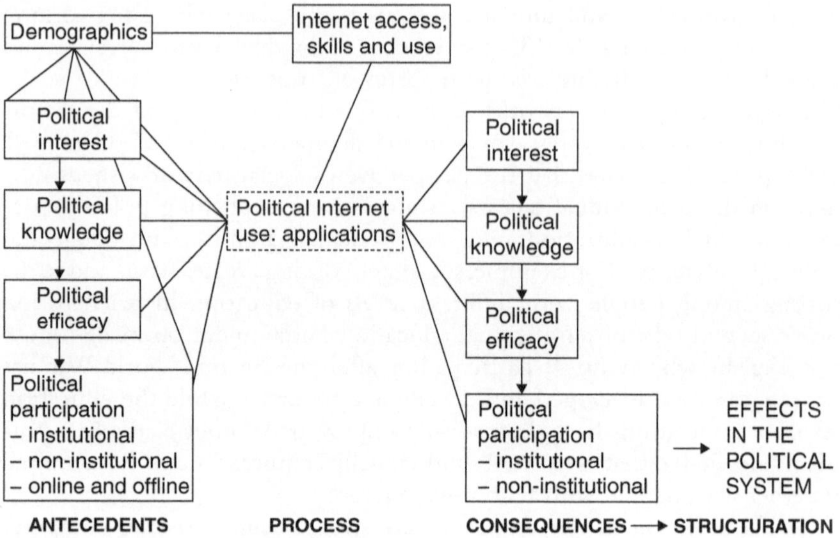

Figure 3.2 Longitudinal model of individual and collective input and output of political Internet use.

survey analysis, most often they decline significantly when controlling for political interest.

While *political knowledge* is necessary for informed participation in a democratic political system, Delli Carpini and Keeter (1996) and Delli Carpini (2000a) note that there are two major competing models concerning Internet usage and political knowledge. In the first model, knowledge increases with Internet usage while the second model assumes insignificant changes to take place.

Internal *political efficacy* concerns believing that you have the ability for political participation that can make a difference, and external political efficacy is the belief that the political system will be responsive to your input (Delli Carpini, 2004). External efficacy is believing that once your voice is heard, meaningful changes will occur. Efficacy and participation are correlated. In accounting for efficacy, you have to realize that citizens do not want to participate only as an activity, but rather as an action that can accomplish political goals.

Claims and Caveats of Political Participation Research

The main claim of political research in terms of digital media use and networking is that they have a significant effect on political engagement, involvement or participation. Most often the claims are that positive effects have been found. Only a few scholars think they have found negative effects, inspired by among others the work of Robert Putnam (1995, 2000), arguing that television and the Internet are more stimulating entertainment and that people prefer to relax at home than take part in civic or political engagement and social capital in the community. Searching for both positive and negative effects, many researchers show an instrumental view of technology (see Introduction) combined with either positive or negative estimations of their effects for society.

The first and principal caveat of these claims is that they are too general. The conclusion that the use of digital media and networking has positive or negative effects on political participation cannot be drawn for three reasons listed by Anduiza et al. (2012, p. 7). First, digital media use in the political system and participation has become common. Both politicians and citizens are increasingly using digital media. For young people, using such media has become natural and they cannot imagine a world, including politics, without this technology. So, currently it is impossible to validly compare a society or politics with and without digital media. We can only compare online and offline participation in a digitized network society. Second, digital media such as the Internet are continually changing. Social media emerged only ten years ago, while beforehand it was websites, online forums and blogs that were discussed everywhere. New claims about the political effects of social media are currently being made while the social media landscape is changing quickly. Third, the context of every political system is different and continually changing in every country. Particular political, constitutional and electoral systems offer different digital channels and applications for political communication.

In assessing research about the relationship between Internet use and political participation or engagement in the last 20 years, another three caveats emerge that are supported by two meta-analyses by Boulianne (2009, 2015). The first meta-analysis comprises 38 American studies about Internet use and civic or political engagement between 1995 and 2005; the second focused on 36 international studies about social media use and participation in civic and political life in the last ten years, mostly after 2008. Bouilianne's first caveat is that when studies predicting engagement by Internet use *control for political interest* – many studies do not – they tend to find that that the effect of Internet use is not statistically significant.

> Only 35% of studies that control for political interest report statistically significant effects. These studies that control for political interest are more likely to report positive effects. However, this pattern might be attributed to tendencies to use online news as a measure of Internet use in these studies
>
> (Boulianne, 2009, p. 202)

Traditionally, Internet use in general, and especially the use of online news, are mostly associated with people with high level of education and political interest.

The second caveat is that research tends to treat Internet use as a predictor of political engagement. However, the reverse association, perhaps as a reciprocal effect, running from political engagement to Internet use, for example looking for political news online, is also found in five studies analyzed (Boulianne, 2009, p. 203). This means that the suggested *causality* is in fact spurious. Issues of causality are most often glossed over while correlations, findings and generalizations about small effects are treated as evidence of large political change, such as more civic and political engagement. Boulianne (2009, 2015, p. 534) observes that nearly all studies are cross-sectional surveys. Few studies employ panel data and none of the studies employ an experimental design, which would help to establish causality.

The third caveat is that many studies use Web surveys in which everybody is using the Internet. Additionally, 8 of the 38 studies use data from self-selected samples of respondents, often American students. Boulianne (2009, p. 205) concludes that the "meta-analysis suggests that the effects of Internet use on engagement are positive" – only 14% of the studies show negative effects – "but does not establish that these effects are substantial". All effects are small (from p = .04 to .13).

We want to add that almost every study concentrates on attitudes and not on behavior. This is the column in the left-hand side of Figure 3.2 above political participation. The middle part of the figure showing Internet use and networking is scarcely and poorly measured, only producing partial measures of Internet and social media use. Measuring actual behavior, such as political activities producing system effects in the right-hand side of the figure, is even more unusual. Our concern is that some scholars neglect the difference between measuring attitudes or beliefs about action and actual action.

The Mobilization and Reinforcement Theses

Some researchers argue that the Internet can draw new participants to political engagement by lowering the barriers to participation and facilitating communication among citizens and between citizens and elected officials (Koc-Michalska et al., 2016, p. 1808). When Internet users come across interesting material they will seek more information, become more political knowledgeable and perhaps engage in political discussions and activism (Barber, 2003; Castells, 2009; Chadwick, 2006; Chadwick, 2013; Delli Carpini, 2000b; Gil de Zúñiga, Veenstra, Vraga, & Shah, 2010; Koc-Michalska et al., 2014; Kriesi, 2008; Krueger, 2002; Jennings & Zeitner, 2003; Anduiza et al., 2012; Wang 2009; Xenos and Moy, 2007). They can also achieve greater certainty in their voting choice (Vedel & Koc-Mischalska, 2009). This mobilization process is mainly observed among young people (Jensen et al., 2012). This impressive list of authors supporting this thesis cannot deny that when the data is controlled (showing relatively weak mobilization effects) for interest for politics and for offline political activities, the effect largely disappears. Jorba and Bimber (2012, p. 23) conclude that:

> [A]fter controlling for those effects, a small but robust effect in the direction from Internet use to participation remains. More politically interested citizens are more likely to use digital media, and they benefit from its use with even more participation. Internet use appears to intensify the salience of interest for political participation.

Following this conclusion we move on to the competing reinforcement thesis. This states that the use of digital media and networking activates those citizens already predisposed to or interested in politics, and who have greater access to and skills in using these media. The argument of the mobilization thesis that the Internet and other digital media reduce the effort needed to find political information for people without political interest is now used to argue that it supports those who are politically interested even more. The new opportunities of information, discussion and action on digital media and networking are especially attractive to those people who are interested, knowledgeable, and already engaged in the political process (Boulianne, 2009, p. 194). The reinforcement thesis is backed by a similar impressive list of authors (Bimber, 1999, 2003; Bonfadelli, 2002; Boulianne, 2011; Brundidge & Rice, 2009; DiMaggio, Hargittai, & Shafer, 2004; Jensen, 2006; Krueger, 2002; Norris, 2001, 2003; van Deursen, Helsper, Eynon, & van Dijk, 2017; van Dijk, 2005).

The core of the reinforcement thesis is the impact of two main background factors: differences in political interest and in access, skills and use of digital media. The latter factor will be discussed below. Theoretical support for the thesis can be found in network theory, especially two so-called laws of the Web: the power law and the law of trend amplification (van Dijk, 2012). See Chapter 2.

Social Media and Political Participation

Before discussing the effect of social media use on political participation, we want to list the advantages and disadvantages of using social media for political action. We found four advantages and five disadvantages in the literature. Of course, the evaluation is related to the view of democracy of those listing features positively or negatively.

The first advantage of social media in politics is that a *new channel is offered* for finding and reading political news, discussion and organization (Howard & Parks, 2012). At the time of writing, more than half of social media users in most developed countries use social media as one of the most important sources for reading the news (see Pew, 2016 for the U.S.). The most popular news is entertainment news, but political news is also popular, and is the fourth most popular type of news in the US (Pew, 2014). In comparison to the news in traditional media, social media users can directly like, share and react to this news. Sharing the news on social networks makes the news more trustworthy and persuasive for the receiver as the news is shared with commentary by friends or other personal contacts and perhaps followed by a call for action. In using social networking for news, an accessible and easy method of participation is offered by means of sending posts, (re)tweets, likes and other reactions by all parts of the population, including people with a low level of education and few writing skills. In this way, voices are entering the political debate that previously were not often heard in the traditional media.

A second advantage of social media for participation is that they can serve as a *direct intermediary* between citizens, representatives and politicians. In this way, these actors are able to bypass the traditional mass media with their gatekeeping role for news and public communication. The potential interaction between politicians and citizens that social media offer could support the political participation of citizens. It is also attractive for politicians with a weak or broiled relation with the traditional media and their gatekeeping journalists. Donald Trump primarily used Twitter as a direct channel to reach his audience in the presidential campaign of 2016. After his name, character, image and statements were made big by the traditional media, he shifted to social media when many of the newspapers and broadcast channels did not endorse his candidacy. As president-elect, his first press conference was a YouTube video. Afterwards, the 'Twitter President' continued to address the people and to respond to the mass media directly via Twitter, Facebook and Snapchat.

A very strong characteristic of social media is their *mobilization power*, as has been shown in many demonstrations, rallies and events in the last ten years (Youmans & York, 2012). Both strong or weak ties of interpersonal communication and mass communication via Facebook pages or Twitter messages can be activated via these media very quickly, even creating a flash(mob). Trump always used Twitter to mobilize people to go the crowded rallies where he spoke.

A final advantage of social media for political participation to be listed here is their role as *campaign organizational tools.* With their growing popularity, social media have become the smarter (targeted) and cheaper alternative to traditional media advertising (Hwang, 2016). Barack Obama explored their role in his campaigns of 2008 and 2012 (Bimber, 2014). Social media were also used to recruit and organize old and new volunteers for the campaign to be used for both online and offline activities. The third purpose was to raise new donations for small amounts to a level not seen before, although the familiar big donations of the business world and the Democratic party still accounted for the majority of donations (Bimber, 2014; Karpf, 2013).

The first disadvantage of social media for political participation is that people can be persuaded, activated and mobilized on false grounds. While truth telling has always been questionable in politics, on the current social media truth is even more problematic. The social media providers *do not edit* the messages created and shared. They only filter for content that is not permissible according to the law or prevailing norms. In this way, the difference between fact and opinion or fact and fiction vanishes. This might be a general trend in contemporary mass media, but social media are especially vulnerable to this. In the year 2016, *post-truth* was announced as the word of the year by the *Oxford English Dictionary*. The term means that objective facts have less impact on public opinion than emotions, norms, estimations and personal considerations. In the 2016 presidential campaign in the U.S., the term *fake news* made the headlines. In pro-Trump news messages in particular, a large portion was evidently false information, such as the Pope endorsing Trump. Fake news was fed to the pages and timelines of his followers because in this way both American and foreign websites obtained a part of the advertisement revenue for Facebook or another provider. One of the consequences is that currently only 3% of Americans have high trust, and 31% some trust, in social media as a source of information (Rainie, 2017).

After the public commotion following the fake news about Trump and Clinton, Facebook reluctantly accepted some editorial responsibility and implemented three measures. First, users were allowed to report fake news messages. Then Facebook offered two options to deal with these messages in 2017. The first was to develop new filter software with its own (secret) algorithms as a fact-checker. This could be used for simple spam and for messages only created to earn advertising money. The second was to ask a number of neutral news agencies and universities to become fact-checkers. This could be used for fake news or troll actions with social and political motives. When all these agencies called the message fake, it would be removed.

A second cause of unreliable news or social media interaction in general is the *manipulation* of message exchange by robots such as Twitterbots. These robots are social media accounts that automate interaction with human users. According to research by the University of Oxford on the evening of the third Presidential Debate in October 2016, Twitter traffic on pro-Trump hashtags was roughly double that of the pro-Clinton hashtags. However, about one-third of the pro-Trump Tweets were written by these robots, compared to one-fifth of the pro-Clinton Tweets (Kollanyi, 2016). We already knew of the practice of simply buying a vast number of followers and likes on social media. The automatization of micro-blogs and posts sends the manipulation of social media exchange to an even higher level. This will certainly harm the trust of many citizens in social media for citizen or voter participation.

The potential for manipulation and disinformation by social media messages allows political powers, such as foreign states, to interfere in national elections. During and after the Clinton and Trump presidential contest it became increasingly evident that Russian hackers linked to the Kremlin were interfering in this election by releasing private e-mails of the candidates and fabricating false social media messages addressing millions of American voters. After the elections an official Congressional investigation was launched. Interference in elections by hackers with false messages and other disinformation will harm democracy in every view and decrease voters' trust in fair elections.

Another cause for losing trust in social media for political participation is when providers themselves ignore their claim to not be editors. Most social media users think that these providers are a neutral go-between of their messages. However, in the American elections of 2010 and 2012, Facebook sprinkled people's news feeds with 'I voted' updates. In this experiment of manipulation, more than 60 million American voters were encouraged to vote via their Facebook friends. According to a Facebook internal investigation, in one of these elections turnout increased by 340,000 people (O'Neil, 2016). Social media providers are certainly not neutral go-betweens (see Chapter 2).

In fact, social media are a combination of so-called Web 2.0 and Web 3.0 (see Figure 3.3). They are mass communication and social network communication. In the first phase of the evolution of the Internet, it only contained electronic files edited by senders for receivers. After the advent of the World Wide Web, editors became suppliers and users were able to give feedback with content created themselves in Web 2.0. With the arrival of social media, users became networkers in the social and semantic Web 3.0. Suppliers pretended to be neutral providers for social networking and content creation. This is the role that social media providers such as Facebook want to serve, realizing their business model of advertisement revenue. However, social media also offer mass communication, for example news organizations having social media pages and users reacting to them after a provider has put messages in a timeline. This means that social media providers are co-responsible for the editing work of both news suppliers and the feedback of users.

A third characteristic of social media use that has both positive and negative effects for political participation is the *personal and emotional style* of

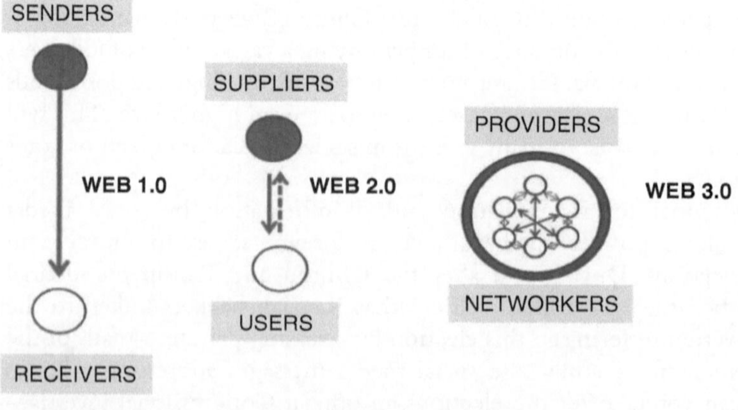

Figure 3.3 Social media as a combination of Web 2.0 and Web 3.0.

expression and debate. Social media are interpersonal channels. This has the advantage of bringing politics to the people in everyday language and meaning because public or political communication reaches a private tenor everybody understands (Highfield, 2016). With this characteristic social media enhance the epochal trends of personalization of politics, the growing importance of imagery and personality for politicians, the rise of a politics of scandals and a type of democracy which has been called emotional, drama or entertainment democracy. The disadvantage is, however, that the classical view or norm of political communication as a rational practice for either decision making or opinion making is weakened. In particular, the deliberation view of democracy based on rational debate in a free, equal and reasoned public space becomes less realistic.

One of the results of this emotional and personal style on social media is that all kinds of emotions are driving the conversation, including scolding, jeering and other abusive behavior. Participants rejecting these types of conversation will escape these discussion outlets. It adds to the commonly held view that politics is a filthy affair inhabited by people you cannot trust.

Another result of using a technology that was invented for another purpose (personal and social networking) for public and political discourse is that the quality and political complexity of this discourse can be degraded. Social media might increase the volume of political discourse while diminishing its depth (Hwang, 2016). Candidates have to be succinct (as in Tweets) and entertaining. They have most success with trivialized and sensationalist messages (Carr, 2015).

Another downside of social media use for politics is that they are able to set people against each other. Although digital media and networks also can have a conciliatory function (see Chapter 5), the emotional and personal character of the social media and their online communication, which often is fragmented into subgroups with the same views and a lack of feedback cues or moderation, more often enhance political disagreement. In this way, existing *polarization* is amplified. This was a clear observation in the last three presidential campaigns in the U.S. The already extremely polarized American society and politics were only reinforced by the use of digital and social media. Democrats and Republicans were chiefly discussing issues with each other and picking at the other party or candidate (Hindman, 2008). In the 2016 presidential race between Clinton and Trump in particular, the role of social media was probably more destructive than constructive (see the figures in Rainie, 2017). Polarized political conversation on social media, and elsewhere, is chasing people away that find politics disgusting; this means less political participation.

One of the causes of polarization in social media discourse is the fragmented nature of online political communication. This is affected by a combination of social and media trends. A post-modern network society is characterized by individualization and social segmentation. Digital media and networking allow actors to select their relations and (re)sources better than ever before. In political communication this might mean that people tend to follow news, views and political representatives or candidates they favor because they are akin or are similar in their opinions and interests. When this is observed in social media news use and discussion, it is backed by the *habitual exposure thesis*. Here, people habitually expose themselves to news and debate in search of support for their own individual or group views.

Searching for an attractive personal cue in online groups and networking that supports the views of individuals is a well-known social-psychological behavior (Eagly & Chaiken, 1993; Lundgren & Prislin, 1998). In the digital media and Internet era, the habitual exposure thesis is known as the phenomena of turning round in so-called 'echo chambers' (Sunstein, 2001, 2007) and staying in a 'filter bubble' first selected by and then continually fed to users (Pariser, 2011). In the political communication literature this thesis is theoretically and empirically supported by Sunstein (2001), Mutz and Martin (2001), Galston, (2002), Mutz (2006), Iyengar and Hahn (2009), and partially by Brundidge (2010) and Brundidge, Gartrett, Rojas, and de Zúñiga (2014).

However, there is an opposite *accidental exposure thesis*, which states that people encounter news, views and persons that they did not previously know, expect to find or look for. Brundidge (2010) observed that people may be exposed to at least some additional political difference online, if only inadvertently. However, she found that users/citizens experience only a small increase in the heterogeneity of their political discussion networks (Brundidge, 2010, p. 695). This second thesis is also supported by Gil de Zúñiga et al. (2010), Kim, Hsue, and Gil de Zúñiga (2013), Lee, Choi, Kim, and Kim (2014), Barberá (2015), Diehl, Weeks, and de Zúñiga (2016) and Karlsen, Steen-Johnsen, Wollebæk, and Enjolras (2017).

As the effects of accidental exposure are relatively small in all studies referred to, as compared to the habitual exposure studies, we estimate that the habitual exposure thesis is stronger than the accidental exposure thesis. It is not warranted and very optimistic to conclude that people looking for connections and news on social media are "more likely to reconsider their political views in light of content they came across" (Diehl et al., 2016, p.1889). According to the Pew Research Center (2016), only 20% of American social media users say they have modified their stance on a social or political issue because of material they saw on social media.

Inclusion and Participation

Participation will always be limited when some people are excluded from having the access or resources needed for the activity concerned. A condition of participation using digital networks is having access to these networks and being able to use them. This is the theme of *the digital divide*. It is a crucial problem for political participation because here it is assumed that all citizens would be able to have access to a technology that is expected to have better opportunities for practicing democracy than older means. In the first part of this chapter we provided a realistic view about the effects of using these technologies on political participation. However, when this technology is much more expensive and more complex compared to older means, it might become an obstacle instead of a driver for political participation. Another effect might be a relative one, in cases where some citizens benefit more than others in using technologies.

The crucial question is whether digital technology and networks are reducing or increasing the costs of political participation. Anduiza, Cantijoch, & Gallego (2009) suggest that they are reducing the costs of participation. Indeed, access to digital political applications and events seems to be easier. It is faster and new information tools are available, such as search engines, voting guides and communication tools such as blogs, posts and Tweets. However, in this section we will show that using digital technology for political participation also increases the costs of participation, at least for considerable parts of the population.

According to structuration and resource theory, being able to reduce or increase the costs of political participation depends on the resources people have. Relevant resources are income, educational level, having cognitive abilities, existing social networks and time to spend. According to Krueger (2002), there are two opposite hypotheses concerning how resources affect political participation that have already been introduced. The *reinforcement hypothesis* claims that available resources reinforce existing participation patterns. In the digital divide literature this thesis is known as the Matthew effect. This means that people who are already rich in information and communication resources and who show high levels of participation tend to become richer in using digital technology and networks (Brundidge & Rice, 2009; Hargittai & Shaw, 2013; Hill & Hughes, 1999; Krueger, 2006; Norris, 2001; van Dijk, 2005). The basis of this thesis is that the distribution of resources determining political participation is the same as that determining access and use of digital technology.

The opposing *expansionist hypothesis* argues that people with fewer resources for effecting political participation are able to rely on new and distinct resources of digital technology to compensate for their deprivation in other resources. These are the information and communication tools mentioned above. This thesis assumes that digital technology and networks draw new segments of the population into political participation (expansion). Examples are young people who are often called 'digital natives', people with a low level of education encountering political views on social media and activists in horizontally organized networks (Anduiza et al., 2009; Castells, 1997, 2012; Gil de Zúñiga & Valenzuela, 2011; Krueger, 2002).

To determine which of these hypotheses is best grounded, we need to first list and evaluate the costs of online and offline political activities. Table 3.1 shows a list of comparable online and offline political communication and organizational activities. The advanced technology needed to give access to and to use the online activities in this table might be an additional obstacle for users or citizens. However, they also benefit because traditional civil skills in politics are less needed for citizens. These skills are being able to speak and ask questions, persuade people and give presentations, to plan or chair meetings, to act effectively in meetings and to contact government officials (Krueger, 2002). Instead, online political activities require skills that are partly similar to and partly different from the traditional skills (see below). Evidently, digital skills are needed. But in addition, general access to digital technology is required. Van Dijk (2005) developed a model of four successive types of access in the appropriation of digital technology: motivation, physical access, skills and usage.

Motivation and Attitude

We have seen that political interest or motivation is the core driver of online and offline political participation. In online participation, an additional interest or motivation is needed to get access to the digital technology needed. This is the motivation or attitude to use digital media as channels for political participation (van Deursen & van Dijk, 2015). Motivation is goal directed: are particular digital media suitable means to achieve political goals such as to inform people about candidates, parties and issues or to communicate with politicians and citizens about issues? Part of the broad concept of motivation is attitude. Attitudes are object directed: are digital media attractive tools in this respect? Some people do not like computers or do not want to use them for political information and communication. They have no interest in computers or the Internet, do not need them, do not know them, have no time to learn how to use them or they view themselves as too old to use them (Selwyn, 2006). They might also suffer from computer anxiety (Chua, Chen, & Wong, 1999). When these people also hate politics or politicians, we have an insurmountable problem for online political participation. They will probably not participate at all. People with particular personal and positional categories have negative attitudes toward both politics and digital media. You can frequently find them among people with low education, low jobs or without a job, low intelligence and living in working-class and minority ethnic cultures.

A second possibility is that people like digital media and have relatively less interest in politics. This might be the case in a part of the younger generations that in many Western countries in the last three decades has shown less interest in traditional politics than the former ('protest') generation. For these generations online political participation tools might be more attractive than traditional offline participation meetings or channels. For this generation, these tools might even be necessary to generate any appeal in political affairs.

A third possibility is that people do not like and use digital media but have interest in traditional offline politics. The elderly generations are often represented here. This category is able to participate but in fact does not encounter the new opportunities of online participation. In this case these generations will be excluded from taking up these opportunities.

The final possibility is that people have interest in both digital media and politics. These are the people that show the highest amount and level of online participation. Here, citizens with the highest material, mental, social, cultural and time resources are the forerunners. People with a high level of education, jobs and income are even more advanced in using online than offline participation activities (for the U.S., see the Pew Research Center, 2013). The first important factor causing this difference is the motivation and attitude to use digital media for political participation.

Physical Access

The second phase of technology appropriation is physical access: having or being able to use digital media and having a connection to the Internet. This is what most people perceive as access. In physical access the most important factors are income and having a job or a course that requires these media (van Deursen & van Dijk, 2015). Age is the second factor because younger people are more motivated to obtain physical access than seniors and are more likely to be studying or looking for a job.

Obviously, physical access is a necessary condition for online participation. In developed countries with advanced technology such as North America, North-West Europe, South Korea and Japan, more than 80% to 95% of the population have computers and Internet connections (ITU, 2017). By chance (?) they are also advanced democracies. In developing countries where digital technology is relatively expensive, only half, a quarter or perhaps less than 10% of the population have computers and Internet connections. The potential for online democracy in these countries is limited. In this book we will discuss the Arab world and the People's Republic of China. For online democracy in China it matters that only about 50% had access to the Internet in 2016 and that in the glorified Arab Spring, depending on the country, only between 10% to a third of the Arab population had access to the Internet and its assumed powerful social media (ITU, 2017).

Digital Skills

According to a series of American surveys, having digital or Internet skills is the most important factor affecting online political participation, and is even more important than political interest (Best & Krueger, 2005; Hargittai & Shaw, 2013; Krueger, 2002, Best & Krueger, 2006). Motivation and physical access might be necessary conditions but digital skills are needed to make online participation work.

In a series of Dutch surveys and experiments by van Deursen and van Dijk (2010, 2012, 2015), a conceptual framework was developed and tested that contains six types of digital skills. The first type is the basic media-related skills of operational and formal skills. *Operational skills* are needed to operate a digital medium. In popular speech they known as 'button knowledge'. *Formal skills* are being able to handle the formal structures of the medium; in computers they involve working with folders and files and on the Internet with websites and hyperlinks to browse and to navigate. Without these medium-related skills, people have no access to the online political activities listed in Table 3.1.

However, having these skills is a necessary but not sufficient condition to actually practice these online activities. To achieve this aim people also require four content-related digital skills. The first is having sufficient *information skills*: to search, select and evaluate information, in this case political information, for example by using search engines and by understanding complex governmental and political statements and regulations. The second is to develop the *communication skills* increasingly needed to participate in online discussions, creating profiles and posts on social media and addressing politicians and government officials with questions, demands or petitions. For these more active political applications *content-creating skills* are required too. This means being able to write effective texts, design web applications and film videos for political use. The final and more advanced skills are *strategic skills*. This means the ability to use digital media as means to achieve a particular personal or professional goal. In this case, this goal might be to be able to contact, question or persuade a political or government representative or to find out for whom or what to vote for. For the last goal, the very strategic decision-support system of voting aiding applications might be used.

Content-related digital skills are crucial to be effective in using online political activities: to get in contact, to be heard, to persuade and to vote or be elected. People with a high level of education have been shown to be better in all these skills than people with a low level of education (Hargittai, 2002; van Deursen & van Dijk, 2010). In terms of age, young people perform better in medium-related digital skills, but not in content-related skills. On the condition that they have sufficient medium-related digital skills, middle-aged and older people have been observed to be better at laboratory assessment tests than the youngest generation (van Deursen & van Dijk, 2010, 2015). While in self-reports and survey questions about digital technology males pretend to be better than females in digital skills overall (see Krueger, 2002), in laboratory performance tests no gender differences have been observed (van Deursen & van Dijk, 2010).

Usage

In the usage of offline and offline political participation activities, frequency and variety can be registered. Generally, political activities on the Internet are not as popular as economic (shopping, jobs), social (networking) and cultural (entertainment) activities. Political activities are carried out by roughly 10% to 20% of Internet users. Communication political activities are more common on the Web than organizational ones, except for online support by donations (see Table 3.1 for the U.S.). Currently, comparable political activities are still more widespread offline than online except for comments on online news articles and blog posts (see also Table 3.1).

There is a bigger variety of online political activities to choose from than traditional offline activities, but in general users use this variety mostly at election time. Variety is most popular among people with strong political interest.

In terms of inclusion and inequality political participation is even more pronounced online than offline. Online political participation is most popular among the well-educated and the financially well-off, probably in all countries; see for example Pew (2013) in the U.S. The gap in using a large proportion of the online activities in Table 3.1.between people with the lowest and the highest household income and educational attainment is bigger than in the comparable offline activities. An age gap is also evident in online activities as the young Americans (18–24) are using them twice as frequently as American seniors (65+) (Pew, 2013). These are clear signs of a digital divide in online political participation. However, there is no bigger gap in online political activity compared to offline activity in America in terms of gender and party identification or ideology, and only a slightly bigger gap in ethnicity (Pew, 2013). The same distributions in 2012 were found by an Internet trend survey in the Netherlands (van Deursen & van Dijk, 2012).

Benefits

The consequences of access or exclusion to digital media for participation in general and political participation in particular are seldom observed. What are the benefits or disadvantages of more or less access? In political participation, the benefits might be being able to find who to vote for, to contact a political representative, to find strategic information for personal or professional use, to persuade politicians and government information through a personal appeal or by engagement in discussions and perhaps to be encouraged to become a member of a political organization. Van Deursen and van Dijk (2012) and Helsper, van Deursen, & Eynon (2015) have investigated this in the UK and the Netherlands. These authors found that in 2012 and 2013 most benefits from Internet use came in the domains of economic and social participation (e.g. finding cheaper products, more jobs and more contacts). The benefits in the political domain were modest. Nevertheless, in 2012, 28% of Dutch Internet users affirmed the statement "Via the Internet I have discovered which political party I would like to vote for". Another benefit observed was that 6% of Dutch users have become a member of a political organization via the Internet. In the UK, 58% of Internet users confirmed that "Online, I have better contact with my MP, local councillor, or political party" (Helsper et al., 2015, p. 62). In both the Dutch and British general surveys, all of the political benefits listed were significantly acquired most by people with a high level of education and by young people (age 16–35). This is the final confirmation that inclusion or exclusion to digital media matters in political participation.

The Outcomes of Online Political Participation

In the introduction of this chapter we argued that online and offline political participation are not necessarily democratic. Participation is behavior and not the outcome of behavior. We have seen that many pundits on digital political communication think that online political news, taking part in online discussion, liking or sharing and petitioning already change democracy. Whether this is true first depends on the basic view of democracy one holds. So far, the view of democracy as opinion making finds more support in the practice of online political activity than the view of democracy as decision making. The first view focuses on the individual and political communication activities in Table 3.1. Online discussion, comments on the news, liking or sharing political messages and candidates are the most popular activities, at least in the U.S. The second view concentrates on collective and organizational political activities. In the latter view, the examples just mentioned of people finding a party to vote for online and working, volunteering or donating for a party or an online political organization are the only real benefits of using digital media for democracy as a contribution to decision making. Not voting, as we will find out soon.

To provide a preliminary summary of outcomes of online political activities for the political system and democracy, we will now look to provide a brief account of institutional, non-institutional (political opinion and activism) and subjective outcomes of online political participation only. In the conclusion chapter of this book we will try to formulate a complete balance sheet.

So far, the most important potential institutional outcome of online political participation, higher *voter turnout*, has not appeared in any country, not even in Estonia, the early adopter of electrical voting (Bochsler, 2013). Over the last 40 years, voter turnout has been declining in established democracies (Nabatchi & Leighninger, 2015; Niemi & Weisberg, 2001). There are many causes for this trend. It seems fairly unlikely that using the Internet and other digital media has stopped or even mitigated this trend. Bruce Bimber (2001) noticed early on that at least in the 1990s, people obtaining political information from the Internet were no more or less likely to vote than those who did not. Following this, Baumgartner and Morris (2010) and Hargittai and Shaw (2015) found that American students using digital media all day were negative in their political attitudes and in intention to vote. In a meta-analysis of a large number of studies on social media use and political participation, Boulianne concluded that greater use of social media did not affect people's likelihood of voting or participating in campaigns (Boulianne, 2015, p. 534).

Indeed, voter turnout in American presidential elections since the arrival of social media and massive Internet use in 2004 has declined from 55.3% (2004), 58.2% (2008) and 54.9% (2012) to 52.5% (2016). In the 2016 campaign, Trump had an assumed number of 22.7 million likes and followers on Facebook, Twitter and Instagram achieved by his own account or by a robot, while Clinton had only 15 million combined (Graham, 2016). However, the turnout in November 2016 for both was more than 60 million voters, and Clinton won the popular vote.

Flanigan, Zingale, Theiss-Morse, & Wagner (2014) have noted how participation in American elections is partially related to the question of how stimulating elections are to voters. Factors which affect voter turnout are the significance of the office concerned, the importance of the issues for voters, the attractiveness of the candidates running, and how exciting and competitive the election is (Flanigan et al., 2014).

All these observations do not rule out that without using digital and social media, the decline of voter turnout would be even greater. However, we did not find any conclusive evidence for this assumption in the literature and the available data. Digital media might improve the chances for a particular candidate or party to win elections but not for one of the most important outcomes of democracy: voter turnout. The only exception might be the turnout of young people, who in most established democracies are voting in lower numbers than elderly people, also in the era of social media. For this portion of the population, it is necessary to address and use digital and social media for politics. Without this option, voting by young people would probably be even lower. Feezell, Conroy, and Guerrero (2016) found that among Americans aged 18 to 30, dutiful citizen norms regarding the need to vote are decreasing while other norms such as engagement and attention to actualizing issues are growing. This means there are more "individualistic, expressive avenues of participation such as volunteerism, public protest and boycotting" (Feezell et al., 2016, p. 95).

The turnout in referenda, which might differ to general elections where voter turnout is in decline, is not higher on account of using social and digital media. Usually the turnout for referenda is much lower than for general elections. Turnout is only relatively high for issues which are found to very important in a society, such as the Brexit referendum in the UK and the Constitutional referendum in Italy in 2016, or when they are combined with general elections. Not surprisingly, activity on the Internet and the social media was high close to these UK and Italian referenda, but we have found no conclusive evidence that this activity significantly increased turnout.

The same experience is now unfolding in Switzerland, a country that has a long history of frequent referenda. In some cantons of this country in 2011, experiments were conducted with the option to use the Internet for voting.

The average electronic turnout was high among expats (more than 50% in some referenda), but among homeland citizens it was relatively low, often about 20% (Federal Chancellery of Switzerland, 2013). So far, there is no evidence that the total turnout in Swiss referenda has been increased by e-voting.

Another potential institutional outcome of online participation might be a reform of the political, constitutional and electoral *system of representation*. Almost nothing has changed in these systems worldwide as a result of the rise of digital media and networking. In many constitutions, referenda are difficult to be accepted, both online and offline. Instruments of direct democracy such as official petitions are rarely permitted. Only in the UK have electronic petitions addressing parliament reached a particular official status. An effective opportunity for using digital media is to more easily reach a minimum number of signatures to ask for a referendum in most countries via the Internet compared to using traditional means. In the U.S. exploding web and social media activity has resulted in no change in the political and electoral system at all. Perhaps President Trump won the election more by the age-old electoral system of electors in (swing) states overturning the popular vote, than by his assumed superior campaign on social media. More of these changes and continuities of political systems and democracies will be discussed in the conclusion chapter of this book.

The picture might be different regarding non-institutional outcomes of online political activities. The Web and social media provide more opportunities and consequences for *collective action or activism* (Castells, 2012; Bennett & Segerberg, 2013). We have argued that young citizens prefer participation such as volunteering, public protest, and boycotting. Anderson (2013) concludes that one of the most promising aspects of online political communication is issue advocacy. We can acknowledge that online communication may not significantly increase voting turnout or other factors of institutional participation while it may contribute to activism. Digital media can help activists find each other and facilitate their organizational activities and reach into various spheres of deliberation or debate.

However, we cannot observe and conclude that increasing digital and social media use is resulting in a global increase in the frequency and level of collective action. In the 1960s to the 1980s, the time of the protest generation, demonstrations, manifestations, strikes and other forms of activism were frequent. In the 1990s we witnessed the anti-globalization movement. But after 2000, when the Web became popular and social media emerged, these activities did not take place more frequently than before. There were bursts of contestation and uprisings in particular countries, such as the Arab Spring, to be discussed in Chapter 6 of this book. The Occupy movement inspired by the banking and economic crisis, the Arab Spring and other events were extinguished in one and a half years despite massive social media and Web attention. Social media are able to create 'flash mobs' in political action that temporarily impact public opinion, but often have no effects on government action or democratic change in the political system at all.

The third and last type of outcome of online political participation are *subjective effects* such as trust in government, politicians or parliament. In a trend study of all American presidential elections (1992–2012), Bucy and Groshek (2017) observed that citizens using a blend of new and traditional media revealed more subjective political system efficacy (a perception of positive responsiveness by government, thinking that the government cares for what people think and that they have a say in what the government does) but less political trust. The latter observation is a clear trend. In most established democracies in the last few decades, trust in government and politicians is fluctuating and is declining in the long run (Dalton, 2005; Thomassen, Andeweg, & Van Ham, 2017). However, support for democracy and the system of representation has on average stayed at the same level, as will be claimed below (Norris, 2011).

In the U.S. the trust of Americans in the government in Washington DC declined from almost 80% to less than 20% over the course of 69 years (see Figure 3.4). After the massive diffusion of the Web and the emergence of social media in 2004, trust has only declined. Similar figures can be illustrated for other (at least) Western countries. Of course, this does not mean that digital media have caused this decline, but the conclusion that they would have boosted trust in government by providing political and government information online and the transparency of governance and politics created in online discussion cannot be supported. The assumption that without the

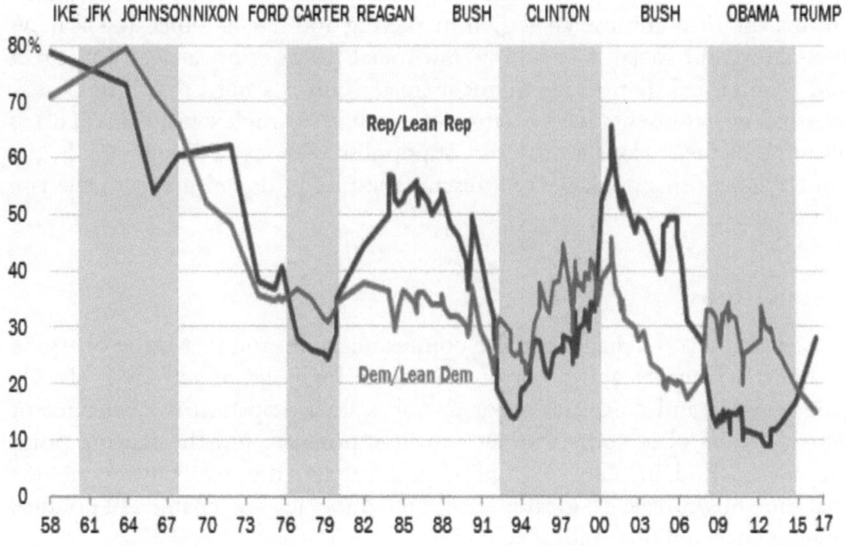

Figure 3.4 Trust in the American government by Republican and Democratic voters between 1958 and 2017.

(*Source*: Pew, 2017)

arrival of these media trust would even been lower is also very unlikely to be true. On the contrary, in this book we will reveal arguments that a wrong use of the Internet for e-participation by governments and negative actions and expressions on social media have harmed citizens' trust in governments.

Despite the widely claimed decline in trust in governments, political parties and institutions worldwide (Dalton, 2005; Norris, 1999), sinking membership and identification with political parties and the volatility of voting turnout and choices, *support and trust in democracy and the political system* have *not* decreased globally. Following a cross-national comparison of more than 50 surveys worldwide, Pippa Norris (2011, p. 337) concluded that "public support for the political system has not eroded consistently in established democracies, not across a wide range of countries". Annual global surveys by www.worldvaluessurvey.com consistently find overwhelming support for democracy worldwide (Shin, 2015; Welzel, 2013). Only the interpretation and the type of democracy desired is different across countries, and globally the support for authoritarian versions of democracy (searching for a strong state and leadership) is becoming more popular compared to the liberal versions (Shin, 2015).

However, Norris (2011, p. 338) also concludes that "in many states today, satisfaction with the performance of democracy continues to diverge from public aspirations". One of the causes of this *democratic deficit*, as she calls it, is that media use, such as using the Internet, strengthens democratic aspirations. Therefore, an important subjective effect of the use of digital media and networking on democracy today might be that it contributes to a widening gap between democratic aspirations and performance of the political system. In this age of e-commerce, digital marketing and fast or short digital news messaging and social networking and social networking, a need for direct and a simplified democracy might increase. This is a need that is not easily satisfied by representative systems dealing with complex problems. This is also one of the reasons for the rise of populist versions of democracy. In the conclusion of this book we will discuss the role of digital media in the rise of populism.

Conclusions

In this chapter, we challenged the common assumption that using or trying to use the Internet and other digital media for political activity is already participatory and democratic. For us political participation is a behavior or activity to be observed. Attitudes and intentions are just the starting point for this. Second, in observing online political activities we had to conclude that they might have no greater effect on democracy and changes of political systems than offline political activities.

The less demanding assumption that the use of digital media has a positive role in political participation can also be challenged. This depends on the existing political context and the political interest, motivation, access and digital media skills of citizens. In the research reviewed, more positive than negative effects for political and civic participation were found, but these positive effects are very weak and often disappear after controlling for the causal assumptions. A longitudinal process model that observes not only individual characteristics but also relational or network properties and also takes into account the systemic results of political behavior is needed to formulate a better research design.

Most effects found are spurious because similar political activities are simply transformed from offline to online activities with continuous technological and political change. In this way, no general conclusions can be drawn. This transformation might perhaps only change the forms of political participation and not the substance. Anyway, the most realistic conclusion of this chapter is that, so far, online political participation has created no, or only negligible, effects on democracy and the political system of advanced democracies. However, changing forms matter. The transformation of traditional political practices into digital political practices might benefit some political actors, parties or candidates more than others. As television changed politics after the Second World War, the Internet is now changing politics in the 21st century. The question is whether it will improve democracy. We have seen that, for instance, social media have both advantages and disadvantages for political participation and democracy – which will prevail depends on politics, political goals and the political context. Politics come first and media second, digital media likewise.

References

Aichholzer, G., & Allhutter, D. (2011). Online forms of political participation and their impact on democracy. *ITA Manuscript*, June 2011. Vienna: Austrian Academy of Science.

Anderson, C. W. (2013). *Rebuilding the news: Metropolitan journalism in the digital age*. Philadelphia, PA: Temple University Press.

Anduiza, E., Cantijoch, M., & Gallego, A. (2009). Participation and the internet: A field essay. *Information, Communication and Society*, *12*(6), 860–878.

Anduiza, E., Jensen, M. J., & Jorba, L. (2012). Digital media and political engagement worldwide. New York: Cambridge University Press.

Barber, B. (2003). *Strong democracy: Participatory politics for a new age*. Twentieth anniversary edition. Berkeley, CA: University of California Press.

Barberá, P. (2015). *How social media reduces mass political polarization*. Evidence from Germany, Spain, and the U.S. Working paper. Retrieved from http://rubenson.org/wp-content/uploads/2015/10/barbera-tpbw.pdf

Baumgartner, J. C., & Morris, J. S. (2009). MyFaceTube politics: Social networking web sites and political engagement of young adults. *Social Science Computer Review*, *28*(1), 24–44.

Bennett, W. L., & Segerberg, A. (2013). The logic of connective action: Digital media and the personalization of contentious politics. *Information, Communication & Society*, *15*(5), 739–768.

Best, S., & Krueger, B. (2005). Analyzing the representativeness of Internet political participation. *Political Behavior*, *27*(2), 183–216.

Best, S. J., & Krueger, B. S. (2006). Online interactions and social capital: Distinguishing between new and existing ties. *Social Science Computer Review, 24*, 395–410.

Bimber, B. (1999). The internet and citizen communication with government: Does the medium matter? *Journal of Political Communication, 16*(4), 409–428.

Bimber, B. (2001). Information and political engagement in America: The search for effects of information technology at the individual level. *Political Research Quarterly, 54*(1), 53–67.

Bimber, B. (2003). *Information and American democracy: Technology in the evolution of political power*. Cambridge, UK: Cambridge University Press.

Bimber, B. (2014). Digital media in the Obama campaigns of 2008 and 2012: Adaptation to the personalized political communication environment. *Journal of Information Technology & Politics, 11*(2), 130–150.

Bochsler, D. (2013). *Can Internet voting increase political participation? Remote electronic voting and turnout in the Estonian 2007 parliamentary elections*. Presentation at the Internet and Voting Conference, Fiesole, 2010.

Bonfadelli, H. (2002). The internet and knowledge gaps: A theoretical and empirical investigation. *European Journal of Communication, 17*(1), 65–84.

Boulianne, S. (2009). Does Internet use affect engagement? A meta-analysis of research. *Political Communication, 26*(2), 193–211.

Boulianne, S. (2011). Stimulating of reinforcing political interest: Using panel data to examine reciprocal effects between news media and political interest. *Political Communication, 28(2)*, 147–162.

Boulianne, S. (2015). Social media use and participation: A meta-analysis of current research. *Information, Communication & Society, 18*(5), 524–538.

Brundidge, J. (2010). Encountering "difference" in the contemporary public sphere: The contribution of the internet to the heterogeneity of political discussion networks. *Journal of Communication, 60*(4), 680–700.

Brundidge, J., & Rice, R. (2009). Political engagement online: Do the information rich get richer and the like-minded more similar? In A. Chadwick & P. H. Howard (Eds.), *Routledge handbook of Internet politics* (pp. 144–156). London; New York: Routledge.

Brundidge, J., Gartrett, R. K., Rojas, H., & Gil de Zúñiga, H. (2014). Political participation and ideological news online: 'Differential gains'and 'differential losses' in a presidential election cycle. *Mass Communication and Society, 17*(4), 464–486.

Bucy, E. P., & Groshek, J. (2017). Empirical support for the media participation hypothesis: Trends across presidential elections, 1992–2012. *New Media & Society*, doi:1461444817709281

Campbell, D. E. (2013). Social networks and political participation. *Annual Review of Political Science, 16*, 33–48.

Carr, N. (2015). How social media is ruining politics. *Politico Magazine*, September 2, 2015. Retrieved from www.politico.com/magazine/story/2015/09/2016-election-social-media-ruining-politics-213104

Castells, M. (1997). *The information age: Economy, society and culture. Vol. II: The power of identity*. Oxford: Blackwell.

Castells, M. (2009). *Communication power*. Oxford, UK: Oxford University Press.

Castells, M. (2012). *Networks of outrage and hope: Social movements in the Internet age*. Cambridge, UK: Polity Press.

Chadwick, A. (2006). *Internet politics, states, citizens, and new communication technologies*. Oxford, UK: Oxford University Press.

Chadwick, A. (2013). *The hybrid media system: Politics and power.* Oxford, UK; New York: Oxford University Press.

Chua, S. L., Chen, D., & Wong, A. F. L. (1999). Computer anxiety and its correlates: A meta-analysis. *Computers in Human Behavior, 15*, 609–623.

Dalton, R. J. (2005). The social transformation of trust in government. *International Review of Sociology, 15*(1), 133–154.

Delli Carpini, M. X. (2000a). In search of the informed citizen: What Americans know about politics and why it matters. *The Communication Review, 4*(1), 129–164.

Delli Carpini, M. X. (2000b). Gen.com: Youth, civic engagement, and the new information environment. *Political Communication, 17*(4), 341–349.

Delli Carpini, M. X.(2004). Mediating democratic engagement: The impact of communications on citizen's involvement in political and civic life. In L. L. Kaid (Ed.), *Handbook of political communication research* (pp. 395–434). Mahwah, NJ: Lawrence Erlbaum Associates.

Delli Carpini, M. X., & Keeter, S.(1996). *What Americans know about politics and why it matters.* New Haven, CT: Yale University Press.

Diehl, T., Weeks, B., & Gil de Zúñiga, H. (2016). Political persuasion on social media: Tracing direct and indirect effects of news use and social interaction. *New Media & Society, 18*(19), 1875–1895.

DiMaggio, P., Hargittai, E, Celeste, C., & Shafer, S. (2004). *From unequal access to differentiated use: A literature review and agenda for research on digital inequality.* Report for the Russell Sage Foundation. New York: Russell Sage Foundation.

Duggan, M., & Smith, A. (2016). *The political environment on social media. Pew Research Center,* Report 25. Retrieved from www.pewinternet.org/2016/10/25/the-political-environment-on-social-media/

Eagly A., & Chaiken, S. (1993). *The psychology of attitudes.* Orlando, FL: Harcourt Brace Jovanovich College.

Feezell, J. T., Conroy, M., & Guerrero, M. (2016). Internet use and political participation: Engaging citizenship norms through online activities. *Journal of Information Technology & Politics, 13*(2), 95–107.

Federal Chancellery of Switzerland (2013). Bericht des Bundestages zu Vote électronique. Retrieved from www.e-voting-cc.ch/index.php/de-DE/component/content/article/1-aktuelle-nachrichten/169-br-bericht-vote-electronique

Flanigan, W. H., Zingale, N. H., Theiss-Morse, E. A., & Wagner, M. W. (2014). *Political behavior of the American electorate.* Los Angeles; London; New Delhi: Sage and CQ Press.

Galston, W.A. (2002). Receiving the political: Notes toward a new pluralism. *Philosophy & Public Policy Quarterly, 22(3)*, 15–20.

Gil de Zúñiga, H., & Valenzuela, S. (2011). The mediating path to a stronger citizenship: Online and offline networks, weak ties, and civic engagement. *Communication Research, 38*(3), 397–421.

Gil de Zúñiga, H., Veenstra, A., Vraga, E., & Shah, D. (2010). Digital democracy: Reimagining pathways to political participation. *Journal of Information Technology & Politics*, 7(1), 36–51.

Graham, J. (2016) Trump vs. Clinton: How the rivals rank on Twitter, Facebook. *USA Today, August 12, 2016.* Retrieved from www.wgal.com/article/trump-vs-clinton-how-they-ranked-on-social-media/8281184

Hargittai, E. (2002). Beyond logs and surveys: In-depth measures of people's web use skills. *Journal of the Association for Information Science and Technology, 53*(14), 1239–1244.

Hargittai, E., & Shaw, A. (2013). Digitally savvy citizenship: The role of internet skills and engagement in young adults' political participation around the 2008 presidential election. *Journal of Broadcasting & Electronic Media, 57*(2), 115–134.

Hargittai, E., & Shaw, A. (2015). Mind the skills gap: The role of Internet know-how and gender in differentiated contributions to Wikipedia. *Information, Communication & Society, 18*(4), 424–442.

Helsper, E. J., van Deursen, A. J. A. M., & Eynon, R. (2015). *Tangible outcomes of internet use*. From Digital Skills to Tangible Outcomes project report. Oxford, UK; Enschede, the Netherlands: Oxford Internet Institute and University of Twente. Retrieved from www.oii.ox.ac.uk/research/projects/?id=112

Highfield, T. (2016). *Social media and everyday politics*. Cambridge, UK; Malden, MA: Polity Press.

Hindman, M. (2008). *The myth of digital democracy*. Princeton, NJ: Princeton University Press.

Hill, K. A., & Hughes, J. E. (1999). *Cyberpolitics: Citizen activism in the age of the Internet*. Lanham, MD: Rowman & Littlefield Publishers, Inc.

Howard, P. N., & Parks, M. R. (2012). Social media and political change: Capacity, constraint, and consequence. *Journal of Communication, 62*(2), 359–362.

Hwang, A. S. (2016). *Social media and the future of U.S. presidential campaigning*. CMC Senior Theses. Paper 1231. Retrieved from http://scholarship.claremont.edu/cmc_theses/1231

ITU. (2017). *Measuring the information society report* (Vol. 1). Geneva: ITU; International Telecommunication Union.

Iyengar, S., & Hahn, K. S. (2009). Red media, blue media: Evidence of ideological selectivity in media use. *Journal of Communication, 59*(1), 19–39.

Jennings, M. K., & Zeitner, V. (2003). Internet use and civic engagement: A longitudinal analysis. *Public Opinion Quarterly, 67*(3), 311–334.

Jensen, M. (2006). Minnesota e-democracy: Mobilizing the mobilized? In S. Oates, D. M. Owen, & R. Gibson (Eds.), *The internet and politics: Citizens, voters, and activists* (pp. 39–58). New York: Routledge.

Jorba, L., & Binber B. (2012). The impact of digital media on citizenship from a global perspective. In M. J. Jensen, L. Jorba, & E. Anduiza (Eds.), *Digital media and political engagement worldwide* (pp. 16–38). New York: Cambridge University Press.

Karlsen, R., Steen-Johnsen, K., Wollebæk, D., & Enjolras, B. (2017). Echo chamber and trench warfare dynamics in online debates. *European Journal of Communication*, doi:0267323117695734

Karpf, D. (2013). The internet and American political campaigns. *The Forum: A Journal of Applied Research in Contemporary Politics, 11(3)*, 413–428.

Kim, Y., Hsue, S-H., & Gil de Zúñiga, H. (2013). Influence of social media use on discussion network heterogeneity and civic engagement: The moderating role of personality traits. *Journal of Communication, 63*(3), 498–516.

Klandermans, B., & Stekelenburg, J. (2013). Social movements and the dynamics of collective action. In L. Huddy, D. Sears, & J, Levy (Eds.), *The Oxford handbook of political psychology*. (pp. 774–811). New York: Oxford University Press.

Koc-Michalska, K., Gibson, R., & Vedel, T. (2014). Online campaigning in France, 2007–2012: Political actors and citizens in the aftermath of the Web.2.0 evolution. *Journal of Information Technology and Politics, 11*(2), 220–244.

Koc-Michalska, K., Lilleker, & D. Vedel, T. (2016). Editorial: Civic political engagement and social change in the new digital age. *New Media & Society, 18*(9), 1807–1816.

Kollanyi, B. (2016). Where do bots come from? An analysis of bot codes shared on GitHub. *International Journal of Communication, 10*, 4932–4951.

Kriesi, H. (2008). Political mobilisation, political participation and the power of the vote. *West European Politics*, *31*(1), 147–168.

Krueger, B. S. (2002). Assessing the potential of internet political participation in the United States: A resource approach. *American Politics Research*, *30*(5), 476–498.

Krueger, B. S. (2006). A comparison of conventional and internet political mobilization. *American Politics Research*, *34*(6), 759–776.

Lee, J. K., Choi, J., Kim, C., & Kim, Y. (2014). Social media, network heterogeneity, and opinion polarization. *Journal of Communication*, *64*(4), 702–722.

Lundgren, S., & Prislin, R. (1998). Motivated cognitive processing and attitude change. *Personality and Social Psychology Bulletin*, *24*(7), 715–726.

McDonald, J. (2008). The benefits of society online: Civic engagement. In K. Mossberger, C. Tolbert, & R. McNeal (Eds.), *Digital citizenship: The Internet, society, and participation* (pp. 47–66). Cambridge, MA: The MIT Press.

Morozov, E. (2013). *To save everything, click here: The folly of technological solutionism*. New York: PublicAffairs.

Mutz, D. (2006). *Hearing the other side: Deliberative versus participatory democracy*. Cambridge, UK: Cambridge University Press.

Mutz, D. C., & Martin, P. S. (2001). Facilitating communication across lines of political difference: The role of mass media. *American Political Science Review*, *95*(1), 97–114.

Nabatchi, T., & Leighninger, M. (2015). *Public participation for 21st century democracy*. Hoboken, NJ: John Wiley & Sons.

Niemi, R. G., & Weisberg, H. F. (Eds.) (2001). *Controversies in voting behavior*. Washington, DC: CQ Press.

Norris, P. (Ed.). (1999). *Critical citizens: Global support for democratic government*. Oxford, UK: Oxford University Press.

Norris, P. (2001). *Digital divide: Civic engagement, information poverty, and the Internet worldwide*. Cambridge, UK: Cambridge University Press.

Norris, P. (2003). Preaching to the converted? Pluralism, participation and party websites. *Party Politics*, *9*(1), 21–45.

Norris, P. (2011). *Democratic deficit: Critical citizens revisited*. New York: Cambridge University Press.

O'Neil, C. (2016). *Weapons of math destruction: How big data increases inequality and threatens democracy*. New York: Broadway Books.

Pariser, E. (2011). *The filter bubble: What the Internet is hiding from you*. London: Viking (Penguin).

Pew Research Center, authored by A. Smith (2013). *Civic engagement in the digital age*. Retrieved from http://pewinternet.org/Reports/2013/Civic-Engagement.aspx

Pew Research Center, authored by M. Anderson and A. Caumont (2014). How social media is reshaping news. Retrieved from www.pewresearch.org/fact-tank/2014/09/24/how-social-media-is-reshaping-news/

Pew Research Center (2015). *Public trust in the government: 1958–2017*. Retrieved from www.people-press.org/2017/05/03/public-trust-in-government-1958-2017/

Pew Research Center, authored by M. Anderson (2016). Social media causes some users to rethink their views on an issue. Retrieved from www.pewresearch.org/fact-tank/2016/11/07/social-media-causes-some-users-to-rethink-their-views-on-an-issue/

Pew Research Center (2017). Public trust in government remains near historic lows as partisan attitudes shift. Retrieved from http://assets.pewresearch.org/wp-content/uploads/sites/5/2017/05/03145544/05-03-17-Trust-release.pdf

Putnam, R. D. (1995). Bowling alone: America's declining social capital. *Journal of Democracy*, *6*(1), 65–78.

Putnam, R. D. (2000). *Bowling alone: America's declining social capital*. New York; London: Simon & Schuster.

Rainie, L. (2017). *The reckoning for social media*. Key note speech at the New Media and Society Conference in Toronto, July 29, 2017. Retrieved from www.pewinternet.org/2017/08/01/the-reckoning-for-social-media/.

Selwyn, N. (2006). Digital division or digital decision? A study of non-users and low-users of computers. *Poetics, 34*(4–5), 273–292.

Shin, D. C. (2015). *Assessing citizen responses to democracy: A review and synthesis of recent public opinion research*. CSD Working Paper Center for the Study of Democracy, University of California-Irvine.

Sunstein, C. R. (2001). *Republic.com*. Princeton, NJ: Princeton University Press.

Sunstein, C. R. (2007). *Republic.com 2.0*. Princeton, NJ: Princeton University Press.

Thomassen, J. J. A., Andeweg, R. B., & Van Ham, C. (2017). Political trust and the decline of legitimacy debate. In S. Zmerli and T. van der Meer (Eds.), *Handbook on Political Trust* (pp. 509–525). Cheltenham, UK: Edward Elgar Publishing Group.

van Deth, J. W. (2014). A conceptual map of political participation. *Acta Politica, 49*(3), 349–367.

van Deursen, A. J. A. M., & van Dijk, J. A. G. M. (2010). Using the Internet: Skill related problems in users' online behavior. *Interacting with Computers, 21*(5–6), 393–402.

van Deursen, A. J. A. M., & van Dijk, J. A. G. M. (2012). *Trendrapport internetgebruik 2012: Een Nederlands en Europees perspectief*. Enschede, the Netherlands: University of Twente.

van Deursen, A. J. A. M., & van Dijk, J. A. G. M. (2015). Internet skill levels increase, but gaps widen: A longitudinal cross-sectional analysis (2010–2013) among the Dutch population. *Information, Communication & Society, 18*(7), 782–797.

van Deursen, A. J. A. M., Helsper, E. J., Eynon, R., & van Dijk, J. A. G. M. (2017). The compoundness and sequentiality of digital inequality. *International Journal of Communication, 11*, 452–473.

van Dijk, J. A. G. M. (2005). *The deepening divide: Inequality in the information society*. Thousand Oaks, CA; London; New Delhi: Sage.

van Dijk, J. (2012). *The network society* (3rd ed.). London; New Delhi; Thousand Oaks, CA; Singapore: Sage.

Vedel, T., & Koc-Michalska, K. (2009, September). *The Internet and French political communication in the aftermath of the 2007 presidential election*. 5th ECPR general conference panel on "Parties, Campaigns and Media Technologies". Potsdam, Germany.

Wang, X. (2009). Seeking channels for engagement: Media use and political communication by China's rising middle class. *China: An International Journal*, 7(1), 31–56.

Welzel, C. (2013). *Freedom rising: Human empowerment and the quest for emancipation* (*World Values Surveys*). New York: Cambridge University Press.

Xenos, M. A., & Moy, P. (2007). Direct and differential effects of the Internet on political participation and civic engagement. *Journal of Communication, 57*(4), 704–718.

Youmans, W. L., & York, J. C. (2012). Social media and the activist toolkit: User agreements, corporate interests, and the information infrastructure of modern social movements. *Journal of Communication, 62*(2), 315–329.

4 The Reconstruction of Public Space in Democracy

From Public Sphere to Public Space

Every democracy needs communication channels for citizens to publicly express their views on issues of society and to address them to the polity of this society when decisions are needed. These settings or channels are often called the public sphere of a society. This concept is commonly marked by the work of Jürgen Habermas. The concept has several connotations. For Habermas it is both a *functional system* of society with flows of information and communication and a *forum* or arena for ideal free speech for citizens. It is "an intermediary system of communication between formally organized and informal face-to-face deliberations in arenas both at the top and at the bottom of the political system" (Habermas, 2006, p. 10). However, perhaps the most popular connotation of the public sphere is a third one: *spatial* conceptions of domains accessible to the public for discourse.

Papacharissi (2010) argues that Habermas's public sphere concept can best be understood as a metaphor because its actual existence is in doubt (p. 115). Below we will also argue that Habermas's concept is more normative than empirical. For Papacharissi, the public sphere must be understood as an abstraction that can be materialized in coffee houses, parliaments, street markets and many other settings (2010, p. 114). She makes a relevant distinction between public sphere and public space:

> The public sphere must not be confused with public space. While public space provides the expanse that allows the public sphere to convene, it does not guarantee a healthy public sphere. The public sphere also serves as a forum for, but is conceptually distinct from, the public, public affairs, or public opinion.
>
> (Papacharissi, 2010, p. 115)

Here, she primarily uses the connotation of public sphere as a forum and as a normative concept ('healthy') while in the rest of her book the connotation of spatial domains reigns.

With all this confusion Manuel Castells, in our view, has given the most neutral definition of the concept of public sphere to be made operational in empirical research: "The public sphere is the space of communication of ideas and projects that emerge from society and are addressed to the decision makers in the institutions of society" (Castells, 2008, p. 78). Departing from the spatial connotation of this definition, we will transform the public sphere concept into a collection of public spaces in this chapter.

In Chapter 1 we distinguished between six views or models of democracy that have different views of the role of the public sphere in a democracy. For an elaborate discussion of these views, see Held (1987) and Hacker and van Dijk (2000). These views are certainly normative. In some views, the principal goal of democracy is to form opinions; in others it is to make decisions. The concept of public sphere is most important for the goal of opinion making. This relates to the connotation of a forum. Pluralist and participatory views of democracy expect and advocate a properly working public sphere. However, the views of democracy with a primary goal of decision making also want an effective public sphere. Castells' definition notes that it addresses the decision makers in society.

We will now briefly summarize the views of democracy in relation to the public sphere. We start with the views of democracy as opinion making. In the *pluralist* view of democracy, the intermediary organizations between the government and individual citizens are vital; they comprise the civil society. In this view, the public sphere is seen as the mediator between the civil society and the government. This consists of *a forum* for a plurality of interests, pressures, religious and ethnic groups or political parties. The pluralist view is a substantial rather than a procedural conception of democracy. The substance is opinion making by a plurality of interests and groups. Deliberative democracy in free speech discussion settings, as proposed by Habermas, is one of the versions of pluralist democracy. It is offered as a way for a working and free (autonomous) public sphere.

Participatory democracy is another substantial view of democracy with a goal of opinion making and citizen activity affecting governance and political decision making. Here, the focus is not on groups but on individuals and their citizenship. They are supposed to become active citizens and to participate in the public sphere. Citizens should have access to the settings, channels and institutions of the public sphere and they have to be educated to become active citizens. Here, the public sphere is a *social and media environment* where citizens have more or less access.

Legalist democracy is a procedural view that focuses on decision making. This view counts on representatives being decision makers on behalf of citizens. Here, the public sphere is an instrument: a *system of information* for representatives where they can find the input of the heterogeneous interests of society and where they themselves can offer their reaction to the interests and proposals of citizens by means of solutions.

Competitive democracy also focuses on decision making. In this view, leaders and representatives are competing for electoral support. To achieve this aim, they want a public sphere to function as an *information domain* for representatives and citizens with competing views of both leaders and followers.

In *plebiscitary* democracy, a public sphere is considered as *a forum with voting or opinion facilities* for direct democracy. Here, the means are facilities of both opinion and decision making, but the goal is decision making by plebiscites such as referenda and petitions.

Finally, *libertarian* democracy primarily advocates a public sphere as an *autonomous domain of opinion and decision making* of citizens between civil society and the government. Here, the public sphere consists of autonomously communicating associations of citizens in between the government and civil society or the market.

From these definitions and views, it appears that the concept of a public sphere is conceived as a *forum*, a *system or domain* of information, media and organizations, or a *spatial structure* separated from private space. Most authors use these three concepts simultaneously. As mentioned above, Habermas uses the concept both as a (part of a) functional system and a forum. Castells calls the public sphere both a "space of communication" and an "essential component of sociopolitical organization" (Castells, 2008, p. 78).

In this book, the public sphere will primarily be conceived as *a spatial structure of public, private and social spaces in society linked by networks.* The public sphere can be located somewhere on a scale between the macro and micro levels of public and private affairs. These affairs can be distinguished from economic and cultural affairs. See Figure 4.1.

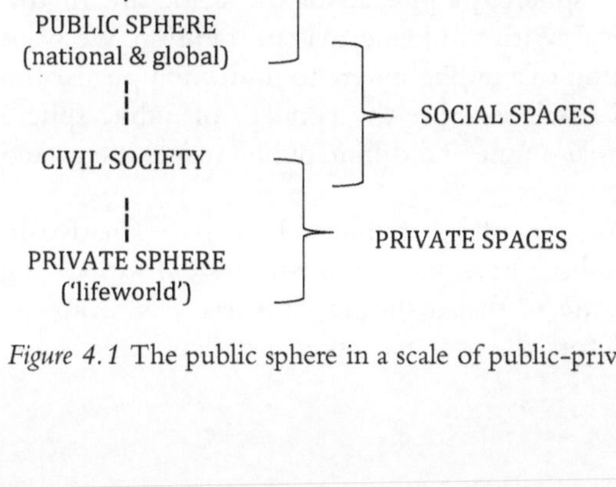

Figure 4.1 The public sphere in a scale of public-private affairs and spaces.

In Figure 4.1 the public sphere is located between civil society and the government, and is the primary decision-making actor in society concerning public affairs. According to Friedland, Hove, and Rojas (2006), following Habermas (2006), the public sphere consists of two parts: a formally organized political public sphere with mass media and political associations and an informal public sphere of face-to-face deliberation by citizens. Similarly, for Castells (2008, p. 78) the public sphere is "the space where people come together as citizens and articulate their autonomous views to influence the political institutions of society".

However, the main distinction of the public sphere is the private sphere. Papacharissi (2010, p. 27) defines this as "the realm of the *personal* or *domestic*, possibly considered *unofficial*, and involving actions and consequences structured around the *self*". Habermas called it the lifeworld. Contrary to this traditional distinction, Paparachissi observes a merging of public and private spheres in contemporary society and even shifts the locus of democracy from the public to the private sphere: "I argue that citizens feel more powerful in negotiating their place in democracy via the nexus of a private sphere" (p. 24). Whether this is true will be discussed below, but we have to affirm the fact that the distinction between the public and private (including the commercial) spheres is at least partly blurred in the network society.

This affirmation is best backed by a spatial conception of the public and private spheres. Wolfe (1997) and Papacharissi (2010) highlight a relevant difference between public, private and social space. In public space we make decisions for society. In private space we seek self-interest and individual freedom. In social space we transform self-interest and individual freedom into collective interest via association and social networking. Here, semi-private and semi-public social needs come together. In the contemporary network society, social media in particular are bridging private and public space in carrying these needs. They are both private/commercial and public, and they host discussion of all kinds of everyday issues with political relevance.

Habermas and Beyond

All of the authors cited in the previous section are still influenced by Habermas's concept of public sphere, despite all of the criticism. In this chapter we want to force a break with the Habermasian tradition. We want to escape a normative conception of a public sphere to find an empirical and more or less objective one. We will redefine the concept of public sphere into a variety of observable actual online and offline public spaces integrated in a network structure.

Habermas's most recent concept of the public sphere is normative in two related ways. First, the public sphere and the media system supporting it should be *self-regulating*; this means that it should be *independent* from the administrative power of state actors, the monetary power of economic actors and the social power of special interest groups or institutions (Habermas, 2006, p. 415). Second, the public sphere needs *communicative reflexivity working on its own norms of rational-critical debate.* With these norms "the public sphere functions as a filtering mechanism. If it works, only considered public opinions pass through it" (ibid., p. 418).

Many critics of Habermas's public sphere concept label it as idealistic and unrealistic. They do not perceive the existence of an autonomous public sphere with inclusion of all social categories and without political, economic and cultural powers. Habermas's 18th and 19th-century ideal public sphere settings of Britain's coffee houses, France's salons and Germany's *Tischgesellschaften* were in fact bourgeois male elite meetings that were unfriendly to workers, farmers and women (Fraser, 1992). Similarly, the 20th-century mass media and discussion meeting rooms were in fact dominated by upper and middle-class intellectuals. "The notion of the public sphere as a neutral space for the production of meaning runs against all historical evidence", argues Castells (2008, p. 80), referring to the work of Michael Mann. Below we will argue that public spaces may require freedom of assembly, association, expression and publication of opinions, but cannot be expected to be free from any economic and political control.

The norm of communicative reflexivity in idealized speech situations of rational-critical debate is also called into question by many critics that do not support pluralist deliberative democracy. Below we will observe that it does not work in online and offline discussions of the network society.

Habermas's concept was inspired by the era of the mass society and mass media, and is less valid for the network society and for a networked public sphere (Friedland et al., 2006; Rasmussen, 2008). "In the contemporary networked public sphere, however, Habermas's requirement of media independence and autonomy may no longer be either possible or necessary"; "the public sphere will not be able to carry out its proper deliberative functions" (Friedland et al., 2006, p. 12).

What is a networked public sphere? In our view, it is an infrastructure of online and offline public spaces linked to each other. We will define what is needed to use this infrastructure for public discourse for every political and democratic goal we know. It will not serve as a structure for particular views or ideals, such as deliberative or participatory democracy only. Public spaces are locations which are open to everybody and are shared in common. Private spaces are locations which are closed and only shared by individuals and their fellow human beings who are invited into these spaces. The concept of the public sphere can be transformed in public spaces with old and new characteristics, belonging to the mass society and the network society, respectively. The characteristics to compared are summarized in Table 4.1.

The spaces in the mass society, as described by Habermas and others, are mostly described as particular places. They are either physical settings for meetings such as coffee houses, rallies, street demonstrations or festivals or media environments such as print media, radio and TV channels. There are

Table 4.1 Evolution from old and new public spaces in the mass and network society.

Old public space (mass society)	*New public space (network society)*
Alliance of public space with a **particular place** or territory	Public space as a **multitude** of online and offline spaces
Supposedly **unitary** character of public space	A **mosaic of different,** but overlapping, public spaces
National and local public space	**Global, national and local** public space
Relatively sharp **public-private distinction**	**Public-private distinction blurred** by individualization in public space

so few of these places in the mass society that people know most of these places and refer to them in conversation with other people. In the network society public spaces multiply because a new series of online public spaces is added and because every physical setting can also be connected to these new online spaces. Additionally, existing mass media channels are also going online. Many observers suppose that this multitude of public spaces is fragmenting public communication in society.

Fragmentation of public communication can also be concluded by people who observe a differentiation of public spaces in the network society as compared to the supposed unitary character of public spaces in the mass society. The traditional idea of a public sphere held by Habermas and other modernist observers after the Second World War was a unitary space serving as a common ground for all members of society. However, contemporary society is a mosaic of public spaces that are different. Post-modernist observers see them as distinct, while others (see for example Keane, 1995, 2000) still see them as partly overlapping, maintaining a common ground for public communication that is more complex than before.

In the course of the 20th century, the national and local public spaces of individual countries have been accompanied by global public spaces. In a new wave of globalization in history, an international civil society is emerging that is increasingly constructed around global communication networks (Castells, 2008). This global civil society and public sphere (places) were carried by the international press, radio and satellite TV in the middle of the 20th century and were significantly enhanced by the appearance of the World Wide Web at the end of the century. They were institutionalized by the United Nations and their organizations, the WTO, the IMF, the World Bank, the ITU, the International Court of Justice and many other global or regional organizations at the state level. At the civil society level, international NGOs such as Amnesty International, Greenpeace and Doctors Without Borders have become bigger and stronger than before. Finally, international social movements have also become larger such as movements against wars in Vietnam and Iraq, the anti- or other globalization movements and many movements for solidarity of any kind. Currently, public spaces can be local, national or global, and sometimes deal with the same issue such as environmental and climate problems.

Finally, public spaces in the mass society were characterized by sharp distinctions between the public and the private. In the network society, public and private communication and behavior are merging by means of networking directly linking private and public spaces. This shift will be elaborated below.

The reconstruction of the public sphere in the network society can spatially be portrayed in a map (see Figure 3.2). The first characteristic of this sphere in the network society is that it *consists of both offline and online spaces*. In this way, manifold spaces are added. They are mostly online public spaces in websites, weblogs, virtual communities and meetings, social media pages and tags and group exchange in (mobile) telecom-media. The second characteristic is that the public spaces of the network society are *less separated from private spaces* and are in fact merging. The most important reasons for this are a number of social and media trends. They are part of network individualism (Wellman, 2000) or network individualization (van Dijk, 1999) in which individuals are simultaneously behaving individually or privately and socially or publically. This social trend of the network society is supported by media networks that offer both personal and public communication.

The third characteristic of the networked public sphere is that *social spaces are multiplied and are increasingly linking public and private spaces*. The most striking example is, of course, the rise of social media. However, social networks are also appearing offline in more and more physical spaces, in spite of the perspective of 'bowling alone' described by scholars such as Putnam (2000). Even in individualized societies, physical cultural, social and political mass meetings satisfy particular social needs. Central squares and streets or public camps and festivals, actually traditional and historical settings of mass protest, are still remarkably frequently used for political activity and communication.

In all these spaces of the network society political communication can be observed. They are more numerous and manifold than before. Mass media, mass meetings, streets and cafes or coffee houses are no longer privileged as they were in the mass society analyzed by Habermas. Political conversations can take place in all of the spaces listed in Figure 4.2. Their reception and creation can also be take place by means of mobile media. Even more important is the fact that political information and communication flows between these spaces.

The dominance of the mass media with an allocation pattern in the mass society gives room for consultation, registration and conversation patterns of spreadable digital media in the network society (van Dijk, 2012). Moreover, the single, distinct and separate media of the mass society have made way for the integrated, interconnected and hybrid media of the network society. Fixed media are accompanied by mobile media. In this way, a vast universe of political communication can be created where an insignificant gaffe by a politician in an instant message can be transferred to a Tweet by someone

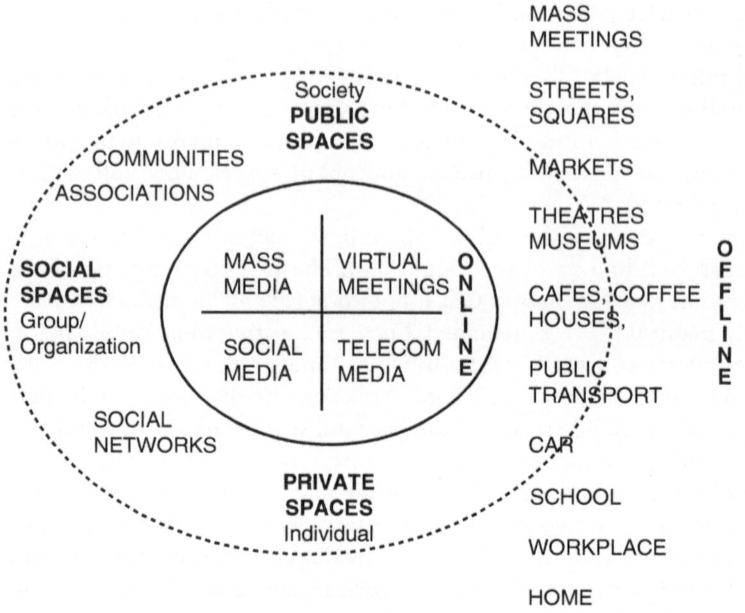

Figure 4.2 Online and offline public, private and social spaces in the network society.

who received it, discussed in a blog and a Facebook page and finally attract the attention of a newspaper. Conversely, every television news item can be discussed in any other spaces linked by social and telecommunication media or physical meetings.

The result of the media appearance and support of the public sphere is a mosaic of overlapping and linked public, social and private spaces in a cross-media constellation, as portrayed in Figure 4.3. These spaces can be very broad, reaching millions of people, such as with a television program, a movie or a YouTube video, or they can be very small, such as with a WhatsApp group chat. In between we can find medium-sized spaces such as Twitter-tag spaces or online discussion forums.

In this cross-media constellation, political communication is freely flowing everywhere and carried by all media available. This means that Habermas's model of the public sphere as a system with fixed components (mass media, civil society, lifeworld, political and economic institutions and others) and gatekeepers or sluices between them is no longer valid in the network society (see Friedland et al., 2006, p. 23). This does not mean that freedom or democracy reign in the network society. Open access to digital media is not assured and content circulates in accordance with power laws and other network properties (Chapter 2) and in accordance with the marketing mechanisms of social media platforms, the new gatekeepers in the network society.

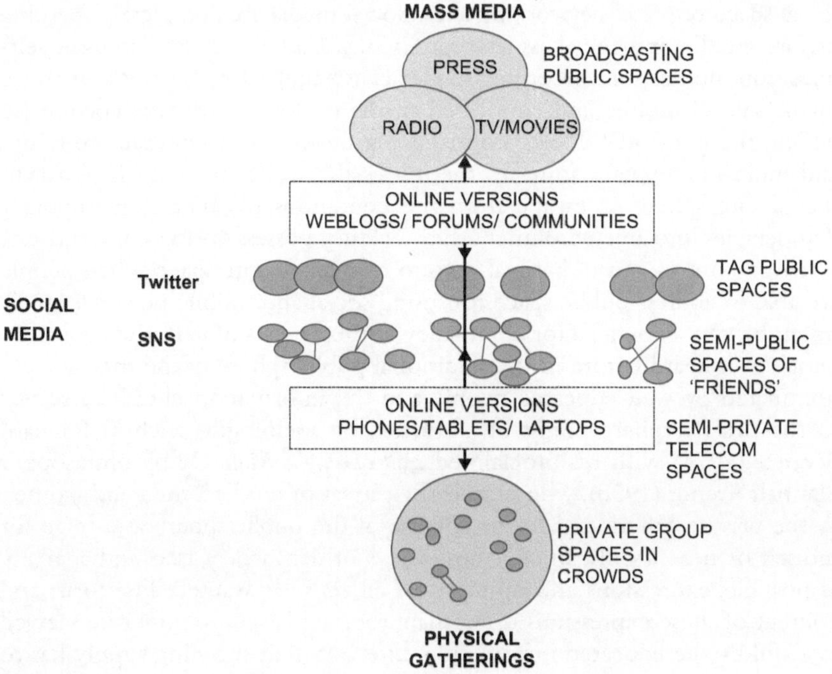

Figure 4.3 A mosaic of overlapping and linked public, private and social spaces.

Trends in the Reconstruction of Public Space

Merging Public and Private Space

Figures 4.2 and 4.3 show that in the network society public and private spaces are easily linked by social spaces and in terms of media by social media. However, the merging of public and private communication found in these spaces had already taken place in the mass society. In (high or late) modern society the self and self-identity are articulating in the context of society (Giddens, 1991). According to Giddens, *reflexive modernization* links self-identity and the actualization of individuals with collective reflexivity of societal issues. This means an increase of interconnections between collective, even globalizing, influences and personal dispositions. Modern and mass society also already showed a link between collective or public politics and a politics of personalization in the rise of *personality politics* enhanced by political communication on television (Hacker, 1995; Hart, 1994).

In the network society, this trend of interconnecting collective or public communication such as political communication, and personalization or life(style) politics, is enhanced by networking and *network individualization* being both a social and a media trend (van Dijk, 1999). Particularly with the rise of social media after 2004, public and private space are supported by the social space of social networking sites. Social media are completely merging private, public and social issues or opinions. Castells (2009) discusses self-mass-communication. According to Papacharissi (2010, p. 21), not only social media but all mobile and connected media enclose a: "private cocoon [in which] the individual directs atomized gestures of social, cultural, economic, and multi-contextual natures to the rest of the world. Individuals retreat to the private sphere to escape from the conditions plaguing contemporary democracies into an environment they feel they possess greater control over".

More control and individual autonomy over private space when people are able to address public space too using social and mobile personal media might be very beneficial for democracy in most views of it. It gives voices to people not heard before in the traditional public sphere of the mass society dominated by well-educated people and the information elite. The retreat to the private sphere might be mourned by sociologists such as Richard Sennett (1974) with his proclaimed *Fall of Public Man*. Or by philosopher Hannah Arendt (1958), who regrets the retreat of modern men and women to the private sphere and his or her use of the public sphere as a stage for himself or herself only. But in most views of democracy, free, and as many as possible, expressions and opinions of citizens are wanted. The form and content of these expressions using inappropriate language might be viewed as awful by the educated information elite, but their meaning simply has to be accepted as the voice of particular citizens in a democracy.

Nevertheless, a basic shift will occur with the merger of private and public space. Marichal (2012) content analyzed 250 Facebook discussion groups and observed that participants mainly postulate statements and do not engage in debate with others. He also noticed primarily personal (self) expression between individuals most often talking to like-minded people in their own set. These individuals express their own perspective, and much less frequently a public perspective. Discussions are concrete, personal and emotional rather than abstract, business-like and rational. The latter type of discussions are the ones we expect in a public debate. They are especially called for in the ideal-speech situation advocated by Habermas and most deliberative views of democracy. However, the first type of discussions might be a valuable extension for public and political debates that most often are normative. A combination of business-like or rational and personal or emotional aspects of discussions is inevitable in public debates in a network society merging public and private spaces.

Opening Public Space

The system of connected public, private and social spaces in the network society portrayed in Figures 4.2 and 4.3 has the potential to be more open for everybody than the public sphere in the mass society. Few professional job requirements for authors in online mass media, few editorial rejections and revisions of user-generated content and less gatekeeper actions are asked for in online mass media. This might be a source of regret for Internet critics such as Andrew Keen (2007, 2015), who calls Internet use a "Cult of the Amateur", but can also be seen as a benefit in terms of enabling inclusion. This might be a particular advantage for participatory and libertarian views of democracy. With digital media applications such as social media, blogging, public chatting and reader replies on online newspapers and magazines, more voices can be raised than in the traditional media (Rasmussen, 2008). In this way, the voices of people with a low level of education and skills of expression such as writing are entering the stage of public space.

Unfortunately, equal *reception* of these expressions is severely limited. These voices of people with a low level of education and skills receive less attention than people with a high level of education (Berkowitz, 1996). "Some citizens are better than others at articulating their views in rational, reasonable terms" (Sanders, 1997, p. 348). "The online public sphere is already a *de facto* aristocracy dominated by those skilled in the 'high deliberative arts'" (Hindman, 2008b, p. 18).

One of the consequences is that the quality and effectiveness of these voices can be questioned. Many observers, primarily people with a high level of education and from an upper or middle-class background, find these voices to be uncivilized or rude. Coe, Kenski, and Rains (2014) define incivility as "features of discussion that convey an unnecessarily disrespectful tone toward the discussion forum, its participants, or its topics". The question is whether the criticism of uncivilized expression is motivated by general norms or rules for proper manners in discussions or by particular biases of social class.

The cause of a lack of quality and effectiveness can also be traced back to the unequal digital skills in expression and discussion. In the previous chapter it was argued that the gap of physical access to digital media is closing in developed countries and that this increases the potential for political participation and including more and different voices from all parts of the population. However, the motivation, positive attitudes and benefits of using digital media for political communication are not necessarily improving with greater access. Additionally, a lack of digital skills is also likely to impair the political efficacy of these new voices.

Extreme Connectivity and Speed in Public Space

Figure 4.3 shows that all current media are linked and partly overlapping in current public, private and social spaces. These spaces are increasingly hosted by the same online infrastructure of the Web and telecommunication. In this way, all spaces and digital media are connected. This leads to an unprecedented *technical connectivity* of media and the people using them. When people are using this connectivity, they might produce *human or social connectedness* (van Dijck, 2013), also to be harnessed for political action and communication. Connectedness means that people have meaningful relationships with other people, in this case to achieve political or democratic goals. It is not certain that the extreme technical connectivity of digital networks will also lead to political connectedness in mobilization, political organization and other public or political activity. This depends or the historical context of these activities and the political motivation of political actors such as citizens.

When highly technical connectivity is used this might have positive consequences for political systems and for democracy. More political actors can be reached than before (when they are motivated to pay attention) and this can be achieved very quickly, using ever more types of media available. Reachability of citizens and representatives might be seen as an encouraging consequence of connectivity in most views of democracy.

However, the accompanying *speed* of the connections also has a downside for political systems and democracy (Hassan, 2009). Just like economic systems have problems with the very fast up-and-down ('yo-yo') movements on the financial and stock markets reinforced by computer networks, political systems are becoming more unstable by using the extreme connectivity and speed of networking. Political systems and democracies need some stability and time to operate (Saward, 2015). They are complex systems that could adapt to their environment when they use networks. However, adaption needs time. The first thing that happens is that a new stimulus comes from the environment and shakes the system. By using social media and other networks, it is relatively easy to call for a demonstration or even a flash mob for a political cause, but it is much more difficult to organize a party or another political organization to change a political system. This is one of the most important political lessons for movements in the Arab Spring. See Chapter 6.

A more general lesson for all views of representative democracy is that representation and deliberation need time (Coleman, 2017). It requires time for representatives to consult grassroots support, to liase with civil associations and businesses, and to deal with other representatives and their parties. In parliaments and other councils politicians have to deliberate and forge compromises that take days, weeks or months to be realized. Imagine that all of a sudden an online petition receives much support, a particular hype arrives, and a rumor or scandal about a politician or party unfolds on the Internet. Then all forged compromises and political strategies might become irrelevant. This happened after the unexpected result of the 2016 Brexit referendum in the UK. The system has to cope with the stimulus immediately. But in fact it sometimes takes years to follow up the one-day vote. The conclusion is that digital media use is fast but acting democratic systems are slow.

Contagion in Public Space

Another reason why political systems are becoming more unstable in spite of being more adaptable than before is that expressions in public space are becoming more and more contagious or viral. One unfortunate Tweet by a politician in charge can be retweeted by a follower to one of his or her contacts, who retweets it to his list of followers, with one person having a blog that is read by a professional journalist. This journalist publishes the message to an online newspaper and all readers share it with their own social media contacts. In one or two hours, 'everybody' knows about this unfortunate expression and a scandal is born. In this way, the trend of a rise of a 'politics of scandals' (Castells, 2008) is supported.

Merging Market and Public Space

In the network society, public space is even more dominated by private business than in the mass society. As a matter of fact, in the mass society privatization of mass communication and telecommunication were already on the rise. However, in the mass society other media organization models than advertisement-led supply only were still available. Examples are state media in socialist and authoritarian societies, public broadcasting and telephony or strongly publically regulated private media in democratic societies. In the 1980s and 1990s, public media were largely privatized and deregulated. After the coming of the World Wide Web, the Internet became dominated by advertisement-led business and revenue models of supply. In this way, users experienced and became accustomed to 'free' usage of web content. This has enormous consequences for democracy and political communication.

The first consequence is that not only are public and private spaces merging, but so too is the private and public *content* produced and exchanged in public spaces. The distinction is barely visible anymore. Today, web supply is largely commercialized and its use is fully surveyed by cookies and other inspections. The main norm for public media advocated by Habermas that they should be independent of business and government now seems to be an utopian ideal. The result might be that users or citizens are becoming vulnerable to manipulation by commercial interests or political propaganda without noticing that this is taking place. Every message accompanied by advertising and manipulated by interfaces designed by producers is loaded with particular commercial or political meaning.

Free Internet access and content are very attractive to users. They support inclusion because otherwise some users could or would not pay for them. However, this option also seduces users to choose only free news and information sources instead of higher-quality paid-for sources . This is an instance of the *usage gap* discussed in Chapter 3. Some people use the Internet for the advantage of obtaining knowledge and to help them in their careers while other people primarily use it for fun, commerce and chat. Similarly, politically motivated citizens might pay for a quality online newspaper while less motivated citizens will only want a free newspaper, but are in fact paying for privacy loss and ad consumption, and perhaps even political propaganda.

Other consequences for democracy of public spaces being primarily designed by public companies are all kinds of manipulation in political communication. In the mass society traditional mass media were deemed to have an enormous effect on political communication by means of agenda setting, framing and gatekeeping content. In the network society, digital media are supposed to be controlled by the users and some say that intermediaries are not needed anymore. Unfortunately, this is a big mistake. On the Internet, intermediaries are in fact *more effective* than in the traditional media. For example, on social media a 'media logic' is at work that is just as operative as the traditional media logic of agenda setting, framing, gatekeeping and professionalism of journalists. Social media logic consists of the strategies, mechanisms and economies underpinning the platforms concerned (van Dijck & Poell, 2013). "Far from being neutral platforms, social media are affecting the conditions and rules of social interaction" (ibid, p. 3).

The first effect of social media, and in fact all digital platforms, is *programmability* (van Dijck & Poell, 2013). Compared to the traditional mass media effects derived from scheduled content in programs, social media platforms have the ability to trigger and steer users' creative or communicative contributions. They achieve this by means of their algorithms and interfaces. Algorithms are a kind of code (see Chapter 2) that shape all kinds of relational activities, such as liking, recommending and sharing (van Dijck & Poell, 2013, p. 5). They are not neutral as they are partly programmed to create as many messages as possible because they contain personal data to be processed for targeting advertisements according to the revenue and business models of the commercial platforms. These platforms are both directed by user choices or actions and by the models of the providers. Unfortunately, the algorithms used by the providers are proprietary and not known by the users. Some providers give more freedom of choice to users than others. "Reddit generally leaves more power to its users in terms of what to post and how to channel attention to a topic than Facebook or YouTube" (van Dijck & Poell, 2013, p. 6).

Another effect of the commercial platforms is the *visibility of popularity*. "As platforms like Facebook and Twitter matured, their techniques for filtering out popular items and influential people became gradually more sophisticated" (van Dijck & Poell, 2013, p. 6). Currently, the number of followers and other items of popularity, so important in politics, can simply be bought.

So, it is possible to conclude that the private digital and social media platforms are the new intermediaries, agenda-setting makers and gatekeepers of the network society. Imagine if these platforms had been created as public utilities primarily managed by users themselves, and for example paid for via subscriptions and without advertisement and personal data selling. Then they could have been more neutral public operators in public space. Similarly, they would be more neutral carriers for political and democratic communication.

Oligopoly in Public Space

In the mass society, media observers and policy makers worried about the monopoly power of big newspapers, television and radio channels. Governments made laws to prevent a newspaper or broadcasting company taking a decisive share of the market. Surprisingly, in the network society governments do not seem to care that a few (American) companies control the Internet exchange. Companies such as Google, Apple, Microsoft, Facebook and Amazon together carry and control the vast proportion of Internet traffic through their interfaces, algorithms and imposed user agreements. This also comprises control over political and government information. In the mass society governments and political parties had a big influence over the media infrastructure and content of the mass media with their spokespersons, lobbyists and spin doctors. In some cases and countries they also had their own public media and information sources. In the network society governments and parties have to follow the rules and conditions of commercial social networking sites and online newspapers. When they provide their information sources, for instance their own Facebook pages, users have to follow the interfaces, algorithms and business models and user agreements about copyright, privacy, publicity and storage conditions imposed by the provider.

At the start of the World Wide Web, people thought that complete freedom of innumerable supplies of senders and sources would be provided on the Internet. Indeed, according to the picture provided by Anderson's long tail, millions of sources and voices have become available to Internet users. However, in fact an oligopoly of the mentioned American Internet companies is by far the biggest carrier of political and government information. In between the innumerable Anderson tail suppliers and these oligopolies, relatively few medium-sized media and sources are available (Hindman, 2008a). This distribution is created by a power law working on the Internet (see Chapter 2). The result is particular oligopolies having enormous power in offering and organizing public space.

Fragmentation and Uniformity, Polarization and Depolarization in Public Space

These oligopolies supplying and hosting public space does not mean that *users* have no choice or less choice in using channels for political and other types of communication. When the Internet and the World Wide Web emerged, people imagined that they would offer a huge space for freely expressing and receiving views and for consuming much more diverse content than at the time was offered by the traditional media. In this way, public space was supposed to become more open and continually expanding. This would give the opportunity for consensus and conciliation (as will be discussed in Chapter 5). These effects would benefit democracy in every view.

After the year 2000, more pessimistic or critical points of view arrived. Sunstein (2001, 2007), Jamieson and Cappella (2008) and Garrett (2009) observed that users in fact selected and preferably discussed views with like-minded people in so-called *echo chambers*. Additionally, online political discussion was likely to lead to polarization instead of conciliation. These effects of bias and polarization would be harmful in most views of democracy, especially pluralist and deliberative democracy.

These opposing views can only be validly assessed by making a clear distinction between the selection, expression and reception of views on the Internet. In *selection*, the question is whether people are processing information in networks selectively or not. Many people experience positive feelings when they find information that confirms their views. This might be explained by the classical theory of cognitive dissonance by Festinger (1954). In this case, network homogeneity would be reinforced as people will preferably look for links and views by like-minded people they know or find. Then 'echo chambers' of discussion could be created.

However, digital networks also have the opportunity to forge network heterogeneity, where people are able to expand the links and views they find. See the discussion about the accidental exposure thesis in Chapter 3. Brundidge (2010) found that some people inadvertently find other views in their own surfing on the Internet. For frequent social media users who also frequently consume news, post news themselves and talk about politics on social networking sites, they show a high level of network heterogeneity (Lee, Choi, Kim, & Kim, 2014). The open, integrated and cross-media public space created by digital networks and described in the first part of this chapter supports the opportunities provided by network heterogeneity. People might come across surprising or unsolicited sources. Barberá (2015) found evidence in the United States, Germany and Spain that social media platforms facilitate exposure to messages from other individuals with whom they have weak ties. This provides novel information not found in offline interactions. Weak ties tend to be with people who are more politically heterogeneous than in people's immediate personal networks. This exposure reduces fragmentation and polarization. This is the opposite of creating 'echo chambers' of Internet discussions.

This discussion was supported by a nationwide representative survey and experiment among 5,677 Norwegian Internet users (Karlsen et al., 2017). 40% of these users were online debaters using social media and online newspaper outlets. Of these debaters, 53% of those who discussed issues with like-minded people said they *as well* (very) often discussed issues with people with opposing views. About one-third (31%) were often contradicted by someone who was in complete disagreement with them. Only 24% of online debaters say they were never contradicted in the debate (Karlsen et al., 2017, p. 9). Of those who have been contradicted, a majority of 71% said that their own views were reinforced. So, there was not only an expected confirmation bias but also a *dis*confirmation basis creating reinforcement of people's own views.

After having refined the echo chamber thesis in this way, the researchers found a *trench warfare* dynamic in the debate. In experiments conducted for the survey (giving three samples different arguments in questions for and against gender inequality) it appeared that prior views were most reinforced with people with the most polarized views (Karlsen et al., 2017, pp. 11–13). This trench warfare dynamic was polarizing the debate. However, 45% of the online debaters in this project also claimed to often learn something new, and only 21% said that this never happens. Karlsen et al. (2017, p. 14) suggest that short-term effects of online debates might show reinforcement, but long-term effects after being confronted with opposing views might nevertheless be learning and modification. This gives opportunities for depolarization.

Selecting information and sources is only the start for people that want to create content themselves in *expression*. Most people only read and do not write political opinion on the Internet. But when they do, they have more outlets than ever before in online public space. The Internet abounds with (semi-) political expressions although it only constitutes a tiny percentage of total web content. The most important outlets are social media, online newspaper reactions, instant messaging and all kinds of online forums and communities. See Table 4.2 below. Every view in the spectrum of views about a particular topic can be found in these outlets. The views are so extensive and dispersed that they tend to fragment political discussion. However, they also come together because the integrated and cross-media system of public space – see Figure 4.3 – easily and swiftly transfers current discussion topics to other places and media because of the extreme connectivity and speed of contemporary public space discussed above (Chadwick, 2013).

This is reinforced by the concentration of *reception* in practice. Selection and expression have boundless opportunities in networked public space, but reception has limits. Audiences have finite attention in taking advantage of these opportunities. The vast majority of political expression on blogs, Tweets and other social media and other online media messages gets no hearing. Instead, users in fact limit their attention to the most popular links and sources or are looking for messages from like-minded people. This results in preferential treatment of links or sources, following the power law of networks (see Chapter 2). The result is that in terms of audience, online content is more concentrated than print and broadcasting content (Hindman, 2008a, 2008b). Reception is unequal in terms of attention:

> Even within the tiny politics niche, top sites have replicated a broadcast-style model of public attention. Moreover, those who get heard in the online public sphere are in many ways *less* representative and *more* elite than those whose voices were carried by traditional media.
>
> (Hindman, 2008b, p. 15)

The conclusion of this section is that the use of online public space for political communication is both simultaneously extended and limited, pluralist and uniform, fragmented and united. The results depend on the goal of political communicators, their use of digital media, the characteristics of these media and the political, economic and social context.

Online and Offline Discussion in Public Space

Over the course of the last 25 to 30 years, research about the comparison between online and offline discussion in public space has been marked by a duality of face-to-face and computer-mediated communication. The advantages and disadvantages of these modes of communication were the focus of attention. These modes are now merging in ubiquitous mobile computing. For example, these days political rallies are combined with permanent mobile telephony, e-mail and search engine use and social media connections such as Twitter and Facebook. Now the perspective focuses on the more or less successful integration of these modes of communication. In this context, the opportunities for online discussion in public space are no longer so distinctive. They are directly linked with more or less traditional offline discussion in political discourse.

A second qualification of political discussion in public space is that its democratic goal is more to support opinion making than decision making. Of course, online public discussion is also engaged in at times of elections in support of particular candidates and parties, but political discussion overwhelmingly focuses on giving general views about social and political issues. Very few examples can be found of Internet discussion that leads to decisions in referenda or other plebiscites. Social and political opinion making goes on outside election times and the sphere of institutional politics. In fact, election and political party discourse is a small part of continuous social and political opinion making.

A third qualification is that online political discussion in public space is more organized in assemblies of individuals than in groups. Most comparisons of online and offline discussion in the literature assume that online discussions are in some kind of group to be observed for group decision making. In fact, they are loose assemblies of individuals that do not meet and do not actually know each other, so they are at best virtual groups. In these assemblies, other social-psychological characteristics apply than in offline groups, or mixed online and offline groups.

In the literature, the type of groups or assemblies in online and offline political discussion are not sufficiently differentiated. Table 4.2 is a proposal to distinguish individual and collective input in online and offline discussion outlets of citizens. The first row in the table contains the input of individuals in online and offline contexts. Individuals give their own views in discussion outlets, which are not organized as a real group with a particular goal, task or identity. Here, individuals participate in offline meetings with another purpose than political discussion only. The second row shows cases of collective input of political discussion in offline and online organized real groups. These groups have specific goals and tasks in debates and a particular group identity. While individual input is oriented to opinion making, collective input might be organized for decision making.

Table 4.2 Offline and online political discussion outlets in groups and assemblies with individual and collective input.

	Offline	*Offline and online*	*Online*
INDIVIDUAL Input, goal, task and identity	Public/private meeting - street - market - café, coffee house - political rally	Public/private meetings streamed online Broadcasting (studio) meeting with online reactions	SNS assemblies Twitter hashtags Facebook/ Google+ pages Online newspaper replies Political site reactions
COLLECTIVE Input, goal, task and identity	Political units or task-groups Party/political organization congress	Political units or groups discussing issues offline and online Congress online	Online for a: government initiative citizen initiative (e.g. Usenet groups or SNS groups) Online congress

When we want to summarize the advantages and disadvantages of offline and online discussion in networked public spaces, we have to carefully distinguish between outlets with individual and collective input. The first advantage of online and integrated online and offline individual input in outlets of public and political discussion is the low threshold for citizens to participate when the public space concerned is open. Access to social media is fairly equal in terms of social status and class. In reading online newspapers and political sites or blogs, medium and highly educated people dominate. In all these outlets sending messages and reactions is easy. The result is that more voices are heard in these outlets than in traditional public outlets and media. They have an expressive function for citizens and their goal is opinion making. In this way, "members of society clarify their own views, learn about the opinions of others, and discover what major problems face the collective" (Stromer-Galley & Wichowski, 2011, p. 169). These advantages also apply in the collective input of discussion groups, to be discussed shortly.

Disadvantages of individual input in meetings and assemblies with political discussion are that interactivity is low. There are very few reactions to reactions such as one or two retweets and social network site replies. They are more individual expressions than collective exchanges. People often repeat their opinion or confirm similar views in a kind of echoing well. This offers mental reassurance and a valve for frustration in airing opinions, but it is not effective as a contribution to political discussion. The best effect might be that these views are taken as serious information about the views of a part of the citizenry by politicians, campaigners and representatives.

A second difficulty is that inputs in these settings frequently contain *flaming* (verbal attacks or insults) and *trolling* (expressions trying to disrupt the conversation). These phenomena occur most frequently in conditions of anonymity, unorganized and unofficial discussion calls and general invitations for comments to online newspaper articles or simply retweeting (Coleman, 2004; Douglas & McGarty, 2001).

Collective input in real groups offline, online or mixed online and offline (second row in Table 4.1) is able to create genuine debate. The advantage is that it bridges the distance between discussants, who will have the time to think about their reactions. In theory, status markers have no effect here. In practice, people also look for status cues online according to SIDE theory (Spears & Lea, 1992). In real groups, online and offline interactive debate with high-quality discussion can be realized. Unfortunately, in practice the quality of online group debates is disappointing (Stromer-Galley & Wichowski, 2011). Interactivity is poor because discussion threads are short and the level of reciprocity or responses to the messages of others, and mutual understanding of others, is low (Davis, 2005; Jankowski & van Os, 2004; Jankowski & van Selm, 2000; Wilhelm, 1998).

A second problem of collective input in real groups is the phenomenon of *group think* that is just as important in online as in offline groups (Price, Nir, & Cappella, 2006). Sunstein (2008) and Sunstein and Hastie (2008) observed four instances of 'group think' in online forums and groups:

- *Amplifying errors:* bias in groups tends to be not reduced but extended; escalation to a course of action that is failing has often been observed;
- *Common knowledge effect:* information and views held by the majority or all group members have far more influence than minority or individual information/views (that tend to remain silent);
- *Cascades:* following the lead of others, people go along with the crowd to maintain a good opinion in the eyes of others even though they know better (they also remain silent);
- *Polarization*: in online groups, initial individual views turn more extreme instead of finding a compromise.

These instances of group think suggest that familiar social-psychological and group-dynamic effects also occur in online collective discussions, perhaps even more so than in offline group discussions. Likewise, some of these group effects might also appear in individual input by assemblies of people they do not meet and do not even know. Here, common knowledge effects and polarization can also be observed.

These effects are no problem for digital democracy unless one supports a view of democracy in which deliberation and ideal-speech situations are the basis for effective political opinion and decision making. This is the case in the deliberative pluralist democracy view of Dahlberg inspired by Habermas. This view advocates "a deliberative public sphere as the ideal for citizen participation in politics, where rational debate or argumentation between citizens over common problems leads to critically informed public opinion that can guide and scrutinize official decision making processes" (Dahlberg, 2007, pp. 48–49).

This deliberative sphere is assumed to work because "the Internet's two-way, relatively low cost, semi-decentralized and global communications, combined with evolving interactive software and moderation techniques, offer the ideal basis (particularly when compared to the mass media) for rational deliberation" (ibid.). Rational debate or argumentation is supposed to be:

> ideally *inclusive* (formally); *free* (non-coercive, including autonomy from state and corporate interests); *equal* (communicatively); *sincere* (as far as this is possible), *respectful* (putting oneself in the position of the other); *reasoned* (framing arguments in terms of why particular claims *ought* to be accepted) and *reflexive* (identity re-constituting).
>
> (Dahlberg, 2007, p. 49)

These assumed properties of rational debate on the Internet have been called into question by many critics (Davis, 2005; Fraser, 1992; Hill & Hughes, 1998; Wilhelm, 1998). In this book we have argued that participation in online communication in general is not inclusive and not equal (see Chapter 3). Online public space is not free concerning the state (surveillance) and corporate interests (social and other social media discourse tainted by commercial interests; see above and Chapter 2). Many contributions in debates are not sincere or respectful. Reasoned and reflexive arguments are a tiny part of popular online discussions.

Furthermore, in terms of the effectiveness online forums for decision making, it has been observed that they do not easily result in consensus and conclusions (van Dijk, 2012, p. 258). In face-to-face discussion, a natural drive exists for members to reach compromise and conclusions, in order to produce results, a drive that is absent in online discussion settings. So, in online discussions careful design of the discussion format, professional moderation and organizational or discussion rules are needed even more than in offline settings (Trénel, 2004; Wright & Street, 2007). "Better discussions seem to occur when there is moderation of the discussions, well-designed software to promote reciprocity and contemplation, and co-mingling of citizens and political elites" (Stromer-Galley & Wichowski, 2011, p. 180).

A final problem concerning political decision making via online forums is that most political representatives and governors do not accept the results of this type of e-participation (van Dijk, 2010). They stick to their representative role and doubt the representativeness of online forums.

Conclusions

In the network society, the public sphere is transformed into a multitude of global, national and local public spaces integrated by both online and offline communication. Habermas's normative concept of the unitary public sphere is outdated. His norm that public media should be self-regulating, rationally reflexive and independent of business and government goes against all trends. In the network society, all kinds of distinctions of Habermas's image of society are blurring. Public and private spaces are merging. Discourse is more concrete, personal and emotional than abstract, business-like and rational. Public spaces are not independent for citizens but partly ruled by private oligopolies. Together with governments they survey both public and private spaces. The big digital and social media platforms are the new intermediaries, agenda-setting makers and gatekeepers of the network society. In the perspective of the audience, online content is more concentrated than print and broadcasting content.

However, public spaces in the network society are more open for everybody who has digital access and skills than the public sphere was previously. New and more voices can be heard. Nevertheless, the quality and effectiveness of these voices can be questioned. Selection and expression have boundless opportunities in networked public space, but reception has limits. Those who are *actually* heard on online public spaces with their refined digital skills might be less representative and more elite than those whose voices were carried by traditional media. Rational debate is far from being free, equal or respectful, and often it is not rational at all.

The extreme connectivity and speed of public spaces in the network society make political systems unstable (van Dijk, 2012). Representative democracy needs some stability and time to deliberate and decide. However, communication in digital media and its effects are relatively quick to emerge. Currently, representative political systems are slow to accommodate these effects.

References

Arendt, H. (1958). *The human condition*. Chicago: University of Chicago Press.

Barberá, P. (2015). *How social media reduces mass political polarization: Evidence from Germany, Spain, and the U.S.* Working paper. Retrieved from http://rubenson.org/wp-content/uploads/2015/10/barbera-tpbw.pdf

Berkowitz, P. (1996). The debating society. *The New Republic*, November 26, 1996, p. 36.

Brundidge, J. (2010). Encountering "difference" in the contemporary public sphere: The contribution of the Internet to the heterogeneity of political discussion networks. *Journal of Communication, 60*(4), 680–700.

Castells, M. (2008). The new public sphere: Global civil society, communication networks, and global governance. *The ANNALS of the American Academy of Political and Social Science, 616*, 78–93.

Castells, M. (2009). *Communication power*. Oxford, UK: Oxford University Press.

Chadwick, A. (2013). *The hybrid media system: Politics and power*. Oxford, UK; New York: Oxford University Press.

Coe, K., Kenski, K., & Rains, S. A. (2014). Online and uncivil? Patterns and determinants of incivility in newspaper website comments. *Journal of Communication, 64*(4), 658–679.

Coleman, S. (2004). Connecting parliament to the public via the Internet: Two case studies of online consultations. *Information, Communication & Society*, 7(1), 1–22.

Coleman, S. (2017). *Can the Internet strengthen democracy?* Cambridge, UK; Malden, MA: Polity Press.

Dahlberg, L. (2007). The Internet, deliberative democracy, and power: Radicalizing the public sphere. *International Journal of Media & Cultural Politics, 3*(1), 47–64.

Davis, R. (2005). *Politics online: Blogs, chatrooms, and discussion groups in American democracy.* New York: Routledge.

Douglas, K. M., & McGarty, C. (2001). Identifiability and self-presentation: Computer-mediated communication and intergroup interaction. *British Journal of Social Psychology, 40*(3), 399–416.

Festinger, L. (1954). A theory of social comparison processes. *Human Relations*, 7(2), 117–140.

Fraser, N. (1992). Rethinking the public sphere: A contribution to the critique of a actually existing democracy. In C. Calhoun (Ed.), *Habermas and the public sphere* (pp. 109–142). Cambridge, MA: The MIT Press.

Friedland, L., Hove, T., & Rojas, H. (2006). The networked public sphere. *Javnost-The Public, 13*(4), 5–26.

Garrett, R. K. (2009). Politically motivated reinforcement seeking: Reframing the selective exposure debate. *Journal of Communication, 59*(4), 676–699.

Giddens, A. (1991) *Modernity and self-identity: Self and society in the late modern age.* Cambridge, UK: Polity Press.

Habermas, J. (2006). Political communication in media society: Does democracy still enjoy an epistemic dimension? The impact of normative theory on empirical research. *Communication Theory, 16*, 411–412.

Hacker, K. L. (1995). *Candidate images in presidential elections.* Westport, CT; London: Greenwood Publishing Group.

Hacker, K. L., & van Dijk, J. (2000). *Digital democracy: Issues of theory and practice.* London; Thousand Oaks, CA; New Delhi: Sage.

Hart, R. P. (1994). *Seducing America: How the television charms the modern voter.* Oxford, UK; New York: Oxford University Press.

Hassan, R. (2009). *Empires of speed: Time and the acceleration of politics and society* (Vol. 4). Leiden: Brill.

Held, D. (1987). Models of democracy. Cambridge, UK: Polity Press.

Hill, K. A., & Hughes, J. E. (1998). *Cyberpolitics: Citizen activism in the age of the Internet.* Lanham, MD: Rowman & Littlefield Publishers, Inc.

Hindman, M. (2008a). *The myth of digital democracy.* Princeton, NJ: Princeton University Press.

Hindman, M. (2008b). What is the online public sphere good for? In J. Turow & T. Lokman (Eds.), *The hyperlinked society: Questioning connections in the digital age* (pp. 268–288). Michigan, WS: Digital Culture Books.

Jamieson, K. H., & Cappella, J. N. (2008). *Echo chamber: Rush Limbaugh and the conservative media establishment.* New York: Oxford University Press.

Jankowski, N., & van Os, R. (2004). Internet-based political discourse: A case study of electronic democracy in Hoogeveen. In P. Shane (Ed.), *Democracy online: The prospects for political renewal through the Internet* (pp. 181–93). New York: Routledge.

Jankowski, N., & van Selm, M. (2000). The promise and practice of public debate in cyberspace. In K. L. Hacker & J. van Dijk (Eds.), *Digital democracy: Issues of theory and practice* (pp 149–65). London; Thousand Oaks, CA; New Delhi: Sage.

Karlsen, R., Steen-Johnsen, K., Wollebæk, D., & Enjolras, B. (2017). Echo chamber and trench warfare dynamics in online debates. *European Journal of Communication, 32*(3), 257–273.

Keane, J. (1995). Structural transformations of the public sphere. *The Communication Review, 1*(1), 1–22.

Keane, J. (2000). Structural transformations of the public sphere. In K. L. Hacker & J. van Dijk (Eds.), *Digital democracy:Issues of theory & practice* (pp. 70–89). London; Thousand Oaks, CA; New Delhi: Sage.

Keane, J. (2009). *The life and death of democracy*. New York: W.W. Norton & Company.

Keen, A. (2007). *The cult of the amateur: How today's Internet is killing our culture*. New York; London: Doubleday/Currency.

Keen, A. (2015). *The Internet is not the answer.* London: Atlantic Monthly Press.

Lee, J. K., Choi, J., Kim, C., & Kim, Y. (2014). Social media, network heterogeneity, and opinion polarization. *Journal of Communication, 64*(4), 702–722.

Marichal, J. (2012). *Facebook democracy: The architecture of disclosure and the threat to public life*. Surrey: Ashgate.

Papacharissi, Z. (2010). *A private sphere: Democracy in a digital age (Digital Media and Society)*. Cambridge, UK, Malden, MA: Polity Press.

Price, V., Nir, L., & Cappella, J. N. (2006). Normative and informational influences in online political discussions. *Communication Theory, 16*(1), 47–74.

Putnam, R. D. (2000). *Bowling alone: America's declining social capital*. New York; London: Simon & Schuster.

Rasmussen, T. (2008). The Internet and differentiation in the political public sphere. *Nordic Review of Research on Media & Communication, 29*(2), 73–84.

Sanders, L. M. (1997). Against deliberation. *Political Theory, 25*(3), 347–376.

Saward, M. (2015). Agency, design and 'slow democracy'. *Time & Society, 26*(3), 362–383.

Sennett, R. (1974). *The fall of public man*. New York: W.W. Norton.

Spears, R., & Lea, M. (1992) Social influence and the influence of the "social" in computer-mediated communication. In M. Lea (Ed.), *Contexts of computer-mediated communication* (pp. 30–65). Hemel Hempstead, UK: Harvester Wheatsheaf.

Sunstein, C. R. (2001). *Republic.com*. Princeton, NJ: Princeton University Press.

Sunstein, C. R. (2007). *Republic.com 2.0*. Princeton, NJ: Princeton University Press.

Sunstein, C. (2008). *Infotopia: How many minds produce knowledge*. Oxford, UK; New York: Oxford University Press.

Sunstein, C. R., & Hastie, R. (2008). *Four failures of deliberating groups*. Olin working paper, University of Chicago Law & Economics.

Stromer-Galley, J., & Wichowski, A. (2011). Political discussion online. In M. Consalvo & C. Ess (Eds.), *The handbook of Internet studies* (pp. 168–187). Chichester: Wiley-Blackwell.

Trénel, M. (2004). *Measuring the deliberativeness of online discussions. Coding scheme 2.4*. Report. Berlin: Social Science Research Centre.

van Dijck, J. (2013). *The culture of connectivity: A critical history of social media*. New York: Oxford University Press.

van Dijck, J., & Poell, T. (2013). Understanding social media logic. *Media and Communication, 1*(1), 2–14.

van Dijk, J. (1999). *The network society*. London; New Delhi; Thousand Oaks, CA; Singapore: Sage.

van Dijk, J. A. G. M. (2010). Participation in policy-making: Study on the social impact of ICT. Final report. In *EU-SMART PROJECT: CPP N 55A – SMART N 2007/0068. Study on the social impact of ICT (Topic Report 3)*. Brussels: European Commission.

van Dijk, J. (2012). *The network society* (3rd ed.). London; New Delhi; Thousand Oaks, CA; Singapore: Sage.

Wellman, B. (2000). Changing connectivity: A future history of Y2.03K. *Sociological Research Online, 4*(4). Retrieved from www.socresonline.org.uk/4/4/wellman.html

Wilhelm, A. G. (1998). Virtual sounding boards: How deliberative is on-line political discussion?. *Information Communication & Society, 1*(3), 313–338.

Wolfe, A. (1997). Public and private in theory and practice: Some implications of an uncertain boundary. In: J. Weintraub & K. Kumar (Eds.), *Public and private in thought and practice* (pp. 182–203). Chicago: University of Chicago Press.

Wright, S., & Street, J. (2007). Democracy, deliberation and design: The case of online discussion forums. *New Media & Society, 9*(5), 849–869.

5 Digital Media and Networking

Opportunities and Constraints for Depolarizing Political Discourse

Co-authored by Ben Mollov, Bar-Ilan University, Israel

Introduction

The task of conflict resolution, which is inherently related to the effort of managing or guiding political discourse, has generally yielded evidence that human nature and society can be at times self-serving and conflictual, but at other times exhibit cooperation toward common goals and constructive communication. In this chapter, we will first seek to discuss the conditions in which human cooperation and moderate political discourse can take place. Somewhat in parallel to the discourse of the conditions in which depolarized political discourse can take place in general, three arguments have been advanced concerning the role that digital communication can play in depolarizing political discourse. In brief, the first suggests that the nature of new technologies can fundamentally and dramatically help to alter, favorably, discourse through use of these new avenues of communication; the second suggests that these new communication technologies will neither necessarily add to or detract from efforts at depolarizing discourse. The third argument however, which we will support, is that under the proper conditions digital communication can contribute to a depolarization of discourse based on appropriate social and technological usage with added value.

Social Psychology and Human Nature

The English philosopher Thomas Hobbes based his views and praise of the Leviathan on the assumption that unrestrained human behavior is crass and barbaric. A strong government must constrain the selfishness of greedy and self-interested individuals. Others like French philosopher Jean-Jacques Rousseau, however, argued that humans can be motivated by more than self-interest and can in fact act on the basis of empathy and moral principles. This latter view has elicited more scientific confirmation than the former today (Benkler, 2011). Simply put, political discourse can be negative, but it can also be positive.

Social psychologist Philip Zimbardo (2007) found over decades of research that all humans are capable of either good or bad behavior, and which they choose often results from social influence. Humans have motives for both positive and negative behavior, including communication behavior. Yochai Benkler (2011) observes that human social systems cannot rely on compensation, control or punishment alone, but must include cooperation. Companies like Toyota deliberately build cooperation among employees by building trust and collaborative networks. The Chicago police force is attempting something similar by having less reliance on swift law enforcement and more reliance on citizens working together with police to prevent criminal activity (Benkler, 2011).

Given this duality of human nature and its susceptibility to the influence of social environmental factors, we will now move on to a discussion of polarization in political discourse in general and the possibilities for its moderation in the sense of guiding it toward civil and cooperative communication.

Polarization in Political Communication

There are numerous admonitions about the power of polarized political discourse to encourage and facilitate violent political actions and to block peaceful international negotiations. For example, Human Rights Watch noted that the 2001 political violence in Haiti occurred in a climate of "extreme political polarization" (December 18). It is generally assumed that polarized discourse contributes to stereotyping, racism and ethnic prejudice, violence and terrorism (Ellis, 2006; Hacker, Coombs, Weaver, & McCulloh, 2006). It is commonly known that polarizing discourse creates polarizing politics.

Recent Pew research polling data in the United States indicates increasing polarization among Democrats and Republicans (Pew Research, 2014). One onerous aspect of this polarization is the finding that political polarization in the United States is highest among those people are who most engaged with politics. More striking, however, is the discovery that people who are highly partisan and polarized think of the other party's members as so misled that they constitute a threat to the wellbeing of the nation. Some scholars argue that political communication has always been extreme and polarized. Evidence from American history shows even more uncivil behavior among politicians in the 19th century. While it is true that the political discourse of the 19th century was vitriolic and mean in presidential elections, these were times when dueling was legal and politicians carried guns and hard liquor into Congress. The point is not that polarization is worse than the 1800s, but that it is dramatically worse than it was just a few decades ago in the 20th century.

Political polarization is a process in which a community becomes divided by one or more of the fault-lines of the human condition (e.g. ethnicity, nation, class, exclusion, income). Conflicts originate as incompatible goals that divide disputants into camps of "Us" and "Them." Social structures within camps are reinforced through discourse that propagates positive beliefs about "Us" (righteous, legitimate, victims, superior, etc.) and negative beliefs about "Them" (evil, illegitimate, aggressors, inferior, etc.). These beliefs manifest in polarized dialogue through discourse features such as: 1) dehumanization of "Them" by naming them with negatively loaded collective nouns (e.g. Zionist); 2) attribution of blame to "Them" for hurting "Us"; 3) reference to a fixed set of highly affectively charged historical incidents in which "They" hurt "Us" (e.g. the Holocaust), or reinforcing expressions of approval at statements that enhance group cohesion and strong disapproval at statements that question the basis for cohesion. Some terrorism experts believe that the reason people become terrorists is rooted in this "Us" versus "Them" way of thinking, which includes the belief that violence must be used to communicate with the out-group (Turk, 2004).

Theories of Social Behavior and Conflict Reduction

Social identity theories such as self-classification theory can be used to describe how people develop positive and intense social identities to the point that they derogate certain out-groups. Hope, however, is found in the fact that strong in-group identity, contrary to what many social psychologists have assumed, does not have to result in out-group derogation. We will argue later that with digital communication (web-based, social media and other digital communication platforms), for example, we can have groups that feel a very intense commitment to their own ethnicity, religion, and political groups, while still respecting the identities and values of others.

As globalization increases, people tend to gain more comfort from their local identities. Contrary to some popular accounts, nationalism and local tribalism do not decline as globalization and communication networking increase. Thickening of identities, whether religious or ethnic, helps people resist what they view as oppressive forces that might endanger them. There is no global culture in globalization, but rather a diversity of sustaining cultures and identities which engage in informational politics and easier communication with technologies (Castells, 1997). People sometimes hold onto tribal or group identities when they feel threatened by other political groups.

Dynamics of Political Discourse

Polarized discourse exhibits some easily recognizable features. First, groups engaged in this discourse often rely on their being separate from and in conflict with the other group's defining feature of their identity. In order to be German in Hitler's Germany, one had to first be "Not Jewish" (Turner et al., 1987). Second, polarization generally devolves into mutual dehumanization (Galtung, Jacobsen & Brand-Jacobsen, 2002; Gergen, McNamee, & Barrett, 2001). That is, both parties engage in polarized discourse regarding the other party as less than human, leading to the potential for justification of violence.

There are six processes commonly used to frame other groups of people in ways that justify violence against them: exaggerated comparison, euphemistic labeling, blame attributions, dehumanization, moral exclusion, and self-perception of victimhood (Ellis, 2006). Likening your opponent to Hitler is an example of exaggerated comparison. Euphemistic labeling of groups allows an avoidance of particulars. An example is calling terrorists "freedom fighters" (Ellis, 2006). Blame attributions mean that blame can be assigned to the "other" (person or situation) instead of one's own responsibility. The process of dehumanization reduces the other group to the extent that it is assumed that they need no moral concern (Ellis, 2006). The extreme versions of this type of discourse, as in the case of the "into the sea" framing of the Israelis by Arabs, can lead to extreme violence like genocide (Ellis, 2006, p. 117). Moral exclusion involves a process of excluding the other group from one's own moral values (Ellis, 2006). Self-perception of victimhood involves arguing from the premise that one's group is always victimized by the other. The Israelis and Palestinians continuously go through cycles of victimhood claims (Ellis, 2006). The victimhood phenomenon can become so extreme that it is taught in school books and used as a theme in TV programs (Ellis, 2006).

Political discourse polarization should be viewed as part of a continuum running from extreme polarization to extreme depolarization. The importance of treating political polarization as a continuum is that discourse may move back and forth between high and low levels of polarization. It is not simply a binary phenomenon but rather one that is dynamic and that changes through time. Polarized discourse can become less polarized and depolarized discourse can become more polarized.

Polarization that moves people into intensifying levels of conflict and violence such as war and terrorism is most likely to occur alongside low levels of what we can consider as depolarizing discourse and communication (conciliation, negotiation, etc.). Escalation of conflict follows cycles of communication which increase polarization in positive feedback loops. Polarization and depolarization are two parts of a dynamic process where social interaction can produce changes in thinking, framing, discourse, and relationship formation, which affect communication and behavior in both directions.

As we will restate later, the argument is that polarization in digital communication is a dynamic process, with the potential to move in the opposite direction, i.e. toward depolarization. Depolarization is a movement toward multiple perspectives or at least the understanding of a competing perspective. It is not simply an intermediate position between alternative points of view in a conflict. Groups that are strongly polarized can be more easily led to engage in the course of action suggested by their leadership (such as violence), as they are convinced that it is the only way to affect change (Kriesberg, 1998). Polarization discourse is more likely to support coercive or forceful political behavior while depolarizing discourse is likely to encourage cooperative political behavior.

Conciliatory Discourse and Democracy

Since language is a differentiating medium, the simple fact of communication between groups is not in itself likely to diminish conflict; they may simply communicate their reasons for not liking each other. Thus, one should expect the normal processes of creating and maintaining social cohesion to lead inevitably to the expression of social polarity. Indeed, the very fabric of democratic civil society is woven through argument in law and politics. Polarization in high-level election campaigns is as normal as the pattern of depolarization once the winner of the election is announced.

Arguments do not only permit the peaceful resolution of differences in values or needs, but also allow a society to adapt to new environmental pressures by the constant creation of variety in its agendas and processes. Thus, the occurrence of political polarization is not inherently bad; it is, indeed, probably a necessary property of a stable, adaptable society (Pribram & Bradley, 1998). Rather, the requirement is for dialogic mechanisms for sustaining relational responsibility (McNamee & Gergen, 1999) between groups that allow a society to benefit from critical deliberation but to avoid the degeneration of arguments into polarizing diatribes. However, conciliatory discourse (depolarizing) involves a consideration of opposing points of view and the merits of the arguments made by one's supposed adversaries.

In this spirit, a perspective for conflict resolution is to encourage cooperative discourse that seeks to build understanding between opponents and to generate fresh conceptual frameworks based on sustained dialogue (Saunders, 1999). This is closer to the transformative perspective envisioned by Gergen, McNamee, and Barrett (2001). This way of looking at political communication is also consistent with the argument put forward by peace activist David Cortright (1997) about the characteristics of communication associated with non-violence. Moreover, Cortright makes a strong case for nonviolent transformative dialogue and opposition to terrorism.

Cooperative Communication and Conflict Reduction

Working toward transformational communication in intractable conflict situations requires some very guided communication changes. First, both sides have to intend to work toward the goal that they will seek solutions that meet the needs of both sides. After that, they must commit to interaction that is responsive to both sides (Ellis, 2006). Work that guides new forms of communication is important for progress. If effective, the communication should move toward identity-widening and shared identity (Ellis, 2006). With identity-widening, groups re-categorize themselves using some features of the competing group (Ellis, 2006).

This type of conflict management requires changes at both micro and macro levels of interaction. At the micro level of interpersonal communication, attitudes and beliefs can be changed as well as various psychological patterns (Ellis, 2006). From there, social structures may emerge which have a basis in the transformed interpersonal communication (Ellis, 2006). For this to work, contact must be intense and long term. Superordinate goals that are valued by both sides are also necessary. For example, the desire for overall peace may be necessary to move violent groups into discussions about differences (Ellis, 2006).

It is ironic that the age of rapid Internet communication and social networking platforms is accompanied by a quick expansion of anti-democratic and even violent movements along with the utilization of these technologies for pro-democracy and beneficial movements. This irony mandates that we understand more about anti-democratic or extremist movements in general.

Culture and Conflict Resolution

It is important to understand that while culture at its most basic and significant level can affect conflict and polarization as it refers to the core values of groups, culture also has an extremely important impact as it affects differing communication styles between groups in conflict; thus, this aspect of communication is extremely relevant for efforts aimed at achieving depolarization. Researchers such as Hall (1959, 1976) and Cohen (1990, 1991) have focused on differing communication styles between groups or nations which can make communication extremely difficult between them.

The key typology of high-context versus low-context cultures and communication styles provides the primary axis of division between global cultures as it can affect communication between them. High-context cultures refer generally to collectivist societies in which there are strong values assigned to elements such as respect, honor, hierarchy and social harmony. Individuals from high-context cultures generally seek to establish relationships before being willing to commence on a discussion of concrete issues, whether in the political or economic sphere. On the other hand, low-context cultures are generally individualistic cultures in which strong values are assigned to individual liberty and achievement and there is a strong emphasis placed on professional merit and equality. Individuals from such cultures will seek to come to the point as quickly as possible as opposed to the more indirect communication approaches predominant in high-context cultures. Cohen (1990, 1991) has described how difficulties have often developed when representatives from the differing cultures have met and tried to advance a discourse.

Given all of these barriers contributing to polarization based on differing core values and communication styles, how can culture have a mediating depolarizing influence on conflict? Experience in offline face-to-face intergroup dialogue on the people-to-people level in a number of protracted conflicts can be instructive. In Northern Ireland, for instance, Knox and Hughes (the former a political scientist, the latter a social anthropologist) reported on the favorable impact of intercultural activities and dialogue, connected to religion and culture, upon Protestant and Catholic participants (Knox & Hughes, 1996, pp. 93–94). And in the deeply intractable Israeli-Palestinian conflict some successes have been reported in utilizing the medium of religion, particularly as it concerns the discovery of commonalities between Islam and Judaism, which has led to improved perceptions and depolarization between the parties involved (Abu-Nimer, 2001; Mollov & Lavie, 2001, 2006).

In the latter examples, Israeli religious Jewish students were able to engage with Palestinian Muslim students, even from extreme camps, and, corroborated by empirical questionnaire-based data, achieved change in perceptions by finding commonalities in the religious practices of Islam and Judaism as the structures of both religions are remarkably similar (Mollov & Lavie, 2001, 2006, 2016). However, the moderation of negative perceptions, as laudable as it may be, is not sufficient to move the conflict toward greater resolution. As suggested by research (Mollov & Lavie, 2001), these changes in perceptions need to be accompanied by a better understanding of the basis of the conflict, with emphasis on the opposing narratives. As discussed earlier in this chapter, traditional identities are becoming stronger in the age of globalization. Still, despite mutually harmful stalemates (Zartman, 1998) it is possible for conflicting parties to move toward steps of reconciliation. For example, intercultural dialogue in the Israeli-Palestinian conflict can lead participants to understanding that an ideological balance of power orstalemate exists between the narratives which connect each side to the same land (Mollov & Lavie, 2001, 2017).

Given an age in which, paradoxically, greater globalization can lead to a strengthening of traditional ties, the challenge is to encourage a 'dialogue of civilizations', in which interpersonal discourse is guided toward self-disclosure and the thoughtful exchange of views rather than incendiary rhetoric and mutual escalation. The previous section has dealt empirically and normatively with this goal. We will now turn our attention to the manner in which digital and social media can better serve as an agent for such depolarization of views and constructive communication.

The Possible Role of Digital Communication in Depolarizing Discourse

Many observers have noted that digital communication appears to contribute to conflict and polarization of political discourse. This is the opposite of what some political communication scholars anticipated.

In 2017, there were constant news stories and commentaries about how divided the U.S. was after the presidential election of 2016 and how social media was not only used for social networking and positive objectives, but also for terrorism and political extremism. Brian Levin, director of the Center for the Study of Hate and Extremism at California State University, San Bernadino, argues that content that is most dramatic and divisive gets the most attention in communication environments where attention spans are already shortening. He claims that "[i]n a very fearful and tribalistic society, we run on emotion, which is the currency of social media" (Schrobsdorff, 2017, p. 19). A study conducted recently in China on 70 million online posts found that anger spreads quicker and more widely than sadness and joy (Schrobsdorff, 2017).

There are three basic arguments about the potential of digital communication for depolarizing discourse. While some scholars claim that digital communication offers little to political communication other than another channel or a set of channels, others view it as having the potential to revolutionize politics. A third view argues that digital communication contributes to an incremental process that creates social structures, and does so through sustained feedback loops. In this view, political power is related to the ways in which agents (human actors) use it to gain more input and effectiveness in social structures that affect political systems (Hacker, 2004; Poole & DeSanctis, 1990). According to this structurational view, under certain conditions digital communication can be used to both increase political participation and to serve as an effective mediation tool to encourage greater conciliatory discourse between parties in conflict. However, as we note in the chapter on China in this book (Chapter 7), such political changes may be gradual and granular enough to remain unnoticed if they are not examined in small spaces of change over time.

Political changes are most likely linked to the platforms being constructed by users who use new technologies to change discourse. In this section we will discuss some of these changes which can be facilitated by digital communications toward more conciliatory discourse. It should be noted that online digital communication aimed at increasing conciliatory discourse cannot be promoted in a vacuum but also should be undertaken with reference to offline approaches which have led to positive results.

The founder and CEO of Facebook, Mark Zuckerberg (2017), has written a 'manifesto' that lists his arguments about how digital communication and social media like Facebook can be used in sociotechnical ways to encourage more civil discourse and less extremist discourse online. His main arguments are:

1. A global community can be built by increasing numbers of people doing social media networking at various levels of society.
2. While there are many globalizing trends, many people in the world are reacting against and going local.
3. While social media can encourage divisiveness, they can also encourage unity.
4. Social media platforms can be used to encourage moral validation and hope for positive changes.
5. Online community formation can be used to help people affiliate both online and offline.

6. Technologies can be created to generate many layers of small and local online communities. Communities are made up of many sub-communities.
7. Encryption can be used to block spam and malice.
8. A social platform can provide more alternatives to filter bubbles than mass media do. Exposure to more diverse content within one's social networks can lead to greater awareness of alternative views.
9. Yet, exposure to divergent views can actually increase polarization. What appears more depolarizing is exposure to a range of views.
10. Getting to know people as individuals works better than interacting with unknown people since they can get to know each other's lives in areas other than politics and get to like them as people even if they disagree with their political arguments.
11. Discussing political subjects from a social rather than ideological starting point is less likely to be polarizing.
12. Artificial intelligence algorithms can be used to enforce pro-civil and depolarizing statements and posts.

This manifesto assumes among other things that new interaction environments will need heavy policing, moderating and control. As Zuckerberg suggests, artificial intelligence algorithms can be used to enforce pro-civil along with depolarizing statements and posts. Indeed, proper moderating approaches designed to promote social and personal relationship building in addition to discourse on substantive issues is an important element to maximize the aim of using digital discourse to achieve the goals which we seek.

However, there is nothing automatic about using online communication, in any form, to depolarize political discourse. Moreover, there are always dual valence (both positive and negative) effects possible with any communication technology (van Dijk, 2012). This suggests that digital communication used for political discussion will likely have both polarizing and depolarizing effects. However, theories of social identity related to structuration theory may make it possible to direct the valence in a more positive (depolarizing) direction. Indeed, while social media can encourage divisiveness, it can also help facilitate unity. Furthermore, encryption can be used to block spam and malice. One might question whether policing, encryption and moderation do anything other than block the most extremist and offensive comments in digital communication while failing to make any significant contribution to depolarization.

Admittedly, there is generally a small amount of empirical literature focusing on the use of online communication for aiding dialogue in situations of intractable conflicts. Using communication to build relationships to lessen conflict is an idea at least as old as the political science theories of Karl Deutsch, who argued that interpersonal ties are critical for good international relations (Deutsch, 1963).

Van Dijk (2012) suggests, however, that online groups do not have as much motivation as offline groups to reach consensus and work together.

We will argue that whether or not this is true, online groups can be coached and steered toward political cooperation and even collaboration. While early online communication researchers found "flaming" to be common, it later appeared to be similar to what is commonly observed in offline communication as rude social behavior. Yet, even if that is true, we need to demonstrate that it is possible for humans, both offline and online, to work together in debating politics and serious political controversies.

Despite limited research in the area of exploring the variable of culture in digital communication dialogue in general, and as a depolarizing influence in particular, some findings can be cited. For instance, Mollov, Schwartz, Steinberg, and Lavie (2001) reported on fieldwork conducted in 1998 and 2000 in Israeli-Palestinian student dialogue via online interaction focusing on the similarities between the Jewish holiday of Rosh Hashana and the Muslim holiday of Ramadan. This reflects the "coexistence" or "joint projects" approach coined by one researcher (Kampf, 2011) and which has achieved greater success as a "learning ground for social and political understanding" than the "confrontational model" (Kampf, 2011, p. 391).

Social information and dialogues such as the one above have the distinct advantage of helping people get to know each other's lives in areas other than politics and to like them as people even if they disagree with their political positions. It should also be noted that students in this dialogue combined the Internet exchanges with initial and final face-to-face meetings, which had the advantage of avoiding the possible disadvantages of strictly digital communication in which participants are deprived of the opportunities to have some perceptions of "social indicators" such as "tone of voice and body gestures accompanying a general conversation" (Kampf, 2011, p. 392) which can include various nuances.

Theories Showing Directions for Depolarization

We suggest that new social media can help to implement change derived from four key theories that can produce and sustain civil deliberative online spaces that tend toward depolarization. The four theories are social identity theory, framing theory, structuration theory and network theory. The directions of these theories for online depolarization are shown in Table 5.1. With our examination of political polarization and depolarization dynamics, we are convinced that a multi-theory and multi-level model of digital communication depolarization is necessary.

Social identity theory (SIT) focuses attention on the relationship between social cohesion and group solidarity and shared attitudes toward other groups. Membership and commitment are central to strong identity. Problems arise when strong in-group identities are directly related to strong out-group derogation. The movement toward cooperation in the presence of high in-group identification appears to be a shared identity that involves multiple groups having one common identity.

Table 5.1 Theories, directions and solutions for online depolarization.

Theory	*Level of analysis*	*Directions*	*Solutions*
Social Identity Theory	Group communication	Safe space for identity thinning and superordinate identity formation.	Changes from in-group vs out-group orientation toward superordinate identities
Structuration Theory	Social structures with rules and resources	Through social interaction over time, new social structures can be formed. Types of rules and resources brought into the interaction affect the results of the process.	Online and offline structures with their rules and resources combined: people knowing each other offline polarize less online
Framing Theory	Linguistic	From conflictual and existential frames to cooperative and negotiated frames.	Decrease negative language and increase conciliatory language
Network Theory	Networking online and offline	Building connections and links among people who share concerns but seek peace rather than violence.	Creation and maintenance of depolarizing norms

The application of structuration theory involves creating new cooperative social structures or making existing social structures less polarizing with their political discourse. This focus on the connections between social structures, systems and communication is a central theme of this book.

Framing theory involves a number of sociolinguistic dynamics, including the possibilities of using more positive and cooperative language to portray and describe political conflicts. The framing of conflicts partially determines how those concepts are debated and responded to with concrete behaviors such as violence or non-violence.

Network theory is central to this book as we relate networking to democracy. Network theory explains how dyads and triads are built through patterns of weak and strong ties, preferential attachment for commonality or desired traits, and flows of cognition, emotions, and messages. It also explains how those who work against network goals, as in the case of polarizing discourse, can be dropped as nodes in a network. We now look at these theories in more detail.

SIDE Theory and Depolarization

A social-psychological theory concerning the relation between computer-mediated and face-to-face communication in the tradition of social identity theory is called social identity and deindividuation theory, abbreviated as SIDE (Postmes & Spears, 1998; Spears & Lea, 1992). The theory states that social identity is so important to people that in conditions of deindividuation, such as a lack of cues in online communication, they attach even more importance to the remaining cues and to the identities they bring in themselves to the online conversation. On the surface, deindividuation with its lack of cues can be used to prevent stereotyping and discrimination because people cannot see the characteristics of the conversation partners (being friend or foe, in-group or out-group). This offers a safe space for 'identity thinning'. Scholars used to think this could lead to depolarization. However, according to SIDE theory, people are in fact "desperately" looking for the cues of the other conversation partners and forcefully reveal their own identities using online cues. However, at that moment they can become aware of their own identity construction, and the conversation process can be directed toward superordinate identity formation, to form a common ground for the group. Polarization can turn to depolarization, moving toward common rather than competing identities. This is a group process that has to be organized by the group itself or by moderators.

This means that contacts and conversations have to be structured appropriately for depolarizing discourse. Indeed, a failure to structure online dialogue appropriately can lead in fact to a further escalation because participants' own identities are articulated even more in conditions of deindividuation because "for the most part … digital communication networks reproduce the social, political, and economic relations that exist in the real world" (Cook, 2004, p. 103).

To advance such structuring, it is relevant to consider some of the key insights from social psychology associated with facilitating positive contact between groups. These include the importance of discovering commonalties in another group as a vehicle for improving intergroup relations and perceptions (Byrne, 1969; Rokeach, Smith, & Evans, 1960), along with critical elements delineated by Amir (1969) as necessary for positive intergroup contact, which include: "equal status contacts"; "intimate" as opposed to merely "casual encounters"; "cooperative" as opposed to "competitive" relationships; and "institutional" support for such efforts. We would also add here the importance of paying attention to differing communication styles representative of the differing cultural typologies (high-context and low-context) in order to maximize possibilities for depolarized discourse. Thus, we would suggest that just as depolarized face-to-face encounters must be conducted while paying attention to some of the conditions indicated here, positive digital communication encounters must also be structured by paying attention to these conditions.

Ellis (2016) shows how intergroup conflicts and polarization can be directly related to what he terms "identity widening" or differences in identities that cannot be reconciled (p. 51). Ellis and Maoz (2012) observe that images of polarized opposites in conflicts can be grounded in viewing competitors as having evil intentions, immorality, and traits that are inferior. Only the in-group is assigned positive traits. They also note that reducing conflict involves communication that closes gaps and bridges identities. This kind of communication is deliberative. Effective deliberation involves learning about the experiences of the other side, critically assessing your own side's contribution to the conflict, empathizing with the experiences of the others, and learning new cooperative behaviors (Ellis & Maoz, 2012).

Structuration Theory and Depolarization

The second theory we can use here is structuration theory, often deployed in this book. It is a sociological theory defining online and offline conversations as social structures with rules and resources. The structures are the design and organization of the conversation, the rules are the norms of the conversation, and the resources are the physical or technological settings and the technical features of the media and settings used. Through social interaction over time, new social structures of online and offline communication can be formed. Moreover, the types of rules and resources brought into the interaction affect the results of the process. This means that online and offline conversations can be organized to create more depolarization and less polarization.

The physical and technological settings of conversation are primary. A combination of online and offline discussion allows people to benefit from the best characteristics and opportunities of both settings. This is also the case for depolarization. While online discussion settings under a condition of anonymity tend to stimulate polarization through uncivil and conflictual communication behavior, combining this with offline discussion settings where people know each other will enable polarization to be reduced. While visual cues are absent in many online settings, they are available in offline settings. While expression is direct in offline settings, easily leading to (verbal) fights, in online conversation people can wait a while to respond.

Rules and resources also are vital for (de)polarization. Through social interaction over time, new social structures can be formed. The types of rules and resources brought into the interaction affect the results of the process. A structured and moderated online discussion will have less polarization and offers the opportunity to organize depolarization. The same goes for technical facilities of video and online content used to prepare fruitful discussions. In general, a plurality of viewpoints and a large number of outlets for discussion can open up the potential for less violent confrontations (Ellis, 2006).

Communication research has shown that social interaction generates social structures, which in turn generates feedback to modify forms of interaction. Polarized and depolarized political structures are likely to be shaped by patterns of discourse and social interaction (van Dijk, 1998). Moreover, discourse feedback loops are an essential part of the polarization process, since it is through feedback that social structures are either reinforced or attenuated (Giddens, 1984; Wiener, 1948). Social structures pattern social interaction through processes that integrate or separate members due to "reciprocity of practices" or the regularizing relations of autonomy and dependence among members (Giddens, 1979, p. 76).

McKenna, Samuel-Azran, and Sutton-Balaban (2009) extensively documented the positive impact of the "Good Neighbors Web project" (http://gnblog.com) in facilitating dialogue and attitudinal change between Middle Eastern participants including Palestinians, Egyptians, Lebanese and Israelis. In earlier work, Amichai-Hamburger and McKenna (2006) argued that the "Internet may be the best tool ... for effectively putting the contact hypothesis into practice". In addition, the informal nature of the discourse, despite the exchanging opinions on heated political issues, can be instructive as it illustrates the importance of discussing political issues from a social rather than an ideological starting point in the effort to decrease polarization.

We are also encouraged by reports and analysis of a significant Internet dialogue held between Christian and Muslim students in Australia, which also gives us insight into "best practices" for the use of digital media to promote intergroup harmony (White, Abu-Raya, Blive, & Faulkner, 2015). The researchers cite the importance of delineating "superordinate goals" which directed the students to discuss the manner in which "their respective religious beliefs and practices could help create an environmentally sustainable Australia." (p. 7). Such goal-directed digital intergroup dialogue and communication, similar to the Israeli-Palestinian student Internet dialogue cited above, has significant advantages compared to more open-ended unstructured dialogue, which at least in the Israeli-Palestinian context can lead to "negative and dead end arguments that do not seek to resolve conflict" (Ellis & Maoz, 2007, p. 304; White, Abu-Raya, Blive, & Faulkner, 2015).

Some researchers believe that digital communication can have a moderating or depolarizing effect on Islamic discourse (Ellis, 2006). The argument is that because there are so many sources available in digital communication, it is easier to challenge religious leaders (Ellis, 2006). A variety of views and sources can encourage cosmopolitanism and this in turn can lead to more positive views of democracy (Ellis, 2006). Mandeville (2001) argues that Internet usage has had a moderating effect on Islamic discourse and this is because the extremes are weakened by more convergence online at the center of Islam (Ellis, 2006). However, plurality does not guarantee less violence, and it is possible that people self-select to the point that they reinforce their violent ideologies.

Framing Theory and Depolarization

Framing theory is a psychological and sociological theory that focuses on concepts of human language revealing meaning (Goffman, 1974; Fodor, 1987; Tversky & Kahneman, 1981), and is analyzed via linguistic analysis. Some of these concepts are *frames*: a set of ideas or perspectives molded in words or images used by individuals, groups and societies to construct, perceive and communicate about reality.

Gergen et al. (2001) propose the fostering of transformative dialogue – dedicated to relational repair. This involves a deeper understanding of each person's individual beliefs and the reasons for those beliefs. It involves using less contentious vocabulary and understanding that there are multiple truths and beliefs. Drawing on experiments on the mediation of contentious public issues (e.g. the Public Conversations Project (PCP); see Chasin et al., 1996), Gergen et al. note the power of a factor such as self-revelation, where an individual reveals both the personal experience behind a contentious belief and any doubts about the consequences of actions arising from the belief, to heal fractured relationships. Group members work to create a new understanding of a problem together, moving from an individual orientation to a co-created "us" orientation through the use of new mutually inclusive language and sympathetic listening. Indeed, the path-breaking work of Martin Buber (1970) in his emphasis on fostering "I-Thou" relationships between individuals falls strongly into this orientation. Here we find directions for depolarization using language and frames.

It is not enough to talk about changing language and framing to deal with intractable political conflicts. This is a painful realization that has returned over and over during at least the past 20 years. Dealing with intractable conflicts is about history, ideology and tangible interests as much as it is about how parties communicate about and with each other. Therefore, it is necessary to design digital communication systems and platforms that deal with political conflict to help to depolarize discourse, as such discourse is realistically guided by structures of interaction that have specific goals and operational guidelines. This enables greater opportunities to tackle these formidable challenges, within the context of civil dialogue.

Network Theory and Depolarization

Network theory, as discussed in Chapter 2, can also explain the results of polarization and depolarization in discussion networks. Networks have several options to build connections and links among people who share concerns and can both seek conflict or seek peace rather than violence. Depolarization in online discussions only works when discussion members are motivated to come together, find a consensus or at least to understand each other, and at a minimum listen to each other. Unfortunately, these conditions are not guaranteed. They have to be organized. Online discussions need just as much discussion leadership as offline discussion (van Dijk, 2012). The discussion has to be moderated with positive and negative feedback according to the setting, design and frame of the discussion and mutually agreed by the participants.

Rather than seeing discussion networks created by digital communication as fixed and predictable, it might be more useful to see them as places of expression and exchange, and as dynamic in terms of shifts in meanings. It is a rather lame view of human communication to assume that people only express themselves in discussions and never learn anything new. There is a network logic that underpins theories of network society and which should inform the analysis here of the conciliatory potential of digital communication networks. This potential is not inherent in the technologies but rather in the networking and influencing that the new media make possible.

Thus, without specific guidance toward depolarization processes, there is little evidence to support the anticipation that digital communication will generate anything more than heated arguments about political events. However, when treated as complex adaptive systems with the potential for self-organizing structures related to depolarizing guidance, there are theoretical reasons to expect success in generating more dialogic forms of political discussion than occur without guidance. This further underlines the importance of having moderators and guidelines to advance communication toward depolarization. And as noted by Adaptive Structuration Theory (AST), effects of technologies are less a matter of software and hardware than of the uses of these technologies.

The type of moderation and correctives needed for network conversation depends on the available application. Table 5.2 shows the most important applications, problems and corrections.

The technological contributions to online deliberation are forums where competing viewpoints can be articulated without fear of censorship but also without fear of irrational attack. This may require signing a user agreement where one recognizes the norms of the discussion space and agrees to abide by them. Users also agree that that they may be removed from the space if they repeatedly violate the norms of cooperative and non-polarized discourse. Assuming a website platform, the space can include a multiplicity of peace-promoting documents that address the political issues at hand. These publications can serve as resources that interact with the rules (norms) of the online space. Cognitive mapping software, automated text analysis, sentiment

Table 5.2 Digital media applications, their potential problems and correctors.

Digital media applications	*Objectives*	*Possible problems*	*Correctors*
Online discussion forums, chats, discussion lists	Political deliberation	Flaming, lack of logic	Moderators, norm reinforcement
Websites	Posting of information, discussion platforms	Lack of civility, ideological competition	Moderators, editors
Blogs	Chronological writing and discussion	Same as above	Public scrutiny and editorial decisions (of blog outlet used)

analysis and other technological tools can be used to show the directions of the deliberations.

Some Specific Uses of Digital and Social Media for Depolarization

Two further case studies of using digital communication and some cases of social media use are described here to illustrate how digital communication design and implementation can be used to encourage more civil and cooperative political communication. The case studies are the website known as Bitter Lemons, and the U.S. State Department initiative called Peer to Peer Countering Extremism.

The Bitter Lemons Israeli-Palestinian website (http://bitterlemons.net) established in 2001 provided a very high-level Israeli-Palestinian social media forum for the exchange of views between Israelis and Palestinians from academia, politics and the media on an array of the most controversial issues facing the Middle East, including outbreaks of Israeli-Palestinian violence, moving toward a two-state solution, refugees, settlements and the Arab Peace Initiative. The website was established by two former Israeli and Palestinian officials, and included a variety of opinions from all sides of the political spectrum in Israel and Palestine. Although it unfortunately closed its operations in 2012, it exposed many thousands of Israelis, Palestinians and others to the possibility of a civilized exchange of views despite a wide gulf between the participants, including the organizers themselves.

The United States' State Department in conjunction with U.S. Homeland Security sponsors university teams who engage in peer-to-peer efforts against online extremism. This initiative is part of American public diplomacy and was established in light of findings which indicate that ISIL and other extremist and terrorist movements actively use social media to recruit members and promote their ideologies, as well as the fact that traditional American mass media and social campaigns failed to stop terrorist appeals online. The goal is for young university students to communicate with other millennials online, offering them positive ways to discuss and deliberate conflicts and to reject violence as an option in these conflicts.

Social media technology and adoption have outpaced the development of positive and enforceable norms to keep digital communication peaceful and cooperative (McLaughlin & Vitak, 2011). Too often, digital communication such as that used on social media platforms like Facebook are used in ways that spread emotional contagion, false narratives, 'memes' and messages that fail to show empathy for competing viewpoints. The technologies and platforms for digital communication today enable one-to-many (e.g. Twitter) and many-to-many interactions (e.g. Facebook) that may or may not encourage thoughtful sharing of ideas and information. The more the focus on personal self-interest and motivations, the less the interest in being sensitive to others' views (Liggett & Ueberall, 2016).

Digital communication is a mixed blend of positive behavior such as activism, social networking with friends and family members, social support networking, and emotional expression, but also includes negative behaviors such as harassment, cyberbullying, prejudice, and promotion of violence (Liggett & Ueberall, 2016). Face-to-face and online norms have in common the basic principle that social interaction produces norms, and people use norms as guides for deciding what constitutes appropriate behavior. These norms are reinforced by laws, policies and social rules. Online norms are enforced by social interaction, community standards, user agreements and platform sanctions (Liggett & Ueberall, 2016). In both online and offline communication, the longer group members interact with each other, the more apparent are the norms.

Offline and online, people generally learn what behaviors are rewarded and punished by observing others. Social media platform providers like Facebook rely on users to report offenders and harmful content so that rules of behavior can be enforced. It is not a perfect method because of inconsistent discovery, reporting and enforcement (Liggett & Ueberall, 2016). Content which elicits strong emotional responses is more likely to gain responses from others – both positive and negative content (Liggett & Ueberall, 2016). This suggests that new media or social platforms designed as places of low polarization of political discourse need to minimize strongly negative emotional postings.

Some scholars assert that online media encourage less impulse control than offline communication (Liggett & Ueberall, 2016). This encourages venting and polarizing comments. The focus can be more on self-expression than on cooperative discussion. If users are more concerned about emotional release than social cooperation, social media communication can serve as tools for expressing anger, frustration, and one-sided political views (Liggett & Ueberall, 2016). Avoiding dealing with conflicting views in social media can make polarization easier than in offline communication.

Studies show that empathy for the views of others (the opposite of polarization) relates to understanding the situations and perspectives of others. Online anonymity makes these problems worse as users feel less inhibited when their personal identities are hidden (Liggett & Ueberall, 2016). However, most online communication, particularly on social media, does not involve anonymity as people post pictures of themselves and continuously self-disclose their interests and backgrounds (Liggett & Ueberall, 2016). Despite this lack of anonymity, however, users can experience deindividuation and a diffusion of responsibility that typify crowd behaviors (Liggett & Ueberall, 2016). All of this suggests the need for strong enforcement of community standards for online networking so that pro-social and non-polarizing norms are less ambiguous and easy to follow.

The accomplishment of positive and depolarizing social norms in online spaces requires platforms to encourage users to take responsibility for posting discourse and thus negate perceptions of diffused responsibilities. Polarizing and negative content needs to be pointed out and discouraged. Critical thinking and rational debate should be encouraged. Facilitators should not be censors as much as they should be encouragers of discourse that shows understanding and respect. Technology features such as delayed posting, to give users a few minutes to think about what they have typed, might encourage more thoughtful and respectful posting.

Social norms emerge and are reinforced in various processes of communication including structuration. Normative influence on individual actions results from both personal judgements and situational constraints (Lapinski & Rimal, 2005). Social networks have collective norms which guide the decisions of individuals in those networks (Lapinski & Rimal, 2005). These collective norms are not aggregations or averages of individual perceived norms. Collective norms can only be observed by examining social behaviors (Lapinski & Rimal, 2005). This might be done by looking at how people in networks like social media form and enact policies about appropriate behaviors.

Both descriptive norms and injunctive norms are important for regulating social constraint in individual behaviors (Lapinski & Rimal, 2005). Certain behaviors can also be encouraged by showing that conforming to norms results in certain benefits. Additionally, relating norm compliance to self-concept and social identify also increases the likelihood of compliance (Lapinski & Rimal, 2005). Fear of losing social acceptance in a network that values contact also can increase compliance (Lapinski & Rimal, 2005). For strong network effects on behavior, individuals must feel committed to their network (Lapinski & Rimal, 2005). Here we see an important mix of strong social identity and high network density effects.

One method of reminding users of online social norms is directing them to policy statements. Severe violators of norms can be expelled from online spaces (McLaughlin & Vitak, 2011).

Conclusions

In this chapter, we have tried to summarize the possibilities and conditions for conflict resolution and non-polarization in discussions to facilitate dialogue between parties in conflict. We then turned our attention to the contribution which digital communication can make to this endeavor. While offering theoretical contours and empirical examples, we combined them with recommendations for the manner in which digital communications can be used to facilitate conciliatory and depolarizing discourse.

While emerging norms, interactive framing and voluntary self-restraint seem idealistic, these are the key ingredients of conflict resolution. If these cannot be aimed at and practiced online, what hope is there for offline and larger-scale depolarization? Old approaches and arguments about online communication are of little use here. We need new thinking and new models that bring a focus on norm development and norm sharing in online structures of deliberation, some examples of which we have included in this chapter.

There are crucial issues to take into consideration in improving digital communication for discourse. The most obvious is how you get polarizing individuals, parties to the conflict and conflict entrepreneurs to become more cooperative. This is not a matter of cognitive or attitudinal change, but of behavioral change. All we can be sure of is that there are general principles of conflict reduction and that digital communication design and implementation can be used to enable, encourage and facilitate these principles. In other words, digital networking can be used to form networks of interaction that encourage positive communication and discourage polarizing communication. The focus is more on the positive building of civil norms, discourse and perceived common goals, and interactive framing of what the issues in conflict are. However, belief in guaranteed positive changes are as artificial as hoping that digital communication will automatically build democracy, and work against authoritarianism. The positive changes made by human agents toward democratization and depolarization can be aided by new media, but are not caused by them. However, we need to advance social media which can encourage moral validation and hope for positive changes; all the more so as extreme groups such as ISIL utilize and exploit social media to promote their highly negative goals.

In sum, using digital communication for increasing conciliatory and cooperative political communication and decreasing polarization does not rely on technological features or affordances as much as it relies on strategic uses of the new media platforms to structurate cooperative and collaborative political discussions and debates. Technological features can be helpful, but they are unlikely to be determinative. Thus, we must combine the best face-to-face approaches for depolarizing discourse with the "best practices" insights for using digital media toward our goal of promoting conciliatory discourse.

References

Abu-Nimer, M. (2001). Conflict resolution, culture and religion: Toward a training model of interreligious peacebuilding. *Journal of Peace Research*, *38*(6), 685–704.

Amichai-Hamburger, Y., & McKenna, K. Y. A. (2006). The contact hypothesis reconsidered: Interacting via the internet, *Journal of Computer-Mediated Communication*, *11*(3), article 7. Retrieved from http://jcmc.Indiana.edu/vol11/issue3/amichahamburger.html

Amir, Y. (1969). Contact hypothesis in ethnic relations. *Psychological Bulletin*, *71*, 319–342.

Benkler, Y. (2011). *The penguin and the leviathan: How cooperation triumphs over self-interest.* New York: Crown Business.

Bitterlemons.net (n.d.). About the bitterlemons family of internet publications. Retrieved from www.bitterlemons.net/about.php

Buber, M. (1970). *I and thou.* With prologue and translation by Walter Kaufman. New York: Charles Scribner's Sons.

Byrne, D. (1969). Attitude and attraction. In L. Berkowitz (Ed.), *Advances in experimental and social psychology* (Vol. 4, pp. 36–89). New York: Academic Press.

Castells, M. (1997). *The information age: Economy, society and culture. Vol. II: The power of identity*. Oxford, UK: Blackwell.

Chasin, R., Herzig, M., Roth, S., Chasin, L., Becker, C., & Stains, R. R. (1996). From diatribe to dialogue on divisive public issues: Approaches drawn from family therapy. *Conflict Resolution Quarterly, 13*(4), 323–344.

Cohen, R. (1990) *Culture and conflict in Israeli-Egyptian relations: A dialogue of the deaf.* Bloomington, IN: Indiana University Press.

Cohen, R. (1991). *Negotiating across cultures*. Washington: United States Institute of Peace.

Cook, S. E. (2004). New technologies and language change: Toward an anthropology of linguistic frontiers. *Annual Review of Anthropology, 33*, 103–115.

Cortright, D. (1997). Gandhi's influence on the US peace movement. *International Studies, 34*(3), 359–375.

Deutsch, K. (1963). *The nervers of government: Models of political communication and control*. New York: The Free Press.

Ellis, D. (2006). *Transforming conflict: Communication and ethnopolitical conflict*. Lanham, MD: Rowman & Littlefield.

Ellis, D. G. (2016). Ethno-political conflict. In C. R. Berger & M. E. Roloff (Eds.), *The international encyclopedia of interpersonal communication*. Chichester, UK: Wiley Blackwell.

Ellis, D. G., and Maoz, I. (2007). Online argument between Israeli Jews and Palestinians. *Human Communication Research, 33*, 291–309.

Ellis, D. G., & Maoz, I. (2012). Communication and reconciling intergroup conflict. In H. Giles (Ed.), *The handbook of intergroup communication* (pp. 153–166). New York: Routledge.

Fodor, J. A. (1987). Modules, frames, fridgeons, sleeping dogs, and the music of the spheres. In Z. W. Pylyshyn (Ed.), *The Robot's Dilemma* (pp. 139–149). Norwood, NJ: Ablex.

Galtung, J., Jacobsen, C. G., & Brand-Jacobsen, K. F. (2002). Searching for peace: The road to TRANSCEND. *Studies in Conflict and Terrorism, 25*(1), 57–65.

Gergen, K. J., & Gergen, M. (2004). *Social construction: Entering the dialogue*. Chagrin Falls, OH: Taos Institute Publications.

Gergen, K. J., McNamee, S., & Barrett, F. J. (2001). Toward transformative dialogue. *International Journal of Public Administration, 24*(7–8), 679–707.

Giddens, A. (1979). *Central problems in social theory: Action, structure, and contradiction in social analysis* (Vol. 241). Berkeley, CA: University of California Press.

Giddens, A. (1984). *The constitution of society*. Cambridge, UK: Polity Press.

Goffman, E. (1974). *Frame analysis*. Cambridge, MA: Harvard University Press.

Hacker, K. L. (Ed.). (2004). *Presidential candidate images*. Lanham, MD: Rowman & Littlefield.

Hacker, K., Coombs, M., Weaver, C., & McCulloh, G. (2006). *Possible uses of blogs and computer-mediated communication (CMC) for depolarizing political discourse*. Communication and Technology division (debate panel), Dresden, Germany.

Hall, E. T. (1959). *The silent language*. New York: Doubleday.

Hall, E. T. (1976). *Beyond culture*. New York: Doubleday.

Human Rights Watch (2001, 18 December). Haiti: Political violence condemned. Retrieved from www.hrw.org/legacy/english/docs/2001/12/18/haiti3433_txt.htm

Kampf, R. (2011). Internet, conflict and dialogue: The Israeli case. *Israel Affairs, 17*(3), 384–400.

Knox, C., & Hughes, J. (1996). Crossing the divide: Community relations in Northern Ireland. *Journal of Peace Research, 33*, 83–98.

Kriesberg, L. (1998). The phases of destructive conflicts: Communal conflicts and proactive solutions. In D. Carment & P. James (Eds.), *Peace in the midst of wars: Preventing and managing international ethnic conflicts* (pp. 33–60). Columbia, SC: University of South Carolina Press.

Lapinski, M. K., & Rimal, R. N. (2005). An explication of social norms. *Communication Theory, 15*(2), 127–147.

Liggett. R., & Ueberall, S. (2016). *Social media impacts behavior and norms*. Citizens Crime Commission of New York City. Retrieved from www.nycrimecommission.org/pdfs/social-mediaimpacts-behavior-norms.pdf

Mandeville, P. (2001). *Transnational Muslim politics. Reimaging the Umma*. London: Routledge.

McLaughlin, C. & Vitak, J. (2011). Norm evolution and violation on Facebook. *New Media and Society*, 1–17.

McKenna, K.Y., Samuel-Azran, T., & Sutton-Balaban, N. (2009). Virtual meetings in the Middle East: Implementing the contact hypothesis on the Internet. *Israel Journal of Conflict Resolution, 1*(1), 63–87.

McNamee, S., & Gergen, K. J. (1998). *Relational responsibility: Resources for sustainable dialogue*. Thousand Oaks, CA: Sage.

Mollov, B., & Lavie, C. (2001). Culture, dialogue and perception change in the Israeli-Palestinian conflict. *The International Journal of Conflict Management, 12*(1), 69–87.

Mollov, B., & Lavie, C.(2006). Arab and Jewish women's inter-religious dialogue evaluated. In Y. Iram (Ed.), *Educating towards a culture of peace* (pp. 247–258). Charlotte, NC: Information Age Publishing Inc.

Mollov, B., & Lavie, C. (2016). The impact of Jewish-Arab intercultural encounters and the discourse of the Holocaust on mutual perceptions. In K. Pandy (Ed.), *Handbook of research on promoting global peace and civic engagement through education* (pp. 166–189). Hershey, PA: IGI Global Publication.

Mollov, B., & Lavie, C. (2017). *The impact of Israeli-Palestinian inter-religious dialogue: Theoretical and empirical perspectives*. Paper presented at Annual Meeting of Association for Israel Studies, Brandeis University, Waltham, MA.

Mollov, B., Schwartz, D., Steinberg, G., & Lavie, C. (2001). *The impact of Israeli-Palestinian intercultural dialogue: Virtual and face to face –an advanced report*. Paper Presented at annual conference of International Association for Conflict Management, June 26, Cergy (Paris), France.

Partners for Progressive Israel (2012). End of Bitterlemons.org: Woe are we. Retrieved from http://progressiveisrael.org/end-of-bitterlemons-org-woe-are-we/

Pew Research Center, authored by M. Anderson & A. Caumont (2014). How social media is reshaping news. www.pewresearch.org/fact-tank/2014/09/24/how-social-media-is-reshaping-news/

Poole, S. M., & DeSanctis, G. (1990). Understanding the use of group decision support systems: The theory of adaptive structuration. In J.Fulk & C. Steinfield (Eds.), *Organizations and communication technology* (pp. 173–193). Newbury Park, CA: Sage.

Postmes, T., & Spears, R. (1998). Breaching or building social boundaries? Side-effects of computer-mediated communication. Paper presented to International Communication Association, annual conference, Jerusalem, 20–24 July.

Pribram, K. H., & Bradley, R. T. (1998). The brain, the me and the I. In M. Ferrari & R. Sternberg (Eds.), *Self-awareness: Its nature and development* (pp. 273–307). New York: The Guilford Press.

Rokeach, M., Smith, P. W., & Evans, R. I. (1960). Two kinds of prejudice or one. In M. Rokeach (Ed.), *The open and closed mind* (pp. 132–168). New York: Basic Books.
Saunders. H (1999). *A public peace process*. New York: St. Martin's Press.
Schrobsdorff, S. (2017). Viral anger spreads like a disease and it's making the country sick. *Time, 190*, 19–20.
Spears, R., & Lea, M. (1992). Social influence and the influence of the "social" in computer-mediated communication. In M. Lea (Ed.), *Contexts of computer-mediated communication* (pp. 30–65). Hemel Hempstead: Harvester Wheatsheaf.
Turk, A. T. (2004). Sociology of terrorism. *Annual Review of Sociology, 30*, 271–286.
Turner, J. C., Hogg, M. A., Oakes, P. J., Reicher, S. D., & Wetherell, M. S. (1987). *Rediscovering the social group: A self-categorization theory*. Cambridge, MA: Basil Blackwell.
Tversky, A., & Kahneman, D. (1981). The framing of decisions and the psychology of choice. *Science, 211*(4481), 453–458.
van Dijk, J. (2012). *The network society* (3rd ed.). London; New Delhi; Thousand Oaks, CA; Singapore: Sage.
van Dijk, T. A. (1998). Discourse and ideology. *Discourse and Society, 9*, 307–308.
White, F. A., Abu-Raya, H. M., Blive, A., & Faulkner, N. (2015). Emotion expression and intergroup bias reduction between Muslims and Christians: Long-term Internet contact. *Computers in Human Behavior, 53*, 435–442.
Wiener, N. (1948). Cybernetics. *Scientific American, 179*(5), 14–19.
Zartman, Z. (1998). *Negotiation as a mechanism for resolution in the Arab-Israeli Conflict*. Paper presented at the conference Peace Making and Negotiations in the Arab-Israeli Conflict, The Leonard Davis Institute, the Hebrew University of Jerusalem, Jerusalem.
Zimbardo, P. G. (2007). *Lucifer effect*. New York: Random House.
Zuckerberg, M. (2017). Building global community. Retrieved from www.facebook.com/notes/mark-zuckerberg/building-global-community/10154544292806634/

6 From Arab Spring to Winter

Democracy in Islamic and Authoritarian States

Introduction

At the start of the year 2011, a wave of uprising suddenly occurred in the Arab region. Starting with particular outrage spurred by anger, people took to the streets and after a short contest managed to topple dictators long in power such as Mubarak in Egypt, Ben Ali in Tunisia and Saleh in Yemen. The Arab region was supposed to have missed the so-called 'third wave of democracy' in the world (Huntington, 1991) when in the mid-1970s new democracies succeeded authoritarian and totalitarian regimes in Southern Europe (Portugal, Spain and Greece) or Eastern Europe and the Soviet Union in the 1980s or 1990s, and spreading to South America and several developing countries (Diamond, 1996; Lutz & du Toit, 2014). For decades long at the end of the 20th and the beginning of the 21st centuries the Arab world was stagnating in its political and economic development (UHDR, 2002–2009) after the times of Independence and the birth of radical republics such as those of Nasser in Egypt, Gadaffi in Libya and the Baath regimes in Syria and Iraq. However, at the turn of the millennium the political legitimation of the Arab regimes was crumbling (UHDR, 2005).

The mass demonstrations and uprisings of popular movements in the Arab world at the end of 2010 and the start of 2011 have been called the *Arab Spring*. At the start they were spontaneous actions. According to Howard and Hussain (2013, p. 3), in the early months they were not driven by "traditional political actors such as unions, political parties, or radical fundamentalists. These protests drew out networks of people, many of whom had not been as successful at political organization before: young entrepreneurs, government workers, women's groups, and the urban middle class".

These networks were using mobile phones and the Internet and were also informed by international satellite television. The most conspicuous role for observers was the use of social media by the protesters. In the popular press, the events in the Arab Spring were called Facebook or Twitter revolutions. Similarly, media and communication scholars were inspired by the use of social media in the protest movement. Many of them emphasized the causal role of social media in the political events at that time in one way or another

(Gladwell & Shirky, 2011; Howard & Hussain, 2013; Howard & Parks, 2012; Lim, 2012). As this is an important topic in this book, we will also discuss the role of social media and digital media in the Arab Spring in this chapter.

However, we intend to do this in another way to the majority of approaches taken by media and communication scholars investigating the role of the Internet and social media in the Arab Spring. These approaches completely focus on the instrumental characteristics of these media. They tend to neglect the political context and political theory. In the Introduction of this book we discussed the pitfall of instrumentalism as a view on technology effects. The popular meaning of instrumentalism for democracy is that media and technology can be both good and bad for democracy. In this chapter we will also observe that social media can similarly be used by protesters for democratization and by Islamic fundamentalists and even terrorists calling for a violent Jihad and against democracy. Instrumentalism focuses on (intended) *first*-order effects of technology and neglects (unintended and unexpected) *second*-order effects. There is also a hint of technological determinism when instrumentalists aim to show that particular digital media have a clear affinity with liberation because they are assumed to contest power (Castells, 2015) or when they are, on the contrary, related to control and surveillance of vested power (Morozov, 2011).

In this book and this chapter, we demonstrate a view of technology in digital media that is primarily determined by the social and political context and by the actual use of the digital media. We do not start with the assumed characteristics of digital technology, but with politics and political theory. We agree with the approach taken by the Israeli scholars Wolfsfeld, Segev, and Sheafer (2013). They have demonstrated two theoretical principles. The first is that politics comes first analytically: one cannot understand the role of digital or social media in collective action without first taking into account the political environment. The second principle is that a significant increase in the use of digital media is more likely to follow than to precede protest activity. For Wolfsfeld, Segev, & Sheafer (2013, p. 120), the theoretical basis of these principles is the general *politics-media-politics principle*: changes in the political environment lead to changes in media performance, which leads to further changes in the environment. In this book and this chapter, we apply a similar dialectical theory: structuration theory applied to political structures and action.

We have completed the general model of political system action inspired by Giddens (1984) presented in the Introduction with all of the factors mediating political action and systems in the Arab Spring. These factors are the guiding line for the argument put forward in this chapter. See Figure 6.1. The axis in this model is the interaction between political action and the structures of the political system at all levels (micro, meso and macro). This interaction is modulated by political facilities (technology and media), political views and political norms. Following this model, one can see that the instrumental hypothesis of the causal role of digital or social media is only

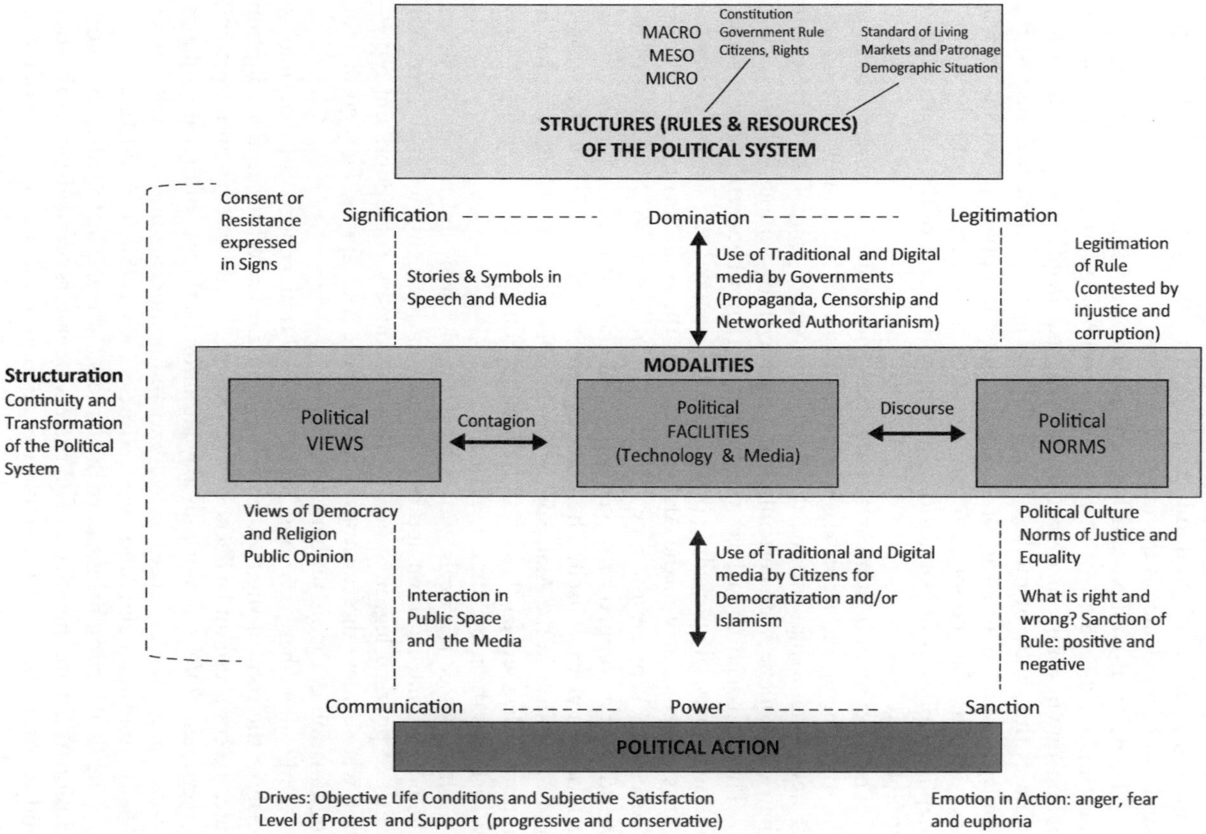

Figure 6.1 A structuration model of Arab political systems and political action.

one of the mediators between political action and structures or systems. The optimist or utopian thesis of digital or social media changing political systems for the aim of democracy with political action is the bottom-up arrow. The pessimist or dystopian thesis of incumbent political systems using digital or social media to dominate political action by domination in propaganda and surveillance is the top-down arrow.

The political context and essential politics are all factors in the model surrounding the core axis of media and technology use, either bottom-up or top-down. With our departure we will start with these political factors (politics first, without media). In the following section, we will discuss the similarities and differences of contemporary Arab political systems. It will also describe the economic (crisis) situation in this region and the demographic explosion of population growth, both causes of discontent motivating the protests.

The next section summarizes the level and nature of political action in the Arab Spring and its backlash: the rise of Islamist extremism and civil war or new dictatorships turning the Arab Spring into winter. The protests and their consequences are certainly not only driven by democratization.

The next section analyzes the first moderation between political action and structures: the prevailing political views in Arab countries. What are the views of democracy in the Arab world? Was the Arab Spring a democratic movement? Why are the views of Islam so important in this region of the world? Is it a competitor of views of democracy or could it be a particular democratic view in itself? The core argument of this section is that protest and opposition in the Arab Spring were driven by both democratization in a more or less secular flavor and by islamization as a religious point of view. Which was the most important one?

The next section deals with Arab political norms and culture. What are the political norms about appropriate rules in this region with an increasing crisis of political legitimation? Injustice, inequality, corruption and repression were evident direct causes of revolt in the Arab Spring. They eroded the legitimation of the incumbent regimes.

Only after these sections about the political context are we able to analyze the role of digital technology and media. What are the adoption rates (access), use and effects of these media used both by protesters and governments? We will not only pay attention to the use of digital media by protesters for the purposes of freedom and democracy but also their use by Islamic fundamentalists and even terrorists such as ISIS and Al Qaida.

The final section brings all of the factors in the model together for a conclusion. What are the effects of all these moderators between political action and structures in the structuration of Arab political systems? The question we find most important in this book is the effect of digital technology and media use. Is it the most important factor or is it only a minor factor? The most important question is, of course, whether all of this political and media activity has transformed Arab political systems.

Arab Political Systems

What are the *rules* of Arab political systems in terms of structuration theory? On the eve of the Arab Spring, almost every Arab state was an authoritarian state or autocracy (Cammett & Diwan, 2013; Chekir & Diwan, 2012; UHDR, 2004, 2009). Although the political background and history of Arab societies in North Africa, the Arab Peninsula and the Middle East differs to a great extent, a number of similarities can also be observed. The 2004 AHD report speaks of an "Arab model of governance" with specific traits common to most Arab political systems. These states have a centralized executive power with a president, king or emir at the top. These autocracies show low levels of democracy in every view with the following traits:

no free and transparent elections;
no parliament independent of the executive;
ruling parties being a piece of the administrative apparatus;
no independent judiciary that is used as a tool for repression of any opposition;
bureaucratic expansion with great state interference in society and the economy;
a weak civil society and feeble civil institutions;
no free public sphere and restricted freedom of the media;
restricted political and human rights and often permanent emergency laws;
dominance of intelligence or security agencies and the national army.

This means that all the rules of the legislative (parliament) and the judiciary are under the control of the rules of the executive. The 2004 UHDR, Arab Human Development Report calls this model a *black-hole state* "which converts its surrounding social environment into a setting in which nothing moves and from which nothing escapes" (p. 126). Of course, there are differences regarding the extremes of these traits and rules. Constitutional monarchies such as Morocco and Jordan have more freedoms for parliaments and citizens than presidential states with only a formal democracy such as Egypt, Algeria and Syria (before the civil war). These presidential states enact more freedoms than absolute monarchies such as Saudi Arabia and complete dictatorships such as Libya, Iraq (under Saddam Hussain) and Tunisia (under Ben Ali).

Arab political organizations are weak and are divided between Islamic parties and liberal or national secular parties. This split marks the fragmentary structure of the social and political systems of Arab societies. Every social and political organization is oriented toward religious, ethnic, tribal, clannish or regional diversity. This makes it easy for the centralized state to divide and rule. When this state is too strongly dominated by one of these interests, the danger of civil war is always imminent in case the national army is also weak and divided.

While the Arab political systems are extremely centralized, the social systems of Arab populations are very decentralized with the (extended) family as the primary unit of society (UHDR, 2004, p. 17). On top of this comes the clan or tribe. This means that personal independence on and support by the family, clan, tribe or religious group are the most important *resources* of the Arab people. They provide security and economic safety, not the army and the security agencies. This occurs in a patronage system of political and social support. Together with the workings of the bureaucracy this creates crony relationships, from petty to big corruption. Often Arab citizens have to depend on personal contacts, called *wasta* in Arabic, and pay a bribe to obtain services or to avoid punishment. The result of both the segmentation of society and the operations of the ubiquitous executive leads to endemic corruption in Arab countries (Transparency International, 2008; UHDR, 2004, 2009).

The economic system is also decentralized in several respects. Local agriculture, trade and services are dominant resources. The biggest economic activity sector is services (constituting at least 50% of the economy), the second is agriculture and the third is industry. A large part of the services sector is the exploitation of oil and gas, which completely dominates the economy of the Arabian peninsula, Iraq, Algeria, Libya and part of Egypt. This is the central habitat of the economy. The oil and gas resources not only go to the elite but also to the treasury, which in this way pays for health, education and public services and provides many subsidies for food, energy and social benefits. This "rentier economy" (UNDP, 2004) supports the political and economic system and parts of the population who depend on it. The remainder comes from employment in the informal labor sector comprising on average 40% of the total workforce. The Arab region has relatively little industry, mostly consisting of small and medium enterprises. Only Morocco, Tunisia, Jordan, Lebanon, and part of Egypt have primarily traditional industrial activities and exports, and the Arabian peninsula and Algeria have an oil and gas industry.

Political Action: From Arab Spring to Winter

The Arab Spring revolts came as a complete surprise to most economists, political scientists and policy makers (Bellin, 2012; Bromly, 2014; Gause 2011). In the first decade of the 21st century the Arab region experienced modest growth rates and relatively low rates of inequality as measured by Gini-indexes (Ianchovichina, Mottaghi, & Devarajan, 2015). However, the financial and economic crisis of 2008 did put some stress on the economies of the Arab region. The result was an upward trend of unemployment in Tunisia and other countries, and lower subsidies for food and energy in Egypt and other countries. The number of Egyptians living below the income poverty line of 1 or 2 dollars a day rose quickly. However, it was not the very poor that dominated the uprising in the Arab Spring; it was more the professional middle class, students and workers with steady jobs or temporary unemployment (Arampatzi et al., 2015; Ianchovichina et al., 2015).

Unemployment in the Arab region is primarily youth unemployment, which is the biggest in the world according to the World Bank, with about at least one-quarter of young people between 16 and 24 having no job. Between 1985 and 2015, the population of the Arab region doubled and more than half of Arabs are under the age of 25.

Arampatzi et al. (2015, p. 9) have shown that "growing dissatisfaction in the wake of the Arab Spring was fueled by a mix of grievances related to the standards of living, unemployment and low quality jobs, and 'wasta' or cronyism". This is not simply a matter of bad objective conditions but of the subjective awareness of shortcomings in these objective conditions. Dissatisfaction alone does not bring political action (Klandermans, 1996). This comes with perceived opportunities for change. Injustice is the social base of revolt (Barrington Moore, 1978).

In this case, the blame was not only placed on bad objective conditions but also on the system responsible. The social contract between obedience and citizens receiving subsidies for basic needs was breaking on the eve of the Arab Spring. Citizens realized the injustice of the system of rampant corruption, luxury of the ruling elites and brutal repression of every resistance by the common man. The Arab Monitor (2012–2014) found the following list of motivations for political action in the Arab Spring by a regional-wide opinion poll: fighting corruption (64%), betterment of the economic situation (63%), social and economic justice (57%), civil and political freedoms, and emancipation from oppression (42%) and dignity (28%). Only the fourth motivation can be labeled as a need for more democracy in a narrow sense.

On December 17, 2010 Mohamed Bouazizi, an unemployed man who made some money by selling fruit at a small roadside stand in Sidi Bouzid, Tunisia, had his wares confiscated by a police inspector. He immediately appealed to three authorities: the police itself, the municipal authorities and the region's governor. At all the offices he turned to he was brutally beaten by security officials. An hour later, he doused himself with gasoline and set himself afire. His death on January 4, 2011 sent masses of people to the streets, such as many unemployed people, workers and trade unionists, students, professionals of all kinds and political and human rights activists. This incident and the Tunisian protests sparked a wave of unrest and protest, demonstrations and occupations of streets, central squares and buildings in North Africa and the Middle East. The most affected countries were Egypt, Libya, Yemen, Bahrain and Syria. Algeria, Morocco, Jordan, Kuwait, Iraq and Sudan were also affected.

Only in Tunisia, Egypt, Yemen and Libya was the head of the state, the president or dictator, removed from office (Ben Ali in Tunisia, Mubarak in Egypt and Saleh in Yemen) or even killed (Gadaffi in Libya). This can be called either a political revolution (Tunisia) or a palace coup (Egypt). Only in Tunisia was a democracy born with a more or less working parliament after five years. In some countries, minor reforms were made in political governance and a few governments or prime ministers were sacked by the king or the emir (Jordan and Kuwait). In Bahrain, the revolt was smashed by the regime with the help of the Saudi army. In Egypt, the freely elected new president, the leader of the victorious Muslim Brotherhood Morsi in 2012, was ousted from office in 2013 by a coup of the army chief general el-Sisi who managed to become elected as president himself. Most observers now perceive that political oppression under el-Sisi is harder than under Mubarak. Finally, in three major Arab Spring countries a violent and devastating civil war or anarchy has started: Syria, Yemen and Libya.

After 2012, another reaction to the political and economic crisis of legitimacy in the Arab world emerged: violent rebellion by Islamist extremists. While first peaceful fundamental Islamic popular parties won the elections in Tunisia and Egypt, in other countries openly anti-democratic currents of Islamist belief prevailed after some time. Al Qaeda, ISIS, Al-Nusra and other extremist or even terrorist movements spread in the Middle East and North Africa. In 2014 ISIS proclaimed an Islamic State, conquering territories in Iraq, Syria, Libya, Egypt and other countries. The Middle East and part of North Africa is now in complete turmoil, anarchy and even civil war. Not much is left from the Arab Spring. Even Tunisia is under attack by Islamist extremists. The Arab Spring seems to have turned into winter. How could the observers, most journalists and even scholars be so wrong about the democratic perspectives of the Arab Spring? We think it is because they primarily saw the superficial phenomena of demonstrations, occupancies and ousting of dictators or using new tools such as social media, and not the political, economic and cultural foundations of contemporary Arab states. For them we also have to look at the left and right-hand margins of the model in Figure 6.1.

Modalities: Arab Political Views

The relation between political action and political system change is modulated by current political views in the Middle East and North Africa, first of all, views of democracy (see the left-hand-side section of Figure 6.1). Most views of democracy listed in the Introduction are not popular in the Arab region. They have evolved in Western democracies. Views of pluralist, participative and libertarian democracy are foreign to the Arab world, which is fragmented into competing ethnic, religious and regional divisions. As argued before, the public sphere and civil society at the level of the nation are weak. As a long history of elections is also negligible, competitive and plebiscitary democracy also seem to be exotic in the Arab world. Only a kind of legalist view of democracy might perhaps be a perspective for secular political views looking for an alternative to authoritarianism. We have seen that the three powers of the legislative, executive and the judiciary are not separated. The state is not small but big, and civil society, political parties and parliaments are weak. A more or less functional legal representative system for democracy with regular elections would at least be a starting point for an alternative to authoritarian rule.

However, what actually are the views toward democracy in the Arab world? In many regional-wide surveys, an overwhelming majority of Arab citizens express support for democracy as a type of governance. However, they have an inadequate understanding of what it means (Shin, 2015). Between 2005 and 2008, more than 65% of these citizens had an ill-informed understanding because they were not able to make a distinction between democracy and autocracy although they knew some basic properties of democracy. An additional 5.8% did not even know any of these properties while only 19% of the Arab population was well informed about what democracy means (Shin, 2015, p. 22, citing 2005–2008 World Values Surveys). Only one or two properties were mentioned by Arabs: holding elections being the most frequently mentioned property (29%), economic security (28%) in second place, while the third, economic equality (23%) and a fourth, freedom (20%), were less frequently indicated.

It has been observed that Arabs, just like many other peoples in the world, usually do not think of democracy in terms of procedural or institutional terms such as elections, majority rule and having free political parties. They think more in terms of substantial outcomes such as economic benefits or social security and freedom or rights (Dalton, Shin, & Jou, 2007). Jamal and Tessler (2008, p. 99, citing recent Arab Barometers) argue that Arab citizens have an *instrumental* conception of democracy, wanting positive social and economic outcomes. These citizens "were more likely to be critical of their government for poor economic performance than for a lack of freedom" (Jamal & Tessler, 2008, p. 99). Extending this argument, Shin (2015, p. 18) states "that people in the non-Western world tend to understand democracy more as government *for* the people than as government *by* the people". This would explain why the majority of citizens in the Arab world is not able to make a distinction between democracy and autocracy. For them the broken social contract of social support with fewer public services and economic subsidies, together with rising unemployment and lower economic growth after the crisis starting in 2008, are a bigger problem than the repression of authoritarian rule (Arampatzi et al., 2015).

Modalities: Arab Political Norms

An instrumental view of democracy and the broken social contract between Arab autocracies and citizens touches the prevailing political norms in the Arab region (see the right-hand section of Figure 6.1). This is a matter of political culture. Arab societies have a political culture that is characterized by patronage in relations between politicians or civil servants and citizens and by religion (Islam). Patronage relations are marked by mutual agreement and consent about the authority and power of rulers or civil servants by citizens in an informal contract. This takes the appearance of a service offered by a politician or a civil servant in return for a vote or other citizen support (patronage). A second form is the exchange of subsidies and other benefits by governments and their support by citizens. A third form is petty corruption or *wasta* (in Arabic). When these arrangements are working properly for both parties they are sanctioned and legitimated by the daily actions in this particular political culture. When the contract is broken, both the sanctioning and the legitimation of these practices crumble.

In the 2011 Arab Spring this social contract was indeed crumbling in several Arab countries. The legitimation of autocracy was contested by visible and no longer accepted injustice and corruption while severe repression was mounting. In this situation, the incidents of a Tunisian street vendor setting himself on fire after unfair treatment by the authorities and a young Egyptian blogger called Khaled Said being beaten to death by the police were able to cause a spark of protest. In this way, norms are violated and emotions are triggered – emotions of anger and a loss of fear together with euphoria when the protests of the people are not repressed and instead dictators are being toppled.

The second important characteristic of Arab political norms is the dominance of Islam in politics. It is impossible to ignore the role of Islam in Arab politics. Islam has become increasingly influential in Arab cultural and political life during the last quarter of a century (Tessler, 2002, p. 339). While Western political culture has become more secular and less religious, in other parts of the world the opposite has occurred. The rise of Islam and other religions in these parts of the world can be seen as a local reaction to globalization (Barber & Schulz, 1996). While in more secular parts of the world religions tend to push toward political conservatism, it does so less consistently in religious societies (Tessler, 2002, p. 350). The believers of Islam can support both conservative and progressive politics, both often called 'political Islam'.

The big question is whether Islam can support democracy or not? Many Western observers argue that democracy requires the norms of openness, competition, pluralism and tolerance of diversity, while Islam stimulates intellectual conformity and uncritical acceptance of authority (Tessler, 2002). Huntington (1997) contends that Islam recognizes no division between church and state and emphasizes community over individualism. Fukuyama (1992) claims that Islam is fundamentally illiberal and creates a normative climate that is hostile to democracy. Unfortunately, these observers are biased by a Western and liberal view of democracy. In this view, individualism is the core of democracy, and is more important than collectivism or community. In other views of democracy, particularly Eastern and Islamist views, community or collectivity come first. Therefore, some political thinkers in the tradition of Islam, or who are knowledgeable about it, argue that Islam is compatible with openness, tolerance and innovation in the community (Esposito & Voll, 1996; Halliday, 1995). So-called 'enlightened Islam' supports a system of good governance with principles of obligatory consultation ('al-shura'), respect for freedoms, questioning rulers and holding them accountable (UHDR, 2009, p. 69). The influence of Islam depends on how and by whom it is interpreted (Tessler, 2002, p. 340).

The key to understanding the current political situation in the Arab world is understanding that Islam has become more conservative in the direction of theodicy and extremism as a result of the economic crisis, the need to defend the identity of Islam and the crisis of legitimacy of corrupt regimes supported by Western powers. The disastrous interventions of the U.S. and the UK with their allies in Iraq (see Committee of Privy Counsellors of the Iraq Inquiry, 2016), Afghanistan and Libya were not good publicity for democracy. For many Arabs, Islam became the answer, rather than Western views of democracy. This explains why the Arab Spring, starting with protests which at first sight looked like a secular contestation of authoritarian rule and a drive for some kind of democracy, clearly ended in a religious direction. First, the elections forced by the protests in Egypt and Tunisia turned into an overwhelming victory for peaceful Islamist parties. Subsequently, in the countries teared apart by civil war (Libya, Syria and Yemen), the strongest opposition to the regimes came not from democratic forces but from violent Islamist extremists. Lastly, in the countries ruined and teared apart by Western intervention (Iraq and Afghanistan), the barely democratic governments in power are not primarily contested by more democratic forces but by violent Islamist extremists and ethnic or regional minorities fighting for succession with weapons instead of votes, such as the Kurds in Iraq and Syria.

Modalities: The Use of Digital Media

A central axis of structuration between political systems and political action is the use of technology, in the case of this book, the Internet and other digital media (see the middle section of Figure 6.1). A great deal of attention has been given to the use of these media in the Arab Spring, especially social media. The assumption is that they were instruments (modalities) to change political systems for the cause of democracy by using them for political action. This is the bottom-up arrow in the middle section of Figure 6.1. In the opposite direction (top-down), these same instruments are used by governments defending their political systems by means of surveillance, intimidation and manipulation of political action; this has received much less interest.

The use of the Internet for the cause of democracy reveals a number of opportunities. The main goal of autocracies is to control the information and freedom of speech in media and communication. The use of the Internet is a lethal threat to totalitarian rulers. When not filtered, the Internet provides sources of free information and the chance to communicate with fellow citizens directly (by e-mail and messaging via mobile telephony). Governments' grip on the national mass media (the press and broadcasting) is getting weaker. In the Arab Spring, the *combination* of international satellite television that was not under control of the authoritarian regimes (al-Jazeera and al-Arabiya) and the free social media were powerful tools for the opposition (Bellin, 2012). The reverse opportunities, of authoritarian regimes using social media for large-scale surveillance, identifying protesters and manipulating these media with their own messages and tactical maneuverings, we repeat, have received less much attention from observers (Deibert & Rohozinski, 2012; MacKinnon, 2012).

The three main uses of social media for political action are information, discussion and organization. The use of *information* entails the reception, sharing and creation of news and other information. Facebook, Twitter and other social media and the use of mobile phones spread current news across the Arab region, from Tunisia to Algeria, Egypt, Bahrain, Yemen, Jordan and other Arab countries. This news is not only received more quickly but is also completely different in tone and substance to that of the traditional mass media. It contains its own footage and copies of fragments from al-Jazeera and other satellite channels. This news is immediately shared by the receivers together with web links to video, pictures and documents. Finally, social media are also independently used to create news by participants of political action. They produce news for other places and protesters by distributing the current events in the continuing action.

The second use of social media for the protests was *discussion* about the current events and how to deal with them. Blogs by advanced writers in public or political affairs were accompanied by a steeply growing number of views in Tweets and Facebook-page discussions. This was the medium to learn about what was going on and to create strategies and tactics to continue the struggle.

The third application of social media with a substantial effect on the protests was *organizing* the action by mobilizing people to go to demonstrations, occupying squares and to prevent counter-actions by the police and security forces. Social media can be a formidable tool to mobilize and direct masses of people.

Howard and Hussain (2013, p. 23) argue that:

> …it is clear that digital media have had an important role in changing the system of political communication during sensitive moments of regime transition. Images of jubilant protesters in Tunisia and Egypt inspired others across the region. Facebook provided an invaluable logistical infrastructure for the initial stages of protest in each country. Text-messaging systems fed in and out of these countries with information about where the action was, where the abuses were, and what the next steps would be.

The big question is whether this 'important role' means digital media were a significant cause of the events in the Arab Spring? Who were the users, what was their cause and what was the specific use of digital or social media in this social context? What were their effects on the political system? Media and communication scholars were so fascinated by the conspicuous and new appearance of social media on the stage that they only looked at the instrumental, mostly positive, effects and not at the political context we have been describing in this chapter. Journalists were even talking about Facebook and Twitter revolutions. Howard and Hussain barely write about the role of Islam in the Arab Spring and pay no attention at all to the use of digital and social media by Islamist extremists and scarcely talk about their use by authoritarian regimes. So, this brings us to the pivotal question: was the Arab Spring revolt a primarily *democratic* movement anyway? Or was it more a protest about the falling standards of living, (youth) unemployment and injustice (corruption and harsh repression), as suggested earlier in this chapter?

Wolfsfeld, Segev, and Sheafer (2013) have destroyed every bold statement about the causal role of social media in the events and effects of the Arab Spring. Their analysis focuses on the societal level, rather than the individual level of social media use. They observed that the Arab countries with the highest level of Internet and social media penetration (such as the UAE, Oman, Qatar, Kuwait and Morocco) appeared to have the lowest level of protest. Conversely, countries with low Internet and social media penetration (such as Egypt, Libya and Yemen) had the highest level of protest. Only Tunisia and Bahrain had a medium level of social media penetration and a high level of protest. At the beginning of the Arab Spring, Egypt had 15% Internet penetration (low) and Tunisia had 34% (medium). This means that populations with the strongest drive to mobilize had the most difficulties in exploiting digital media (Wolfsfeld et al., 2013 pp. 119, 128). This does not rule out the possibility that on the individual level, an elite of highly educated and young urban digital media users could very well benefit from these media for mobilization in particular places and times, as was the case in Tunisia and Egypt.

The second main observation of Wolfsfeld et al. (p. 128) is that digital and social media use followed a significant amount of protest activity instead of preceding it. In the Arab countries, Facebook penetration was slowing in the early and proximate period before the Arab Spring (November 2009 to November 2010); only during the months of the Arab Spring (December 2010 to April 2011) did it increase. Egypt, Libya and Syria were excluded from the analysis because their governments blocked Internet access during the Arab Spring. There was also no indication of social media messages showing discontent and announcing protest in the months before the Arab Spring (Norris, 2012; Wolfsfeld et al., 2013, pp. 129–130).

In an opposing direction, digital and social media can be used by autocratic governments to change political systems, using these media for surveillance of the opposition, for censorship and manipulation of opposite views and for counter-information campaigns on these same media (Deibert & Rohozinski, 2012). They continually *monitor* and *intervene* in social media use. The security agencies, police and the military of the Arab authoritarian regimes have used these strategies before, during and after the Arab Spring. It is a case of *networked authoritarianism* (MacKinnon, 2012). As a first step, these regimes, for example in Syria, Tunisia and Egypt, tried to shut down the Internet, or parts of it, and even the mobile phone network, for days at the start of the Arab Spring. Usually they preferred to take a less blunt and more smart strategy. Primarily, they tried to benefit from the registration capacity and the persistency of all content on social media (Boyd, 2011). This gave them the opportunity to completely map the membership of the opposition using these media and their online relations. Hundreds, perhaps thousands, of protesters were arrested after online surveillance during the Arab Spring.

Second, severe disruption of the Internet and the mobile phone network has been attempted by hackers employed or hired by Arab regimes. For example, "government-employed hackers in Tunisia attacked dissident websites, taking them offline, hacked into dissidents' computers and stole information, intercepted and even altered people's e-mails, and hacked into webmail and social media accounts" (MacKinnon, 2012, p. 58).

Third, the most 'positive' strategy is for government employees or supporters to intervene in social media discourses with counter-information or views, propaganda or outright lies. They have their own Facebook pages, Twitter hashtags and YouTube videos. The Syrian regime has equipped a complete *Syrian Electronic Army* with sophisticated technologies and propaganda strategies to be used for counter-information, mobilizing pro-government demonstrations, warning people against going to opposition demonstrations or simply showing them a wrong place and time. In February 2011, Bahrain's regime, after having smashed the revolt through brute violence, also struck back on the Internet.

> No long after the protests began pro-government bloggers, Facebook activists, and Twitter users popped up like mushrooms after a rainstorm, posting views and 'evidence' that the protesters were Shiite terrorists in league with Iran, and blaming them for the bloodshed.
>
> (MacKinnon, 2012, p. 62)

Nobody is able to prove that these networked authoritarian strategies have had a lesser or greater influence on the political action during the Arab Spring than the effects of the digital and social media use of the protesters.

The third party benefiting from social media are the other opposition to the incumbent Arab regimes: Islamist extremists, such as ISIS. For ISIS, social media are just as important weapons in the war as their Kalashnikovs. Currently, they are their most important tools for recruiting fighters to the Jihad in Arab countries under attack. Thousands of mostly young Islamist fighters from the West and East have largely been recruited by social media. ISIS deploys the same uses of social media as the more or less secular and democratic opposition that took part in the Arab Spring, although the nature of use is slightly different.

The first use is for the purpose of information, which in this case can be called pure propaganda. ISIS creates imagery and graphics on social media in a Hollywood style, trying to find new supporters. ISIS Facebook and YouTube videos offer viewers a camera eye to imagine themselves shooting Western invaders and unbelievers like in a computer game. In this way, they attract mostly young people in the West and the East yearning for identity and meaning in life, not only Muslims. Only victories are shown or orchestrated in these pictures and videos. Atrocities such as beheadings and stonings are proudly shown. The propaganda is also intended to intimidate opponents with images of gore, beheadings and executions (Farwell, 2014). When Facebook or Twitter removes these pages, ISIS immediately brings them back in another place or simply moves them to Telegram and VKontakte, the Russian social network site which rarely controls its content.

The second use is discussion. Typically, this is not used or is completely differently used by ISIS supporters compared to the Arab Spring protesters. Here, 'discussion' is only affirmation of propaganda statements. No counter-arguments are given, or it would be against the statements of the enemy.

The third use is as a tool for organization such as mobilization and other action. Here, the pattern is similar to the use by protesters. This use is the second most important opportunity offered by social media for extremists: recruitment. Most communication here is anonymous, secret or encrypted. Most action and organization of terrorists and militants happens face to face without any electronic traces. The last phases of recruitment are certainly not organized on social media, or any other digital media.

The conclusion that social media use can be good and bad is too simple. In this chapter, we have argued that the effect of digital media depends on the circumstances, particularly the politics and political action going on, and on particular uses of the social and digital media. Social media are both a new version of mass communication and interpersonal communication, which can occur in a one-way direction or a two-way direction (interaction). The use of social media by networked autocracies and Islamist extremists is primarily mass communication, one way. The use of social media by protesters with a more or less democratic cause is both mass- and interpersonal communication with the ample exchange of information for action and discussions.

Conclusions: The Structuration of Arab Political Systems

Has the political action of the Arab Spring changed the current Arab political systems? And the other way round: have these systems continually changed political action? These questions, inspired by structuration theory (see Figure 6.1), have to be answered more in a negative than a positive sense five years on. Almost every Arab autocracy has survived, only one democracy has been created (Tunisia) and one autocracy has experienced a kind of palace coup (Egypt) where one dictator backed by a very powerful army (Mubarak) was exchanged for another (el-Sisi) after an elected president was removed and arrested. The remainder of the other countries are in the same condition as before the Arab Spring or are in complete turmoil or anarchy with bloody civil wars and terrorist attacks. The remaining autocracies have not been confronted with any uprising comparable to the revolts of the Arab Spring. So, the sober conclusion is that there is more continuity than transformation in Arab political systems. Where there is transformation, the direction is more away from democracy than toward it.

This is the objective situation after the Arab Spring. In subjective terms, almost all Arab people in opinion surveys reject the proposition that the Arab world is better off five years after the Arab Spring. See the Arab Youth Survey 2016 and recent Arab Barometers 2012–2016. In 2012, 72% of Arab young respondents stated that they were better off after the uprisings; in 2016 this figure was only 32%. In 2016, more young Tunesians (86%) confirmed that democracy is the best political system than in 2011 (70%). See Robbins (2016, p. 1). In other Arab countries, the support of young Arabs for democracy is eroding quickly. In 2016, a majority of them (53%) perceived the stability of the system to be more important than democracy (28%). See Arab Youth Survey 2016. Even in Tunisia, the Arab country most in favor of democracy, the confidence of people of all ages in government, parliament and courts has dwindled from between 50% and 60% in 2011 to between 20% and 35% in 2016. In the 2016 Arab Barometer, Tunisians responded that the economic situation (75%), corruption (47%), religious extremism (34%) and internal stability (20%) are the biggest challenges faced by Tunisia in 2016, with democracy as the last on the list (only 4%). See Robbins (2016, p. 6).

These figures support the suspicion expressed above that the Arab Spring was more a movement for social and economic improvement than for democracy. In the discussion about Arab political views, we estimated following surveys that Arabs have an instrumental view of democracy and that in general they have an ill-informed understanding of democracy, scarcely making a distinction between democracy and autocracy. In the ensuing discussion about Arab political norms, it was argued that political culture in this part of the world is based on patronage relationships and links with the social basis of the family, the clan and ethnic or religious origins and not on the citizenship and common good of a nation.

But the most important Arab political norm is the importance of Islam, which is either a competitor to democracy or a particular view of it. For most Arabs, (political) Islam is more of a solution to the current economic and political crisis than Western democracy. For example, according to the Arab Youth Survey (2016, p. 13), a lack of jobs and opportunities was assumed to be the most important reason for young people joining ISIS. Even in Tunisia, 55% of young people between 18 and 24 are thinking about leaving Tunisia (Robbins, 2016, p. 7). For them, escaping to Europe seems to be a better prospect than building an acceptable economy and democracy in their own country.

Turning to the issues focused on in this book, we have to conclude that the role of digital technology in the Arab Spring, its causes and effects was small. The factors to the left and right-hand sides of Figure 6.1 (political views and norms) and at the top and bottom (the political system and political action) are much more influential than the technological axis in the middle of the figure. This statement is a case of putting politics and political theory first and media or technology with their theory second. The balance of the effects of technology from the bottom up (digital media used for political action for change) and top-down (networked authoritarianism) is insecure.

Nevertheless, the advent of the Internet, mobile telephony and new empowering digital media such as social media can be described as a game-changer for the existing authoritarian regimes in the Arab world and around the world (Bellin, 2012, p. 143). Together with free international satellite TV, they are a lethal threat to totalitarian regimes trying to control every source of information. Social media can be a powerful tool for mobilization in political action, as has been shown in the Arab Spring. But they are not a viable tool for steady political organization and working democracy. The whole, partly secular and democratic movement on the streets of Tunis and Cairo in 2011, amply using social media and mobile telephony, was completely wiped away by the victory of very well-organized Islamic parties in free elections afterwards.

Eva Bellin (2012, p. 139) has hit the mark very well:

> Even if social media can facilitate contentious collective action that can bring down an authoritarian regime, this media may be less effective at advancing the subsequent process of building democracy. To the contrary, the very qualities that make social media effective at evading authoritarian repression—anonymity, spontaneity, lack of hierarchy—may be precisely the qualities that undermine its ability to help build the institutional foundation of a working democracy. Without hierarchy, institutionalized longevity, or a clear identity, it becomes difficult for activists to identify collective priorities, negotiate compromises, and make credible commitments to those compromises.

References

Arab Barometer (2012–2014). Retrieved from www.arabbarometer.org/

Arab Youth Survey (2016). 8th Annual ASDA'A Burson-Marsteller Arab Youth Survey, *Inside the hearts and minds of Arab youth*. White paper on the findings. Retrieved from www.gsdrc.org/document-library/arab-youth-survey-2016/

Arampatzi, E., Burger, M., Ianchovichina, E., Röhricht, T., & Veenhoven, R. (2015). *Unhappy development: Dissatisfaction with life on the eve of the Arab spring* (No. 7488). Washington, DC: World Bank Group, Middle East and North Africa Region, Office of the Chief Economist.

Barber, B., & Schulz, A. (1996) *Jihad versus McWorld: How the planet is both falling apart and coming together.* New York: Ballantine Books.

Bellin, E. (2012). Reconsidering the robustness of authoritarianism in the Middle East: Lessons from the Arab Spring. *Comparative Politics, 44*(2), 127–149.

Boyd, D. (2011). Social network sites as networked publics: Affordances, dynamics, and implications. In Z. Papacharissi (Ed.), *A networked self: Identity, community, and culture on social network sites* (pp. 39–58). New York: Routledge.

Bromly, D. W. (2014). *The 'Arab Spring' stress test: Diagnosing reasons for the revolt.* Working paper. University of Wisconsin-Madison, Madison, WI.

Cammett, F. R., & Diwan, I. (2013). *The political economy of the Arab uprisings.* Jackson, TN: Westview Press, c/o The Perseus Books Group.

Castells, M. (2015). *Networks of outrage and hope: Social movements in the Internet age.* Cambridge, UK: Polity Press.

Chekir, H., & Diwan, I. (2012). *Crony capitalism in Egypt.* Center for International Development, Harvard University, Cambridge, MA. CID working paper No. 250, November 2012. Retrieved from http://projects.iq.harvard.edu/files/growthlab/files/cid_working_paper_250.pdf

Committee of Privy Counsellors of The Iraq Inquiry (2016). Report of the Committee of Privy Counsellors of the Iraq War. Retrieved from http://webarchive.nationalarchives.gov.uk/20171123122743/http://www.iraqinquiry.org.uk/the-report/

Dalton, R. J., Shin, T. C., & Jou, W. (2007). Understanding democracy: Data from unlikely places. *Journal of Democracy, 18*(4), 142–156.

Deibert, R., & Rohozinski, R. (2012). Liberation vs. control: The future of cyberspace. In Diamond, L. & Plattner, M. (Eds.), *Liberation technology: Social media and the struggle for democracy.* Baltimore, MD: Johns Hopkins University Press.

Diamond, L. J. (1996). Is the third wave over?. *Journal of Democracy*, 7(3), 20–37.

Esposito, J., & Voll, J. (1996). *Islam and democracy.* Oxford, UK: Oxford University Press.

Farwell, J. (2014). The media strategy of ISIS, *Survival, 56*(6), 49–55.

Fukuyama, F. (1992). By way of an introduction. *The end of history and the last man.* New York: Basic Books.

Gause III, G. F. (2011). Why Middle East studies missed the Arab Spring. *Foreign Affairs, 90*, 81–90.

Giddens, A. (1984). *The constitution of society.* Cambridge, UK: Polity Press.

Gladwell, M., & Shirky, C. (2011). From innovation to revolution: Do social media make protests possible? *Foreign Affairs, 90*(2), 153–154.

Halliday, F. (1995). Relativism and universalism in human rights: The case of the Islamic Middle East. *Political Studies, 43*(1), 152–167.

Howard, P. N., & Parks, M. R. (2012). Social media and political change: Capacity, constraint, and consequence. *Journal of Communication, 62*(2), 359–362.

Howard, P., & Hussain, M. M. (2013). *Democracy's fourth wave?: Digital media and the Arab Spring.* Oxford, UK: Oxford University Press.

Huntington, S. P. (1991). Democracy's third wave. *Journal of Democracy, 2*(2), 12–34.

Huntington, S. P. (1997). *The clash of civilizations and the remaking of world order.* New Delhi: Penguin Books India.

Ianchovichina, E., Mottaghi, L., & Devarajan, S. (2015). Inequality, uprisings, and conflict in the Arab World. Washington, DC: World Bank.

Jamal, A. A., & Tessler, M. A. (2008). Attitudes in the Arab world. *Journal of Democracy, 19*(1), 97–110.

Klandermans, B. (1996). *The social psychology of political protest.* Oxford, UK: Blackwell.

Lim, M. (2012). Clicks, cabs, and coffee houses: Social media and oppositional movements in Egypt, 2004–2011. *Journal of Communication, 62*(2), 231–248.

Lutz, B., & du Toit, P., (2014). *Defining democracy in a digital age: Political support on social media.* New York: Palgrave Macmillan.

MacKinnon, R. (2012). *Consent of the networked: The worldwide struggle for Internet freedom.* New York: Basic Books.

Moore, B. (1978). *Injustice: The social bases of obedience and revolt* (pp. 376–397). White Plains, NY: ME Sharpe.

Morozov, E. (2011). *The net delusion: The dark side of Internet freedom.* New York: PublicAffairs.

Norris, P. (2012). *The impact of social media on the Arab uprisings: The Facebook, Twitter and YouTube revolutions?* Paper presented at Advancing Comparative Political Communication Research. Antwerp, Belgium, April 2012.

Robbins, M. (2016). Five years after the revolution, more and more Tunisians support democracy. *The Washington* Post, May 20, 2016. Retrieved from www.washingtonpost.com/news/monkey-cage/wp/2016/05/20/are-tunisians-more-optimistic-about-democracy-after-5-years-living-under-it/?utm_term=.065acb4f1963

Shin, D. C. (2015). *Assessing citizen responses to democracy: A review and synthesis of recent public opinion research.* CSD working paper. Center for the Study of Democracy, University of California-Irvine.

Tessler, M. (2002). Islam and democracy in the Middle East: The impact of religious orientations on attitudes toward democracy in four Arab countries. *Comparative Politics, 34,* 337–354.

Transparency International (2008). *Global Corruption Report 2008.* Retrieved from www.transparency.org/research/gcr/

UNDP (United Nations Development Programme) (2002–2009). *The Arab human development reports.* New York: United Nations Development Programme, Regional Bureau for Arab States (RBAS).

UNDP (United Nations Development Programme) (2005). *The Arab human development report 2004: Towards freedom in the Arab world.* New York: United Nations Development Programme, Regional Bureau for Arab States (RBAS).

Wolfsfeld, G., Segev, E., & Sheafer, T. (2013). Social media and the Arab Spring: Politics comes first. *The International Journal of Press/Politics, 18*(2), 115–137.

7 Making Sense of China and Digital Democracy

Introduction

For over 30 years, communication scientists and political scientists have awaited the day when the Chinese authoritarian and dictatorial political system would democratize because of rapid Internet adoption by its citizens. The rapidity of Internet adoption in China, of course, has occurred mainly in the past few years despite the fact that, as with other nations, China began using the World Wide Web in the 1990s.

By Western standards, scholars who believe this accelerating and expansive adoption will create democracy in China will have to wait for a long time if they are anticipating cataclysmic changes. Scholarly beliefs that digital communication would be accompanied, almost monotonically, by democratization, have their roots in narratives such as that of Samuel Huntington, which assumed that globalizing communication would ensure political emancipation. Such claims go back to the 1980s (Lagerkvist, 2010). These notions have suffered from weak empirical confirmation. On the other hand, there are empirical case studies which indicate that Chinese citizens are able to use networks to challenge official messages and distribute information about actions of the government that citizens would like to challenge. Additionally, the Chinese government appears willing to encourage certain forms of political participation online, even if within carefully planned boundaries.

While it may be tempting to think that increasing political participation is equivalent to democracy building, this is simply not supported by facts. This is especially true when the system is non-democratic and dictatorial. For the past 25 years, European and American scholars have noted the potential for incipient democracy that is somehow related to expanding Internet usage. Without taking the political, historical and theoretical contexts into consideration, however, such hopes for the emergence of democracy will keep getting pushed into the future.

Participation in a democratic system can be deemed as participatory democracy. Participation without a democratic system does not suddenly make a democracy. Political scientists note that participatory democracy entails: a) a democratic political system, b) citizen participation in governing and forming political opinions, c) more involvement of citizens in governing than in liberal/representative democracies, and d) high regard for citizen deliberation (Fuchs, 2007). What, then, is participatory democracy assuming there is a democratic system? Participatory democracy has its foundation in citizen involvement in political discussion, debate and deliberation, not simply representation by elected leaders (McLaverty & Morris, 2007).

In China, there is a dynamic of expanding opportunities for citizen participation in political communication with a continual governmental system of constraints on that communication imposed and enforced by the Chinese government. The appropriate metaphor is not chess; it is the game of Go. Go is an ancient game in China with many constraints involving 19 vertical lines, 19 horizontal lines, 361 intersections and 360 stones. In contrast, chess has 32 pieces that are moved around 64 squares.

In this chapter, we will aim to show how the Chinese government attempts to use digital communication to reinforce its autocracy at a time when many Chinese citizens attempt to use digital communication to assert their political voices as citizens. It is debatable as to whether the Chinese are consciously seeking democracy in their social and political interactions or are simply producing various forms of political voice that are conducive to more democratic communication. It is possible that the Chinese believe that they already have a form of democracy. The intersectionality of these two countervailing objectives is what makes the future of the Chinese political system in relation to digital communication so complex and difficult to forecast. In this chapter we employ a structuration theory perspective to identify, describe and explain certains aspects of Chinese digital communication that might encourage democracy. Bringing together the historical and cultural context, political theory and communication theory helps to do more than quantifying Internet usage, blogs or chats. It also helps with the important work of discovering where the Chinese people and their government are both enabling and constraining various types of online interactions that look like democratic practices.

We are not attempting to forecast the future of democracy in China because more data that is not yet analyzed is necessary for systemic predictions. Scholars, of course, have made claims about democratization efforts in other nations like Iran and Turkey. Many of these claims speculate that increasing usage of digital communication portends increasing democratization of the societies involved. The goal of forecasting may be a misplaced one as the situation in China is multifaceted and is unlike the development of democracy in many Western nations. Rather than forecasting, we seek to develop a clear understanding of trends, tendencies and indicators which point toward citizen and government efforts in regard to either promoting or muffling democratic practices. As political science has long shown, a democracy depends on both values of democracy and practices of democracy (Flanigan et al., 2014). With that in mind, we must dig deeper than collecting anecdotes about resistance or protests and figures that show rapidly increasing penetration and adoption of connection technologies in China.

Competing Views about Democracy and China

There are competing narratives about how digital communication might affect politics, power and democracy in China. First, the official Chinese government presents control over mediated expression as something that is necessary for order and progress. An American activist narrative views the Internet and digital communication as providing ways for the Chinese people to liberate themselves and become more like the Dutch or the people in New York City. A reinforcement narrative says that the Chinese Communist Party controls all major political communication in the nation, whether online or offline, and this will continue as online communication is forced to travel alongside the dominating political culture. Finally, a structurationist narrative, which we ourselves advocate, says that changes in digital communication at any level of Chinese society can stimulate changes at other levels, even if the changes occur very gradually.

In this chapter, we attempt to take a realistic view of what is occurring in China and other authoritarian societies where Internet penetration, social media usage and communication networking in general are increasing at accelerating rates. Part of our objective here is to sort out what is democratizing and what is a reproduction of existing power relations. This includes sorting out the differences between Western (European, American) views of digital democracy and those of the Chinese. In doing so, it will be useful to examine the differing cultural lenses that affect perceptions of power, ideology, politics, democracy and communication. It is unproductive and ethnocentric to sustain an imposition of European or American models of power and politics on China. This chapter also seeks to identify the empowering aspects of new media networking in China that work dynamically against the disempowering aspects of the surveillance society and the tendencies of the Chinese government to work diligently on detecting and monitoring political dissent and mobilization. While we occasionally refer to other autocracies, we focus most sharply on China.

Understanding the Chinese Political Context

China has been and remains a one-party authoritarian nation. It has been ruled by the Chinese Communist Party since 1949. This party controls all top government and military operations. The National People's Congress follows the directives of the Communist Party (Kalathil & Boas, 2003). The severity of Chinese authoritarianism is not a thing of the past. It should not be underestimated or minimized because of increasing Internet and social media usage. Suppression is not a matter of the nation's far-distant past such as the Cultural Revolution of the 1960s and 1970s and the crush of the Tiananmen Square Beijing revolt in 1989. The most recent Freedom House report on freedom in the nations of the world states that China has been chilling private and public political discussions, increasing Internet surveillance, and giving heavy jail sentences to human rights lawyers, microbloggers and activists (Freedom House, 2017). Control of information and communication is central to the Chinese government's strategies for governance and unity in the nation. Propaganda is openly accepted. Media, including new media, are considered to be tools for economic and cultural development, rather than for political changes that are internal to Chinese society (Kalathil & Boas, 2003). American and European scholars may neglect the fact that Western political theory and Chinese political theory are not the same. Chinese political theory, for example, is not grounded in the Enlightenment, universal rights of humans doctrines, or commitments against propaganda and one-party rule.

Some observers believe that a rising middle class in China portends the rise of democracy. This is akin to linking the rise of European liberalism to the rise of capitalism centuries ago. While capitalism emerged historically along with capitalism, liberalism did not just have one historical cause like capitalism. In the United States, there is a strong belief that increasing market freedom and economic growth will produce more, and stronger, democracies. As shown by Robert Dahl and other political scientists many decades ago, however, this is not accurate. Studies have shown that market growth can occur in dictatorships and problems with democracy can happen in free-market societies.

Economically, the Chinese standard of living has been continually rising in the last 25 years. However, there are still highly visible problems of environmental pollution, governmental corruption and economic poverty in the nation. This is the basis for an implicit contract between the party and the people, especially with the growing middle class: the party can rule alone as long as the economy is growing and inequality does not become too high. The old central planning system has been replaced by state capitalism. This means large-scale privatization of almost half of the public goods to the oligarchs and billionaires. And the result is steepening inequality. American conservatives like Richard Nixon believed that the economic modernization of China would bring about its political liberalism. Shambaugh (2016, p. 153) observes that "[a]s China grows stronger economically, it is becoming more – not less – regressive politically and socially". He also notes that Chinese repression today is the strongest it has been since the Tiananmen Incident of 1989. Today, China has the largest number of millionaires in the world and the second largest number of billionaires (Shambaugh, 2016). The upper and lower-middle-class Chinese households are estimated to constitute about 28% of the population, and currently there are millions of Chinese millionairs (Shambaugh, 2016). Does this mean an increase in social demands for democracy? It means rising expectations for economic and public goods. The latter includes lower crime, better schools, universal health care, and other public goods (Shambaugh, 2016).

The economic development of China has been very impressive and very fast. In the following phase its leadership wants China to become the most innovative economy in the world, and is currently establishing many universities and research centers. The population has achieved a fast-rising level of education. Recent economic analysis shows that while there is a rapidly expanding class of super-rich Chinese and an expanding middle class, there are large problems with poverty and income inequalities (Shambaugh, 2016). The party accepts that the Internet is needed for the economy, and wants to become the second most important economic actor on the Web after the US, if not the first one. To do so, it needs to accepts some room for freedom of oppositional voices as long as they do not question the authority of the party. The Party tries 'to ride the tiger' (a Chinese expression); the tiger is the Internet.

In Chinese political culture, information and communication are considered to be in need of management and control by the government. 'Propaganda' is not viewed as a negative term as it is in many other nations (Shambaugh, 2013). The State Council Information Office works with other government agencies to control political communication in China (Shambaugh, 2013). One of them is the State Council Ministry of Industry and Information Technology, which regulates the postal service, Internet, wireless, broadcasting and information production (Shambaugh, 2013). The Chinese government recently developed an app for cell phones in order to provide Chinese citizens with a one-stop government white paper and party publicity shop (Shambaugh, 2013). Internet service providers in China must register with an information bureau and submit documents about their personnel, goals and content. Sites that do not follow these rules can have their owners fined and the sites can be shut down (Pang, 2008).

One tool of managing the Internet that is used by the government of China is encouraging and supporting as much self-censorship as possible. There is actually an Internet police in China (Pang, 2008). These officers say that Internet users should monitor their own online behavior. Some Chinese are not sure of how far they can go without getting into trouble, with this ambiguity being known as the difficulty of "grasping the yardstick" (Pang, 2008, p. 5). Inappropriate online behavior includes divulging state secrets, disturbing the social order, harming the dignity of the state, and endangering social stability. However, as Pang (2008) observes, the degree of censorship and openness in China fluctuates depending on how problematic the government views open communication at any given moment.

The official Chinese government report on its Internet usage reports the following:

1. In 2015, China had 688 million Internet users. Internet penetration is over 50%.
2. The yearly increase of Internet users in China is 39.51 million.
3. Mobile Internet user netizens account for 90.1% of the total netizen population.

4. In December 2015, China had 4.23 million websites, of which 2.13 million were under ".CN".
5. Mobile phone access to the Internet continues to increase with 90% of the Chinese online accessing the Internet on their phones.
6. Over 90% of Internet users are using Wi-Fi for access.
7. Common uses for digital communication are cited as commerce and education.
8. Instant messaging (IM) applications are the most used.
9. News applications are the next most common, after IM and search engine usage.
10. It is reported that news organizations are pressured to provide more content quality and personalization.
11. QQ Zone is the most common social media platform, followed by Weibo. QQ Zone stresses relationship marketing based on big data analysis. Weibo is placing an emphasis on the expansion of networks based on common interests.

From these observations, we can see that China is clearly becoming more and more of a network society. However, all expression is surveyed by the Chinese government and largely controlled with a kind of censorship that has become much smarter as compared to the early years of the *Great Firewall*, starting in 2003. Many authors have noted how the Chinese government promotes expansion of Internet usage but combines the suppression of digital democracy with the promotion of Communist Party ideology and control. We can observe what MacKinnon (2012) describes as networked authoritarianism in China. It is common knowledge that Internet technology has created what is called the 'Great Firewall of China', but MacKinnon highlights how the Chinese government combines expanding networking with Internet usage to fortify its power.

MacKinnon (2012) argues that classic authoritarianism involved total suppression while networked authoritarianism involves a single-party dictatorship with an allowance of online political discussions that provide citizens with a sense of freedom. The fact that all university students in Beijing have high-speed Internet access does not ensure democracy as much as it ensures that these students have access to lots of information and also read messages seeded by the government (MacKinnon, 2012). There is a multitude of news and scholarly articles about the explosion of Chinese citizen opinions and protests regarding food safety, fraud in medical care, environmental pollution and corruption (Chen, 2017). The government responses to fix some of these problems can be swift (Chen, 2017). On the other hand, in 2014, the Chinese government shut down over 2,000 websites and 20 million online forums, blogs and social media accounts that were viewed as disseminating erotic and illegal content (Chen, 2017).

We might relate the Chinese control or management of digital communication to deliberation within an authoritarian society. The question then arises as to what effects that deliberation has on the authoritarian society. As structuration theory notes, in dualities of structure, social interaction can either reinforce the social structure or challenge it. Significant challenges require continuous change over long periods of time. It is perhaps ironic that some Chinese leaders claim that a movement in their nation toward democracy will occur gradually over the years. However, while individuals may gain a greater voice in Chinese political communication, change at an individual level is not the same as change at an institutional (macro) level (Lagerkvist, 2010). Methodological individualism in social studies of China can conflate the two levels of change.

Despite the authoritarianism, there are challenges to it found in digital communication in some parts of Chinese online interactions. First, there is an increasing number of information sources that can be consulted by citizens. Second, the government practices website blocking and a host of other censorship processes to shape the communication environment online. To some extent, the Chinese government has allowed digital communication to address government corruption, local reforms, and development in poor parts of the nation (Kalathil & Boas, 2003). Apparently, the Chinese can freely discuss these issues, but there is a *clear red line*: questioning the rule of the Communist Party or even suggesting the possibility of more political parties in China is completely forbidden (Shambaugh, 2016). There are various forms of online political communication in China such as discussions, texts and blogs, but citizens who are Internet service providers have to be careful that they do not exceed state limits on speech. Shambaugh (2013, p. 15) calls this "open discourse in a contained environment". There are apparently seven topics that the Chinese one-party government seeks to suppress: universal values, free press, civil society, civil rights, Party mistakes, party-elite capitalism, and judicial independence (Ranade, 2013).

Some scholars argue that increasing uses of digital communication in China draw attention to problems as such as labor and environmental issues, a fact which indicates that expanding digital communication is leading authorities to respond more to public opinion (Qiang, 2013). The argument is made that increasing public opinion expression online is giving more agenda-setting force to ordinary citizens. Of course, one might ask whether greater citizen participation in an authoritarian society is a mark of democratization or simply an improvement in authoritarian e-government. Messages about social service issues in China can spread rapidly through e-mail, instant messaging and texting. Reporting and discussing events and problems online can lead to street demonstrations. The Chinese government reports that digital communication helps people to voice their opinions, and Qiang (2013) notes that many new online users are younger and more educated. When examined critically, these two observations are all well and good but voicing opinion in a dictatorship does not necessarily harm the dictatorship, and younger and more educated voters do not necessarily make more democratic choices than older and less educated voters. Again, assumptions or hopes should not be confused with empirical realities.

As mentioned earlier, there is a dynamic of tension in China between those citizens who attempt to use digital communication to increase their input into political decisions and the Chinese national government that seeks to contain their input and minimize its potential to bring about any major changes. To understand this dynamic, we have to clearly understand: a) how the government attempts and manages to control all major forms of political communication, b) how citizens attempt to gain information and distribute messages that empower citizens more in terms of participation, and c) how these two political forces operate at the same time in terms of effects and possible changes over time. A system wherein challenges by citizens are allowed or even encouraged by government is totally different to a system like the Chinese system where conformity to government is valued more than challenges to government.

The Chinese government constrains challenges with an increasingly smart control over most oppositional voices on the Internet. The big advantage for the regime is that the Internet is its most important source of information to examine the mood and the problems of the people, in order to steer its policies and to purge too corrupt and bad managers among their local party bosses. It looks like a democratic response. In fact, however, this is an attempt to improve the functions of the system. Otherwise, it would be completely stuck in bureaucracy, corruption and the opposite of innovation. This is a typical effect of networked authoritarianism – a concept announced earlier and which will be better explained later.

It is possible for a nation to be non-democratic and to still have a great deal of digital political communication. In China, for example, there are many political sources of information and communication, but there is little press freedom and the government assumes that political censorship is needed for an orderly society. While the quantity of digital communication is soaring, the leadership of Xi Jinping since 2012 has brought about increasing repression, not less (Bell, 2015). There are no strong alternatives to the Chinese Communist Party or to Jinping himself. In 2008, dissident Liu Xiabo wrote the 'Charter 08' manifesto, which called for free speech, freedom of religion and democratic elections. Xiabo won the Nobel Peace Prize but the Chinese government blocked users from searching for his name on the Internet (The Week, 2017). After contracting liver cancer, the government forbade him from going abroad for treatment. He died under guard in a hospital in 2017. His body was cremated and his ashes were scattered at sea so that supporters would have no memorial site for him.

Rising Participation in an Authoritarian System?

Earlier we discussed networked authoritarianism in China and how it forms the political context that one must understand in order to accurately contemplate how digital communication is related to democracy in China. A major realization stemming from the research carried out to write this chapter is that digital communication and its contribution to increasing political participation does not equal increasing democracy. This is due to the simple fact that participation can increase within authoritarian or any other kind of political system. It is also true that an authoritarian system can liberalize and become more democratic without its democracy overpowering its dictatorial power structures and practices. Consider the roles of the citizens of ancient Rome. From then until now, citizen input is often muffled by elitism and others forms of government designed to check against the will of the people. This can also be observed in the American and European systems. Unlike China, of course, these are examples of democratic systems limited by certain degrees of authoritarianism or elitism. China does not have any historical commitments to political progress that we commonly associate with democracy.

There is a point where the state goals of the Chinese ruling class or dictatorship and the discourse of Chinese citizens seeking a more democratic society compete in an interesting way. There is an interesting discourse put forward by the Chinese government that sounds like an acceptance and encouragement of democracy and the desire for citizens to have more input into political decisions. One must wonder how it is possible to have a discourse of freedom coinciding with a political system that is not democratic. It is also paradoxical that there is increased freedom for accessing the Internet in China at the same time that that there is increasing Internet control by the government (Lagerkvist, 2010). Perhaps scholars have too often treated democratization and authoritarianism as binary, zero-sum games. A non-binary or more holistic view of China can entertain the possibility of control and freedom increasing simultaneously.

The Chinese government says that it is concerned with the development of socialism with Chinese goals and characteristics. They refer to the promotion of a socialist market economy, democratic politics and a harmonious society. They state that "[w]e should work harder to accelerate socialist democracy in a systematic way by adopting due standards and procedures" (Central Committee, 2014, p. 3). They also express a need for "multiparty cooperation" that functions under the leadership of the Communist Party. There is also a striking endorsement of improving political communication to "widen the channels for the public to participate in legislative work in an orderly manner through discussion, hearing, assessment, and publicizing draft laws" (Central Committee, 2014, p. 20). Also in this set of policy statements are party endorsements of greater democracy at the community level and more "community-level consultative democracy in various forms" (Central Committee, 2014, p. 21). We can see here that the Chinese government does not reject the concept of democracy, but rather frames a Chinese democracy, kept mainly local, as a good objective for the nation.

The present leaders of China have a view of keeping themselves free from outside influences, and frame too much Internet freedom as dangerous.

The present leader of China, Xi Jinping, openly expresses what he views as a Chinese approach to power and politics. He openly advocates control over information by the Chinese government – control that includes media and education (Lam, 2015). Jinping's administration has recruited millions of citizens to spy on other citizens (Lam, 2015). The city of Beijing has approximately 500,000 surveillance cameras in public places. Technical operators of Internet search engines in China have been ordered to ban more than 60 political terms (Lam, 2015).

As noted earlier, there are indications that Chinese citizens are interested in having more online political discussions. There are more web-based collectives that encourage greater political interaction and participation (Pang, 2008). Pang (2008) argues that these online collectives create an anonymous environment with ways of building mutual trust. Some observers think this is an unlocking of public spaces and civil society practices. From a structurational view, this might be viewed as micro-level politics that might be able to move into higher levels of the political system. Limiting conditions for this development is the fact that online freedom is limited. And for users and providers, there is a threshold for what the government will allow and what they will shut down. Despite so much state control over digital communication, numerous scholars argue that the closed "public sphere" of political communication is becoming less restricted over time.

Tang, Jorba, and Jensen (2012) note, as many scholars do, that digital communication is rapidly diffusing among the Chinese and that such diffusion provides opportunities for non-official political communication. Despite this observation, however, these scholars acknowledge that "control is becoming more efficient and widespread (p. 222)". New online spaces for citizen interaction have been emerging but government projects like the "Golden Shield Project" work to limit information that can found on the Chinese Internet (Tang et al., 2012, p. 228).

Networking Authoritarianism while Increasing Participation

China is not a democratic nation despite the fact that it has seen dramatically rising Internet usage and young Chinese are using more and more social media. About the same as the United States, in China the Internet was commercially available around 1994 (Lagerkvist, 2010). Between 1999 and 2004, chat rooms, bulletin boards and blogs worked as alternative forms of communication but were contained by the Chinese government. After 2004, social media in China were used by citizens to mobilize opinions which affected policies while users became more cautious with the news that the government was planning a registration (real names) system for bloggers together with other new media control strategies (Lagerkvist, 2010).

Anonymity for digital communication is not always possible, as with the requirement by universities using bulletin boards for users to report their real names when registering (Tang et al., 2012). When the Chinese government views posted opinions as too controversial, blogs and web pages can be shut down (Tang et al., 2012). Some users are hired by the state to monitor other users and some are hired by the 50-Cent Party (Wumao Dang) – posters who make comments online that favor the government (Tang et al., 2012). Restrictions on access and usage do not end important political communication in China, but they severely restrict it. At the same time, the state seeks to expand digital communication for economic progress. Despite the non-democratic nature of the Chinese government and political system, the state in China can view citizen-based digital communication as a useful means of gaining feedback on government policies and actions (Tang et al., 2012).

One method of restricting online political communication in China is the use of governmental requests to companies such as Internet service providers and posting sites to remove postings that endanger national security or Chinese culture (Deibert & Rohozinski, 2012). China has worked with American companies like Google, Microsoft, Yahoo, and others to increase its control over Internet information and digital communication. At one time, a Chinese arrangement with a partner company to Skype (Tom-Skype) installed a covert surveillance system to track pro-democracy activists using Skype chat for political outreach (Deibert & Rohozinski, 2012).

In 2013, President Xi Jinping announced that "control over the Internet is a matter of life and death for the Party" (Lam, 2015, p. 124). The Chinese government equates Internet political safety with national security. Xi speaks of promoting Internet expansion and tightening Internet protection with "two wings of a bird" (Lam, 2015, p. 124). Legal action can be threatened against Sina Weibo users for spreading rumors if those rumors are seen by more than 5,000 people (Lam, 2015). Bloggers who have a large following and challenge the government can be detained by the police and charged with creating disturbances, and upsetting the public order. Some may receive jail terms. The government also claims that the Internet is very effective for spreading terrorist ideas (Lam, 2015).

What happens when a system of networked authoritarianism meets cyber collective political communication? When the cyber collective communication is very small, can the effects move upward in meso-level changes? Is it possible to have a top-down macro-level dictatorship with micro-level and local forms of democracy? Addressing these kinds of questions can help us to understand the state of democracy structuration in China.

We do not observe any common or widespread structuration of democracy in China, but we do see indications of increasing political interactivity in how Chinese citizens use the Internet. To see if this has significant tendencies toward the structuration of democracy, we will have to observe how the micro, meso, and macro forms of digital political communication are producing the kinds of social and political conditions that are necessary for the functioning of any democratic system in general.

Political Structuration and Digital Communication in China

Clearly, there is a dialectical tension between citizen political expression on the one hand and government control of communication objectives on the other. Citizens seek agency for political opinion giving and sharing while the government wants to sustain its "harmonious society" of one-party, one-ideology rule. Political communication is most free in democratic societies and scholars struggle with the causal question of whether democracy causes free speech or whether free speech causes democracy. From a structurational perspective, there is no chicken and egg puzzle. It is assumed that democracy and free speech vary together but both are caused by other factors. Wenli Yuan (2010) describes those other factors as being how much citizens participate, the political landscape, the state of political communication, and international influence over the types of political system and practices that characterize the nation.

We can explore the challenges of political discourse emergence in a closed society by employing the structuration model used in earlier chapters (see Figure 7.1).

To look at China from a structurational view, we need to drop the European and American lenses and ideological filters and focus objectively on what the Chinese are accomplishing politically in whatever directions. We can then examine what specific forms of political social influence are developing in China and with what effects. As the Arab Spring results indicate, revolution or revolt do not guarantee democratic ends. With China also, we may be more capable of describing micro-actions and possible broader implications with an allowance for much error in forecasting.

By examining the structurational processes of the Chinese political system, we can begin to study how the system has long-term stability and durability, but also pressures within to reform economic and social problems that can affect politics and how some political decisions are made. Authoritarianism and repression in China are presently normative, but they can be challenged in terms of changes that could bring the nation more economic progress. Thus, continuity and transformation can happen simultaneously. It is often assumed that economic progress and the formation of a market automatically brings about political reforms leaning toward democracy (Shambaugh, 2016). China is an interesting case study that will either confirm or reject this long-standing hypothesis.

The Structures of the Chinese Political System

Structuration theory notes that cycles of communication within social structures can affect larger systems such as a political system. In this analysis, we therefore need to identify the system and social structures which either reinforce or challenge it.

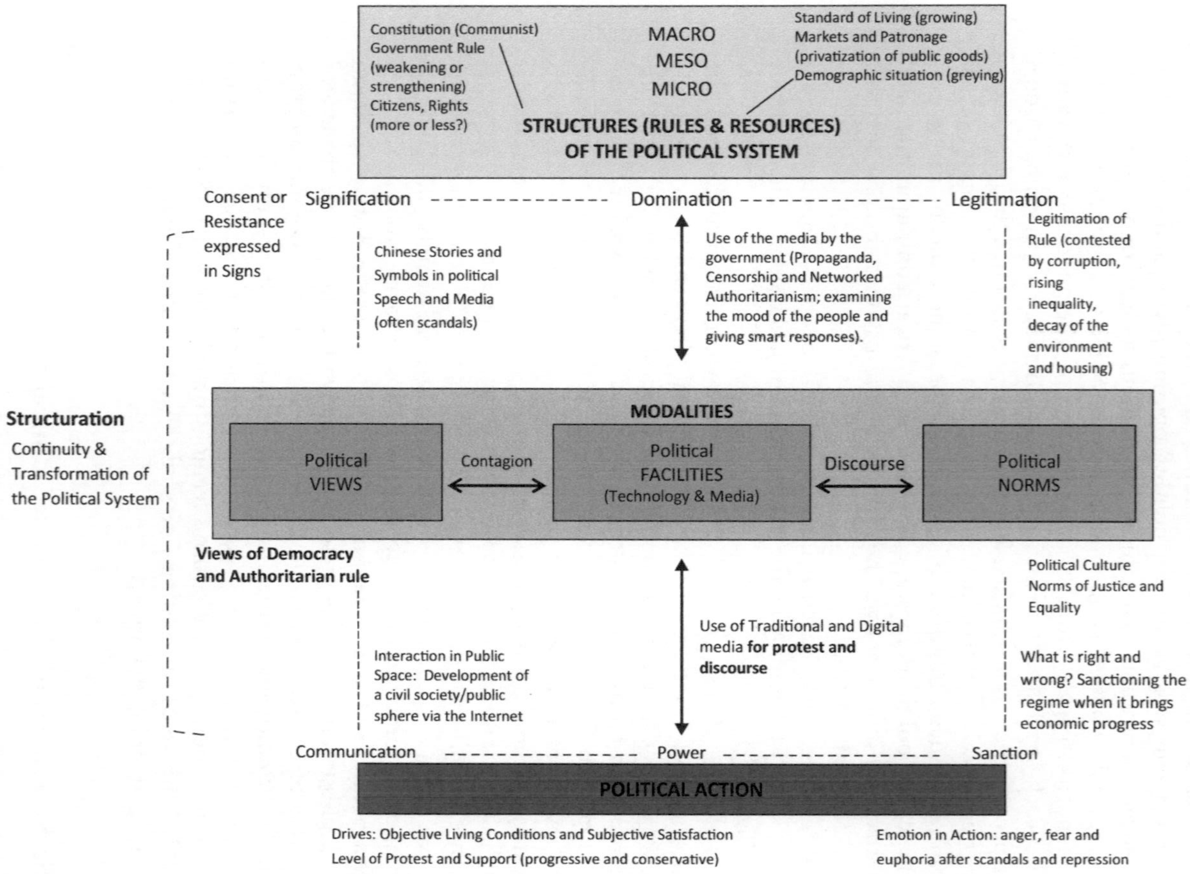

Figure 7.1 Structuration of the Chinese political system by political action.

The hardest question for reform-minded scholars is why such an authoritarian system would want to allow pro-democracy speech and democracy. Certainly, challenges to any dictatorship are possible, if not present, but whether or not they are accomplishing anything significant in terms of increasing or introducing democracy must be empirically examined and resolved. Shambaugh (2016) argues that there are four basic and possible trajectories for China: neo-totalitarianism, hard authoritarianism, soft authoritarianism, and semi-democracy. The present baseline for China is hard authoritarianism (Shambaugh, 2016).

Before introducing possible changes in China, it is necessary to describe the actual state of affairs in the nation. China is a Communist nation state that blended certain forms of capital investment with a one-party command economy. If the nation were to integrate forms of democracy into its system, it would most likely evolve into something of a semi-democratic society in which repression, one-party rule and more open political communication would exist. Shambaugh (2016) argues that this would look like Singapore today, in which there are multiple parties, elections, some degree of openness in the media, and yet a strong ruling party and repression of certain citizen rights.

In various Congress meetings of the top Chinese leaders, reforms have been discussed and prioritized. One such Congress was the Third Plenum in November, 2013. At that meeting, the Chinese leaders agreed on the following necessary reforms for their nation. The leaders describe one of their desired traits as "democratic". A more repeated theme is holding high their objective of "socialism with Chinese characteristics". Values other than democracy are emphasized by these leaders; they include justice, fairness and improving people's lives. It is important, however, that these leaders refer positively to "democratic politics" as a goal. This goal is articulated in discursive contexts of improving economics and the "modern market system". They also talk about the nation being the "masters of the country" and of a need to "accelerate socialist democracy". In this democratic system, the Chinese leaders have referred to "more adequate and sound participation" of their citizens. With no willingness to stop their present system of political suppression, censorship, and propaganda, it appears that the Chinese leaders are attempting to blend some forms of democracy within their existing structure of dictatorship and authoritarianism, as they blended some forms of market capitalism within their national structure of a statist and Communist command economy.

Chinese leaders view democracy in ways that are much different to European and American scholars' views. For example, township mayors can be elected directly by citizens while higher-level government officials are not (Keping, 2008). Thus, we see a system with village-level elections, possibly democratic, and national-level dictatorship. More efficient government and more transparent government are advocated by Chinese leaders. In 2007, the State Council announced open government regulations (Keping,

2008). We should note the danger of conflating efficient and transparent governance with democracy, however. A non-democratic government can have transparency. Transparency involves obtaining opinions from citizens about governmental policies and providing large amounts of information about budgets, judicial actions and political appointments (Keping, 2008).

Political Action

As noted above, official political action is conducted within the state party. The party has to continually deal with the economy (how to maintain the high growth rate), endemic corruption, too much freedom for the oligarchs going their own way as real capitalists, inequality, environmental problems, planning problems (unpopular city building, housing plans, etc.) and many more problems. Outside the party, a lot of political action is going on in this huge country that does not reach the international press and of course not the Chinese press: demonstrations, strikes and the like, sometimes allowed by the leadership of the party and used to purge their own enemies in the party.

As we have stated earlier, the political history, theories and perspectives of China are very different to those of Europe and the United States. It is a major mistake to impose Western political theory on Eastern cultures and societies. We have little knowledge about the political interests, knowledge and attitudes of the Chinese people that are driving their political action. Some scholars have looked at published survey research using barometer studies to surmise Chinese citizens' interests and motivations (Tang et al., 2012). However, we also have thousands of years of history and the writings of Chinese scholars and leaders to examine. These are important because they provide a cultural landscape for how the Chinese perceive their nation and their politics.

If democracy begins to emerge in China, it should be related to many forms of political agency and action initiated at micro levels of social interaction. As Diamond (2012) argues, there are many cases of citizen protests in China that caused the government to take certain actions. Some protests have led to wrongdoing being punished. Diamond draws attention to the pervasive use of texting in China to aid grassroots protests. In 2007, thousands of text messages drew attention to a dangerous chemical plant in Xiamen and the government suspended the project (Diamond, 2012). Text messaging in this case spread to blogging with more political effects. Xiao Qiang (2013) notes that the Chinese government officials are responding increasingly to public opinion created online. Qiang argues that online popular opinion creates a new form of agenda setting in China. More grassroots voicing of opinions online sounds consistent with democracy but we have to ask if public opinion, while being a necessary condition for democracy, is a sufficient one. It is possible that bloggers, those that are allowed to continue, and texters, are forming online political communities and that user clusters and links are forming networks of political information (Qiang, 2013).

From a structurational view, political changes at micro levels can influence changes at larger or higher levels of interaction. The more the government blocks such bottom-up changes, however, the more likely the changes will remain local. Despite the fact that upward political pressure may not change the political system any time soon or in a major way, this not negate the observations that Chinese citizens are creating more digital communication to discuss social issues and that the Chinese government has responded to some public concerns. It is often suggested that there are so many young Chinese netizens that the system must be changing. Such speculations ignore other nations like the United States where more and more young people are using digital communication for political information, discussion and organization, while the political system becomes more regressive. One effective use of digital communication by Chinese citizens may be acting as citizen journalists in reporting criminal actions by government officials or business people. For example, a corrupt real estate manager was revealed on the Internet in 2008. He was sentenced to 11 years in prison (Lagerkvist, 2010). Social media and blogs are used for exposing social and political problems. At times, there is protest mobilization, as in the case of nearly 30,000 people protesting the cover-up of a teenager's death in 2008 (Lagerkvist, 2010).

Modality 1: Digital Media

The main axis in the model, and in the topic of our book, is the core axis of power and domination. Do digital media empower the people (perhaps to reach democracy) or the government? Most authors expect that the people are empowered by digital media such as the Internet and create a future democracy.

Chinese blog portals such as Sina.com and microblogging platforms like Sina Weibo allow some degree of opinion circulation. Within a censored communication environment, Chinese citizens are able to form social connections and networks and encourage collective actions (Link & Qiang, 2013). Link and Qiang (2013) observe that online political discussions in China can be seen as forms of democracy in the citizen assemblies that form online. In other words, actions that are taken in democratic systems are taken in this non-democratic system in forms of communication like debating issues, voting in online polls, and organizing public pressure. As in the case of Guo Meimi, a young Chinese woman involved in a major scandal, Chinese uses of digital communication can expose wrongdoing and corruption (Link & Qiang, 2013). Digital communication appears to be opening certain spaces for increasing expressions of public opinion in China even if these spaces can hardly be deemed public spheres. Increasing opportunities for Chinese citizens to organize and exert public pressure on social issues is facilitated by digital communication (Link & Qiang, 2013). Some scholars believe that this indicates that voices in an ecology of censorship and domination are capable of forming networks of influence and change. Still, we need to sort possibilities from actualities.

We have a very critical and balanced view of this. We see evidence that a modest potential effect of digital media use on the Chinese political system is the best thing to be achieved. Perhaps even a more top-down effect (or networked authoritarianism, see below) than a bottom-up effect. However, the population, at least part of the 50% that has Internet access, try to use digital media for protest and discussion (the Chinese SNS, Twitter and blog platforms). The mass media recently has more room for manoeuver than before (see the trends of de-monopolization [more mass media, partly private], professionalism and more legal protection; see Tang et al., 2012 and Lagerkvist, 2010).

As we stated earlier, Chinese citizens are able to discuss politics and raise protesting views within certain boundaries set by the state. The hopes of post-Mao liberalism and democracy held by scholars in the 1980s were dashed in the bloody repression seen in the 1989 Tiananmen massacre. New hopes arose in academia post-Tiananmen for political censorship to fade while Internet-based activism and pluralism arose. More hopes were dashed. In 2006, Reporters Without Borders rated China 163rd in the world for press freedom, out of 168 nations rated (Baum, 2008). In the structuration process, if agents (citizens in this case) interact with government structures continually attempting to resist suppression but never get any changes in the oppressive message from the state and its government structures, the structures are not likely to change. If the citizens in this process simply repeat the discourse of the state, the structures are reproduced and fortified over time. Perhaps, as Baum (2008) argues, China will not move toward democracy without some degree of political will in the national leadership to allow some types of democratic practices. Since China says it has a Chinese Dream rather than an American Dream and it rejects the politics of Europe and the United States, we should look for distinctly Chinese forms of political liberalization to occur with clearly Chinese characteristics.

Modality 2: Chinese Political Views

The modality of (digital) technology for interaction between political action and systems is not the only one. In this book, we criticize instrumentalism, which presumes that digital media are endemically democratic or participatory. Instrumentalism in this way is not only one-sided (only having bottom-up effects on systems); it also ignores political contexts (and political theory). Political systems and structures, political views and political norms are the context of digital media use. See the politics-media-politics cycle mentioned in the Introduction.

Authoritarianism must be understood before ways to lessen it are understood, and both of these must be explained before any substantive role of digital communication promoting freedom from authoritarian rules can be discerned. The principle applies to moving from disempowerment to empowerment and from low political participation to high participation.

Those leaders who hold authoritarian power, such as those in China and Russia, design a type of rule in their political systems that helps them stay in power. Even before the Leviathan arguments of Thomas Hobbes and the powerful superpowers of the 20th century, people in nations all over the world have had social contracts with strong authoritarian leaders, trading freedoms for securities. This is a true principle of human organization despite whatever communication technologies were in vogue at any given time. There are no pure democracies and there has never been a democratic system that has not had problems.

A second principle of human organization that applies to political changes is the fact that those leaders who hold power generally find ways to hold onto, if not expand, their political power. Even the invention of Greek democracy in Athens was related to royal motivations of keeping in office. Effective leaders learn how to manipulate various forms of citizen empowerment and disempowerment in dynamics that help them stay in control. This was true in ancient Athens and is true in contemporary nation states. This is clearly visible with Chinese political leadership today. There is a dual game of resistance and suppression with the same new media. Governments do not sit idly by while members of their citizenry organize online protests with opposition discourse.

Modality 3: Chinese Political Views

A gross error so easily made when looking at China is the imposition of Western standards of democracy on a non-Western culture with its own values, history and definitions of democracy, and effective citizen participation in governance. Some experts suggest that Americans keep discussing the emergence of democracy as a habit of foreign policy exceptionalism that goes all the way back to Thomas Jefferson in the 19th century and later American presidents like Woodrow Wilson who saw their nation as having to a duty to get other nations to accept their values and ways of doing politics (Mitchell, 2016). One should go so far as to ask why Europeans and Americans are so concerned about there being democracy in China. Digging deeper, one should ask why the Chinese would ever want a democratic system like that of the Europeans or the Americans.

Chinese intellectuals and leaders believe they have a better system and one that is not out of the norm in the way the Euro-Americans assume they are. Shambaugh (2016) argues that Americans are disillusioned with the Chinese and suggests this might be a follow-up to many years of trying to shape China. He says "[i]t is the latest chapter in America's two-century long quest to influence China's evolution" (p. 152) and argues that attempts to shape China in America's image result in "not understanding the complexities on the ground in China" and China very deliberately not wanting to go the American political way (p. 153).

It is useful to examine the differing cultural lenses that affect perceptions of power, ideology, politics, democracy and communication that are found in China. Despite the fact that democracies develop within the context of culture and political systems, many Americans' views show the need to demand that China adopts principles of Westernized democracy. The Chinese believe the China Model is just as good as the American Model. While China criticizes the U.S. for trying to makes its national values universal, China does the same thing. It claims to oppose fairness and justice, oppose hegemony, and also provide universal values which, as Wang (2013) notes, seek to end the crisis and failures of capitalism.

Political views are the modality created and operating in the axis of communication and signification (on the left-hand side in the structuration model). Views are continually discussed and changed in communication channels which are not 100% under the control of the regime. Digital networks offer the opportunity and the effect of contagion (spread on the Internet). Signification of political affairs might be a result when the contagion of Chinese scandals and symbols in current affairs and media discourse are so important (like in the U.S.). See some examples in Tang et al. (2012).

While some observers like to say that the days of the intense suppression and one-party rule of Maoism are part of the past, the very words and actions of today's Chinese leaders show that suppression of human rights and free speech in China are very much in force today. The people may have aspirations that they discuss, but the contemporary state requires that those aspirations must align with the interests of the state and its Communist Party, or else must be banished (Lam, 2015). Chinese leaders are fond of the concept of ideological space and use the word *zhendi* to talk about how people's minds are battlegrounds (Lam, 2015, p. 283). The Chinese leader Xi Jinping has made it clear that he believes that the people must remain loyal to the Party, to Chinese socialism, and to their nation (Lam, 2015).

Modality 4: Chinese Political Norms and Culture

Political norms are the flesh of discourse in political digital media use (see the right-hand side of the model). The legitimation of the Chinese political leadership in governing the country is part of this discourse. This leadership is continually challenged regarding its success or failure in solving problems of corruption, unemployment, inequality, decay of the environment, and city or infrastructure planning and housing. The result is more or less consent to the contract discussed above. Norms of (in)justice, equality and good treatment in public affairs are crucial in sanctioning or rejecting party officials and governors.

Despite its thousands of years of history and traditions, the Chinese say "Change oneself; change the world". They appear to believe that cultural rules of virtue affect political virtue and that the Chinese culture is a learning culture. Thus, self-examination and change can be persuasive to others. The Chinese prefer harmony to conformity. According to Wang (2013), harmony involves both wellbeing and civil rights. Common prosperity is valued, along with long-term peace. Confucian thinking holds that change can stem from individuals up to families and then to societies and the world. Chinese thought does not stress the kind of dualism found in Western thought: us vs. them, good vs. bad, dichotomies, etc. Even the "others" can be viewed as being part of a harmonious coexistence in Chinese thought. The "them" of the "other" can become part of "us".

Some newer data might be found in the form of content analysis of what Chinese leaders, citizens and scholars say in their arguments when analyzing their nation. Shambaugh (2013) documents numerous interesting and current claims made by Chinese scholars. Shi Yinhong of Renmn University, for example, told Shambaugh that Chinese scholars attack each other's ideas but not each other. However, in general, Chinese scholars do not explicitly criticize government policies and are careful about making policy recommendations (Shambaugh, 2013). Ironically, while American and European scholars assume that they know what the Chinese people need to do with their Internet connections to increase democracy, the Chinese government is campaigning against foreign cultural influences on their society (Shambaugh, 2013). Chinese leaders refer to a need for "cultural security" or guarding China from external cultural penetration (Shambaugh, 2013, p. 208).

Clearly, the forces of both revolution and counter-revolution must be considered together. Some current events illustrating strong struggles between autocracies and protests illustrate where new forms of digital communication can compete with older forms of communication that were easier for suppressive forces to employ against revolutionary forces.

Citizen Attempts to Create More Citizen Participation

Chinese citizens' attempts to increase their political voice takes two forms. The first is the occurrence of protests, while the second is the online use of discussion spaces. As we noted above, China is not officially committed to any democratization in its nation despite the fact that it uses language of liberalism and democracy in describing its politics. The government believes that its people have all of the input they need in reporting things locally and engaging with e-government. Political changes are therefore seen more as improving the efficiency and responsiveness of the one-party system than entertaining thoughts or debates about multiple political ideologies and parties. Still, as noted by many communication researchers, Chinese citizens appear capable and somewhat motivated to expand their political influence with digital communication.

Conclusions

Some observers argue that imagined democracy in China facilitated by digital communication can both aid and hinder actual democracy progress (Zhang & Fung, 2013). As in other nations, the spaces or "spheres" for political discussions in Chinese digital communication offer possible resistance to authoritarianism while still being heavily influenced by commercial forces and governmental suppression or control of some sort (Zhang & Fung, 2013). It is now a well-recognized fallacy that economic liberalization is deemed to be equitable with political democratization. China is one example of this non-equivalence (Zhang & Fung, 2013).

As the Chinese economic system has liberalized into a more market-based system, observers have speculated that increased capitalism will bring about increased democratization. Such simplistic thinking, of course, is not consistent with history and political theory. Market participation is not the same thing as political participation or input into governance. The market reforms and liberalism are carefully managed by the Communist government of China. There is no such thing as a fully free mass media or online media system in China.

In this chapter, we have seen that that there is now more online political action and activism, but this is accompanied with increased government online monitoring and suppression. Two dichotomous views are that: a) Chinese authoritarianism will weaken increasingly due to expanding online communication, and b) the Chinese government will continuously use the Internet for surveillance and monitoring that checks pro-democracy traction in the nation. A third view argues that the entire question of whether or how digital communication will affect the emergence of democracy in China is usually framed in over-simplistic terms. As Kalathil and Boas (2003) argue, "[t]he truth is considerably more complex than either extreme or difficult to discern" (p. 14). Many scholars agree with this conclusion since history shows that democratization is related to many determinants, with communication technologies playing an important role along with other causes. The latter include ideologies and political parties that compete with each other. It has been chimerical to think that single causes like new media or good economic growth ensure democratization. Far more than message exchanges and expanding middle classes are involved. Philosophies, ideologies, cultural norms, etc. also affect attitudes about democracy.

In this chapter, we have used structuration theory as a theoretical framework to identify what special levels of political action and communication are positively aided by digital media and networking in ways that can resist authoritarianism. In the other direction, we have observed how the Chinese government continues to use existing means of suppressing democratization and political change at these levels. This framework can explain the dynamic of liberating and oppressing tendencies as well as possible movements toward democratization in the face of anti-democratic pressures.

The central question for us is when theoretically can democracy be recommended in dualities of structure in China? The state social structures will push back on democracy while individual and collective Chinese citizens (agents) are talking about processes that are consistent with democracy. Structuration theory holds that changes can produce results in these dualities of structure when the citizens/agents act outside of the normal constraints of the government and the government does not stop them. In China today, we see massive censorship at the macro and meso levels of political communication, with some degree of latitude at the micro level. It is not rational to think that changes at the micro level, however, will automatically percolate up to higher levels. If there are open upward communication channels, upward influence is possible. China, at present, does not have open upward communication channels on political issues that suggest changes in power or citizen influence on governance.

Social platforms may emerge in Chinese digital communication that allow users to produce content (informal sources) rather than simply consume content (official sources). Still, the fact remains that the majority of digitally initiated political revolts do not succeed (Margetts, John, Hale, & Yasseri, 2016). One can document dramatic mobilization of the Occupy Wall Street movement in the United States and then find no significant political or economic results. Still, we should not pin the political significance of digital communication solely on grand changes in systems. The smaller changes are also important. As Castells (2009) and others have argued, framing effects may occur while revolutionary ones are not occurring. This means that changes in how people think and discuss politics and how they interpret political events can occur with digital communication, while large corporate or governmental forces which own and steer the new media platforms resist changes and slow them down. This is the candle in the dark whereby digital communication may ultimately contribute to social platforms and political interactivity that generate new ideas, connections, networking, framing and demands. To declare this into existence now, of course, is premature.

To look at China from a structurational view, we need to drop the European and American lenses and ideological filters and focus objectively on what the Chinese are accomplishing politically in whatever direction. We can then examine what specific forms of political social influence are developing in China and with what effects.

The consequences of structuration between political action and structures in Chinese society and politics are that there is more continuity than transformation in the Chinese political system. This does not rule out that there might be transformations in the future, when the contract is falling apart, when the population has become so educated that it wants a more advanced, innovative and plural politics, perhaps more freedom and a more responsive government.

Unstable authoritarian or dictatorship governments may or may not become democratic. Some regimes have what are called "democratic moments" with times of relaxed repression and then return to authoritarian rule (Levitsky & Way, 2015, p. 69). We believe that the key questions that need to be asked now regarding digital communication and democracy in China should not be binary questions, such as whether democracy is increasing along with more and more chatting and blogging. Nor should there be a focus on hoping or wishing for change in arguments that say that potential exists. Potential always exists. Additionally, we do not need to spend time attempting to forecast or state likelihood estimates of democracy arising in China. Instead, we conclude that scholars should focus on the observable processes of social interaction and government responses to those social interactions (the dualities of structure) that are affecting where and how the Chinese citizens and their government are allowing or stifling citizen input in political communication and policy making.

References

Baum, R. (2008). Political implications of China's information revolution: The media, the minders, and their message. In C. Li (Ed.), *China's changing political landscape: Prospects for democracy* (pp. 161–184). Washington, DC: Brookings Institution Press.

Bell, D. (2015). Chinese democracy isn't inevitable. *The Atlantic*. Retrieved from www.theatlantic.com/international/archive/2015/05/chinese-democracy-isnt-inevitable/394325/

Castells, M. (2009) *Communication power*. Oxford, UK: Oxford University Press.

Central Committee of the Communist Party of China (2014). *Decision of the Central Committee of the Communist Party of China on some major issues concerning comprehensively deepening the reform*. Retrieved from www.china.org.cn/china/third_plenary_session/2014-01/16/content_31212602.htm

Chen, L. (2017). A preliminary analysis of discourses about China and democracy. *China Media Research*, *13*, 46–53.

Deibert, R., & Rohozinski, R. (2012). Liberation vs. control: The future of cyberspace. In L. Diamond & M. Plattner (Eds.), *Liberation technology: Social media and the struggle for democracy* (pp. 18–32). Baltimore, MD: Johns Hopkins University Press.

Diamond, L. (2012). Liberation technology. In L. Diamond & M. F. Plattner (Eds.), *Liberation technology: Social media and the struggle for democracy* (pp. 3–17). Baltimore, MD: Johns Hopkins University Press.

Diamond, L., & Plattner, M. F. (2012). *Liberation technology: Social media and the struggle for democracy*. Baltimore, MD: Johns Hopkins University Press.

Flanigan, W. H., Zingale, N. H., Theiss-Morse, E. A., & Wagner, M. W. (2014). *Political behavior of the American electorate*. CQ Press.

Freedom House (2017). *Freedom in the world, 2017*. Retrieved from https://freedomhouse.org/report/freedom-world/2017/china

Fuchs, D. (2007). Participatory, liberal, and electronic democracy. In T. Zittel & D. Fuchs (Eds), *Participatory democracy and political participation* (pp. 29–54). London: Routledge.

Kalathil, S., & Boas, T. (2003). *Open networks, closed regimes: The impact of the Internet on authoritarian rule*. Washington, DC: Carnegie Endowment for International Peace.

Keping, Y. (2008). Ideological change and incremental democracy in reform-era China. In C. Li (Ed.), *China's changing political landscape* (pp. 44–58). Washington, DC: Brookings Institution Press.

Lagerkvist, J. (2010). *After the Internet, before democracy: Competing norms in Chinese media and society.* Bern: Peter Lang International Publishers.

Lam, W. (2015). *Chinese politics in the era of Xi Jinping.* New York: Routledge.

Levitsky, S., & Way, L. (2015). The myth of democratic recession. In L. Diamond & M. Plattner (Eds.), *Democracy in decline?* (pp. 58–76). Baltimore, MD, John Hopkins University Press.

Link, P., & Qiang, X. (2013). From "fart people" to citizens. *Journal of Democracy, 24*(1), 79–85.

MacKinnon, R. (2012). China's "networked authoritarianism". In A. Nathan, L. Diamond, & M. Plattner (Eds.), *Will China democratize?* (pp. 256–270). Baltimore, MD: John Hopkins University Press.

Margetts, M., John, P., Hale, S., & Yasseri, T. (2016). *Political turbulence: How social media shape collective action.* Princeton. NJ: Princeton University Press.

McLaverty, P., & Morris, S. (2007). The Scottish parliament: A new era for participatory democracy? In T. Zittel & D. Fuchs (Eds), *Participatory democracy and political participation* (pp. 73–87). London: Routledge.

Mitchell, L. (2016). *The democracy promotion paradox.* Washington, DC: Brookings Institution Press.

Pang, C. (2008). Self-censorship and the rise of cyber collectives: An anthropological study of a Chinese online community. *Intercultural Communication Studies, 17*, 57–76.

Qiang, X. (2013). The battle for the Chinese Internet. In A. Nathan, L. Diamond, & M. Plattner (Eds.), *Will China democratize?* (pp. 234–248). Baltimore, MD: John Hopkins University Press.

Ranade, J. (2013). *China: Document No. 9 and the new propaganda regime.* Institute of Peace and Conflict Studies. Retrieved from www.ipcs.org/article/china/ipcs-special-commentary-china-document-no-9-and-the-new-4175.html

Shambaugh, D. (2013). *China goes global: The partial power.* New York: Oxford University Press.

Shambaugh, D. (2016). *China's future.* Malden, MA: Polity Press.

Tang, M., Jorba, L., & Jensen, M. (2012). Digital media and political attitudes in China. In M. J. Jensen, L. Jorba, & E. Anduiza (Eds.), *Digital media and political engagement worldwide* (pp. 221–239). New York: Cambridge University Press.

The Week (2017). *Was Liu Xiabo a patriot or a patsy?* Retrieved from www.pressreader.com/usa/the-week-us/20170728/281917363135207

Wang, J. (2013). A "gray" transformation. In A. Nathan, L. Diamond, & M. Plattner (Eds.), *Will China democratize?* (pp. 38–43). Baltimore, MD: John Hopkins University Press.

Yuan, W. (2010). E-democracy@China: Does it work? *Chinese Journal of Communication, 3*, 488–503.

Zhang, L., & Fung. A. (2013). The myth of "shanzhai" culture and paradoxes of digital democracy in China. *Inter-Asia Cultural Studies, 14*, 401–416.

8 E-Government and Democracy

Introduction

This chapter is about the relationship between e-government and democracy. This relationship is crucial for the democratic potential of networks. Most discussions about digital democracy or online democracy ignore the role of the state and public administration. Instead, they focus on political communication between citizens and their political representatives in parties and parliaments or among citizens themselves. This is a narrow or simplistic vision of politics and democracy. It assumes that states and governments are mere executors of the decisions of parliament. However, in this chapter we will show that it is justified to maintain the position of the government and public administration at the core of the political system, although networks enable citizens and economic or political organizations to bypass the state as was argued in Chapter 1.

How governments and states should act is a main topic of democratic discourse. People in favor of representative democracy primarily address the democratic and civilian-friendly actions of parliamentary representatives and civil servants.

E-government is commonly defined as the use of information and communication technologies (ICTs) by governments to improve government information or public services and to streamline the internal information systems of government. E-government usually is distinguished from E-gover*nance*. This more general and abstract concept refers to the use of ICTs to improve ways of governing or governance. These ways are political, and include the opportunities of citizen participation and democracy. In this chapter, we relate both uses under the title e-government and democracy.

In this chapter, it will be argued that both the internal computer networks of public administration and the external information networks of public administration and governments for citizens, societal organizations and corporations using the Internet can have a decisive influence on democracy, in every view of it. These networks can both improve democracy by creating an open, transparent and service-oriented government and reduce democracy by generating a closed, bureaucratic government and a surveillance state.

In the next section, several forms of so-called network government and their meaning for democracy will be distinguished. For example, the use of government websites in online democracy is a quite different form of the use of computer networks than the effort to create so-called joined-up government, a system of cooperating government departments that used to work independently. These forms of network govern*ment* will be related to three modes of govern*ance* that are quite important for the analysis in this chapter: the hierarchy, the market and the network (see Powell, 1990 and van Dijk, 1999).

Three alternative strategies of government innovation will then be discussed. In all three strategies computer networks or digital media can be used. These strategies are so-called *Reinvented Government* transforming the hierarchies of public administration, *Government by Market* and *Government by Network* (Kamarck, 2007). The choice of one of these strategies, or a combination of them will have a strong impact on the potential of democracy.

The focus then turns to the form of network government that seems to be most influential on democracy. It consists of digital public services. Are these services a mere instrument of management to improve the efficiency and effectiveness of government or do they also have implications in terms of better citizen consultation and participation?

Forms of Network Government

In the network society, all organizations and institutions increasingly function and communicate on the basis of social and media (computer) networks. This is also the case for individual government departments, political organizations or the state and the democratic constituency more broadly. As we have seen in Chapter 1, all actors of the political system in the broadest sense are connected by networks. This is the case for the core of the political system that comprises the government and public administration and for the relationships of this core with other organizational actors and individual actors (citizens) in the system. Connections are realized by both internal organizational and external networks.

From the perspective of this core of the political system, a *network government* and a *network state* are appearing (van Dijk & Winters-van Beek, 2009). This means that the government and the state are in a process of becoming network governments and network states. No fully developed network governments and states exist yet. Even in current developed high-tech societies, governments and states are still largely ruled by traditional hierarchies that use other operations of control, coordination and communication than those that are evolving in networks. The other alternative rule is that of the market that emerged in the 1980s and 1990s with the trends of privatization and deregulation of government operations.

In this chapter, we will distinguish five forms of network government. To clarify their aim and function we will present them in Figure 8.1.

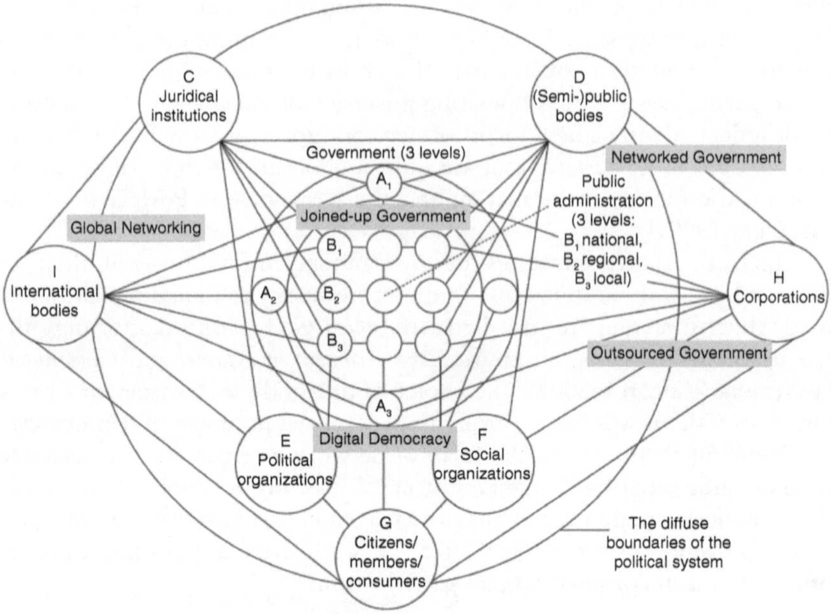

Figure 8.1 Kinds of network government in the political system.
(Adapted from van Dijk (1999, p. 82)

The first form of network government is the form that is discussed in most chapters of this book. It deals with the political relations of the government with citizens or societal organizations and communities. It is called *Online Democracy* or *Digital Democracy* (Chadwick, 2006; Hacker & van Dijk, 2000; Hague & Loader, 1999; Shane, 2004). Here, networks, the Internet in particular, are used as a medium of political communication, the focus of this book

The second form to be distinguished is the cooperation of organizations of the government and the public administration that are using computer networks. This is usually called *Joined-up Government* (Perri, 2004). Here, ministries, provinces, municipalities and administrative or executive departments at every level are linked by computer networks and the services they share. Increasingly, these government departments face common tasks in the field of electronic government. For example, both national and local governments need the same citizen identity and authentication numbers and codes. In collecting taxes, different departments use the same personal and income data on citizens.

Further to the edges of Figure 8.1, other forms of network government are found. First of all, there is a place for so-called *Networked Government* (Goldsmith & Eggers, 2004) or *Government by Network* (Kamarck, 2007).

These terms indicate the growing number of public-private partnerships in government at large that often also have acquired the character of a network. For example, labor and unemployment departments of the government cooperate with private employment agencies and job counseling bureaus to help people in getting a job. In the 1990s, many governments of OECD countries turned regular government departments into (semi-)independent organizations. However, their relationships with the departments of central government have not diminished and a number of coordinating and managing network configurations have been shaped to regulate and account for their activities.

A form of network government that is close to the former is called *Outsourced Government* (Goldsmith & Eggers, 2004, pp. 20–21). Here we are dealing with completely independent or privatized commercial organizations that execute outsourced government tasks. However, they are continually held accountable to central government or to supervisory institutions. Currently, outsourcing in government and in the economy is increasingly practiced by networks of a large number of (sub)contracting corporations and individual businesses.

A last form of network government is so-called *Global Networking* (Slaughter, 2004, 2017). This primarily concerns the networks of national governments and their departments in official associations or unions such as the UN, the WTO, the IMF, the World Bank, NATO and the EU and, second, it refers to the networks of NGOs, global corporations and lobby groups circulating around these international organizations. Increasingly, the internal and external networks of national governments have to compete for power with these global networks. According to Slaughter, the global networks have become ever more powerful compared with national governments.

Not only online democracy but other forms of network government are also significant for democracy. In all views of democracy the role of government as the main executor of the democratic will is important. By using networks as a form of organization and communication, this role of the executive might change. It might both gain and lose power.

Traditionally, tasks of the government charged by parliaments could only be executed by civil servants or be outsourced to the market with a particular contract. In contemporary government, more complex divisions of labor are appearing based on the cooperation of government units or of public-private partnerships (see above: *Joined-up Government* and *Networked Government*).

The consequences of these network forms of government for democracy are that the government and the executive power cannot simply be considered to be an instrument of elected representatives and leaders. There is no simple departmental authority or market contract. This is the assumption of views of democracy based upon constitutional law and the separation of powers, such as legalist and competitive democracy. Instead, the executive spreads into society by means of networks of public-private partnerships. According to the pluralist and participatory views of democracy, this might also mean progress for democracy as governance moves from unelected government bureaucracies to organizations of civil society.

So, the executive branches of government cannot simply be regarded as an instrument of political government and parliamentary representation any more. In the era of powerful government bureaucracy, covering the 20th century, the executive was criticized as a power escaping democratic control. In the age of network government, relationships of power between the executive and the legislation are becoming more diffuse, and not necessarily more democratic. This can be shown when we observe three basic strategies of contemporary government innovation, one of which is government by network.

Strategies of Government Innovation and Democracy

In the 1970s and 1980s, the bureaucratic state in Western democracies ran into difficulties because the trust of citizens in governments deteriorated. Increasingly, citizens compared the relatively efficient business activities and services with the inflexible, slow and inefficient operations and services of government (Kettl, 2002). Apparently, the governments of those days were not able to confront the rising complexity of societies and the quickly evolving demands of citizens. A lack of trust in government threatened to usher in a legitimation crisis of politics and democracy in general. Governments responded with experiments in at least three basic strategies of government innovation: (1) Reinvented Government; (2) New Public Management or Government by Market; and (3) Government by Network (Kamarck, 2007) or New Public Governance (Osborne, 2010). To support these innovations, information and communication technology was used on a massive scale. In this section, we will observe how the emerging forms of post-bureaucratic government that were the product of these strategies and technologies relate to (views of) democracy. These innovations will be evaluated in relation to the different views of democracy, with a particular emphasis on one or more of the following performance criteria.

1. *efficiency*: executive governments should use the fewest means as possible to realize the decisions of parliaments and elected governments as faithful servants;
2. *accountability*: all operations of executive government should be held accountable to elected representatives and governors;
3. *transparency*: the operations of executive government should be transparent for the citizens and their representatives;
4. *accessibility*: all services of executive governments and public administrations should be accessible to every citizen on an equal basis.

The following government innovation strategies have tried to meet these performance criteria more or less successfully.

Reinvented Government

In the 1990s, Reinvented Government first appeared in the U.S. in the years of the Clinton-Gore administration. In this strategy government departments try to replace fixed bureaucratic government rules and operations with *performance measures* for civil servants that should be as close as possible to the prices and profits as measures of efficiency in business corporations. The most important measure is improved customer service in which citizens are approached as consumers.

Following a similar strategy ten years later, in December 2009 President Obama launched the Open Government Directive, of which principles of transparency, participation and collaboration were supposed to be the cornerstones.

Whether transparency, accountability and accessibility really increase with reinvented government depends on the democratic motives and views behind this strategy. According to Kettl (2002, pp. 91–92):

> ...some reinvented government reforms were Jeffersonian style bottom-up initiatives, like 'empowering' lower level employees and pursuing a major customer-service initiative to make government programs more responsive to citizen needs. For the most part, however, reinventing government was a Wilsonian-Hamiltonian initiative that sought to strengthen bureaucracy and reduce the number of levels to strengthen hierarchy.

These strategies are apparently directly linked to views of democracy labeled with American presidents' names. Jeffersonian democracy is similar to participatory, pluralist and libertarian views of democracy, while Wilsonian-Hamiltonian democracy has an affinity with legalist and competitive democracy which aims for a small but efficient state and a strict separation between politics and the administration. In the last two views of democracy, empowering lower-level civil servants might mean more accessibility, but less transparency and less accountability to legislative power.

Reinvented Government is strongly supported by information and communication technology processing the results of performance measures and helping to create efficient and accessible electronic public services via user data.

Government by Market

A significant step further is made in Government by Market. In this strategy citizens are not treated as customers; they really are customers. Government operations are privatized and executed by business corporations. This strategy appeared in the 1980s, not only in the U.S. but also in other Western countries, Anglo-Saxon countries in particular. Here it first received the name of New Public Management (Pollitt & Bouckaert, 2004).

In this strategy the main mechanism is having prices instead of formal rules and regulations or performance measures. Price stimuli can be used when the government wants to manipulate the compliance of citizens to duties and when a high level of flexibility and innovation is required (Kamarck, 2007). For example, environmental policies can be realized by selling emission rights and calculating environmental costs in consumer prices.

Government by Market is deemed to be the most efficient strategy by many people in this age of liberalization. However, this certainly does not apply for government tasks and products that have a system character and are not flexible in demand. For example, privatizing governments have discovered that some transport or energy systems and other complex infrastructures might be better off not being split into privately run parts as coordination might be lost. Additionally, they must have noticed that bringing down costs by privatizing services with inflexible demand, such as healthcare, is not easy.

However, the most important disadvantage of Government by Market is that government services tend to become less accessible for people with low incomes and more accessible for people with high incomes. This kind of inequality will be rejected by proponents of a participatory and pluralist view of democracy. Advocates of legalist and libertarian views might accept this when governments at least become more efficient.

The transparency and accountability of government operations do not have to improve with this strategy either. The results of government privatization can only be measured after some time, substantially longer than on the market. Moreover, it is impossible to monitor all market actions in the government domain (Kamarck, 2007, p. 40), not even with information technology.

Government by Network

The most recent government innovation strategy is Government by Network (Goldsmith & Eggers, 2004). "In government by network the state makes a conscious decision to implement policy by creating a network of nongovernmental organizations maintaining its power to contract, fund or coerce" (Kamarck, 2007, p. 100). All kinds of non-profit and for-profit organizations are invited to perform the work of the government together with national and local government agencies. This is done for government operations that are too complex and too innovative to be executed by a single bureaucracy. These operations would also not be produced by the private market to the extent required (Kamarck, 2007, p. 17). Examples are large-scale emergency operations after a disaster, homeland security involving a multitude of police and information agencies, and the creation of shared services centers for e-government applications requiring the cooperation of many departments and IT companies.

The most important goal of this innovation is to increase efficiency in terms of speed, flexibility and innovativeness as compared to the operations of traditional single-government bureaucracies. When the network is sensibly designed with the right actors, tasks and responsibilities and when it is well managed, government services such as those mentioned above might be delivered at a high quantity and quality. Information and communication technology is able to support network design and management. However, when the management of a network fails, results can be disastrous. This happened, for example, in the American Federal government response to the 2005 hurricane Katrina in New Orleans. Most networked government agencies appeared to work alongside each other and the coordination required for a fast response clearly was inadequate (see a summary of the criticism, see Wikipedia, 2007 and Kamarck, 2007, p. 121).

This means that in actual government these strategies could best be combined in one way or another. The choice of combination can be a rational one, adopting government strategies that are appropriate for particular government tasks (see Kamarck, 2007). Or it could be a normative one, favoring a combination that fits with a particular view of democracy. Generalizing to a large extent, it would be possible to summarize that proponents of a legalist and competitive view of democracy favor Government by Market and Reinvented Government, while advocates of a pluralist and a participatory view of democracy prefer Government by Network and Reinvented Government in the bottom-up version described above. From the views of plebiscitary and libertarian democracy no preference can be derived. This is no surprise as these views care less about the management of government. Instead, they emphasize the needs, voice and autonomy of citizens.

Online Government Services and Democracy

Following the definition of e-government, one of the main tasks in using digital media is to improve government information and public services. These are extremely important for democracy as no democracy can function without adequate government information about laws, regulations, decisions of parliament and accounts of the work of the executive. Further, accessible, user-friendly and appropriate online government services increase the public's trust in the government and the political system.

In this section we will argue that online government services are able to support and to undermine democracy and that these pros and cons also depend on the view of democracy one takes. A communication- and citizen-centered service perspective is chosen to describe the development of e-government services. These services evolve from supply-side oriented information services published in a one-way direction by governments to a demand-side oriented exchange of participation and personalized communication services in two directions. This evolution is portrayed in Figure 8.2.

The following phases from the left to the right of Figure 8.2 can be explained:

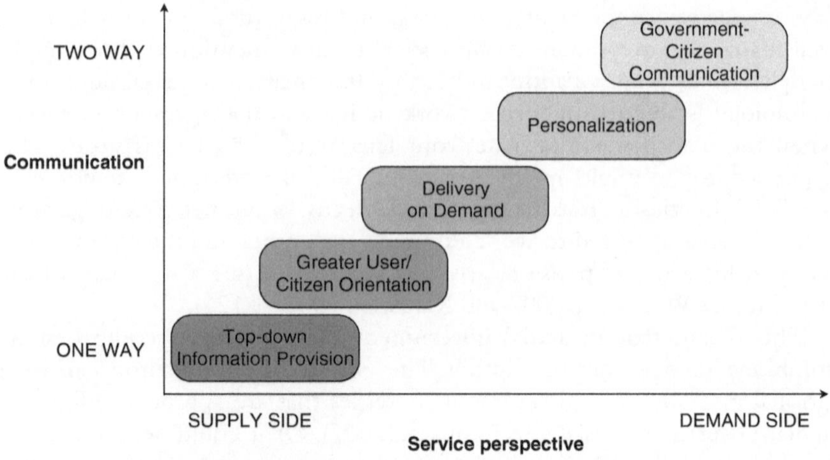

Figure 8.2 Evolution of e-government services in a communication and service perspective.
(*Source*: van Dijk, van de Wijngaert, & Ebbers, 2015)

Phase I – Top-Down Information Provision: The evolution has started with information services, primarily on websites that originally were no more than electronic presentations of printed brochures and administrative forms. In this first phase, top-down information provision is the focus of all activities. Services are implemented while using the existing governmental infrastructure.

Phase II – Greater User/ Citizen Orientation: In the second phase, the attention shifts to service provision. Building upon the lessons learned from e-commerce, Reinvention of Government and New Public Management, governments attempt to develop a more corporate way of working with services. A user or citizen orientation becomes the focus of attention. Governments start to listen to citizen needs in the domain of services. After some years with a focus on downloading and uploading forms to complete, it becomes possible to perform real-time online transactions.

Phase III – Delivery on User Demand: In this third phase, services start to be delivered on user demand. So, governments not only listen to citizen and company needs but also develop a supply of services following the actual demands of citizens and companies. This means that governments need to monitor the actual use of services, an activity that was previously neglected in the supply-side orientation of governments. One of the instruments is to develop multifunctional portals. By clustering services in portals, governments hope to connect more closely to the real demands of citizens and companies.

Phase IV – Personalization: In the fourth phase, feedback is realized through personalization. Governments are developing personalized portals where users can perform and view all of their transactions with multiple government agencies. The aim of this phase is to achieve cost reductions through a decrease of the administrative burden of governments and an increase in self-service by citizens and companies. The provision of personalized and proactive services is an innovative way to increase effective and efficient governmental processes. The final goal is to create a networked government in which all parties seamlessly exchange data, information and services.

Phase V – Communication between Governments and Citizens: In the fifth and final phase, two-way communication between governments, citizens and organizations is anticipated. For example, social media offer new possibilities to support this interaction. The goal in this phase is two-fold: to improve service quality by means of citizen feedback and participatory design of new services and to advance democracy and citizen participation through e-participation. Early experiments show that on average citizens are less interested in forms of classical political participation and more interested in asking for solutions and offering suggestions that help to improve their own daily lives and environment. This activity is called e-participation (Hagen et al., 2015; Macintosh, 2004).

The drive for governments to offer online public services is to keep up with the services e-commerce is offering to consumers and to improve the efficiency and effectiveness of these services. The positive side of this market-driven model of supply is that the service quality of governments for citizens is able to increase and that they learn to listen to their demands and discover their capabilities in using services. Offering online government services is a more difficult task than the supply of e-commerce services. Governments have to treat citizens on an equal basis, they are limited in only targeting particular groups of citizens and they have to maintain not only rights but also many more duties than just offering services. Moreover, the government is not a single company but a collection of departments, with very different tasks, that do not fully cooperate.

A narrow consumer-oriented vision of e-government service has nothing to do with democracy: "*choice* should not be confused with *voice*" (Chadwick, 2006, p. 200, italics added). It should be granted that citizen and user-oriented government services increase the trust of citizens in government as an effective and reliable executor of the democratic decisions of their representatives, as has been argued above. However, some citizens want more than just convenience of service delivery; they want to influence the design and opportunities of online government services and to use the growing interactive features of these services, such as social media, to have a say in government matters. At the very least, many citizens want to supply information for an improvement of their living environment, for the struggle with crime and inconvenience in neighborhoods and for other purposes. This means the intention to open up online government services for participation, which is part of e-participation to be discussed shortly.

The opportunity of participation brings us to the most fundamental change that e-government is able to bring to democracy. Whether this opportunity is taken or not, in online government services the interaction and communication of citizens with civil servants, and in this way directly with the government, is becoming just as important as communication and interaction of citizens with their political representatives. All citizens use government services, but only a minority is engaged in personal communication with representatives. However, in some views of democracy, elected representatives are supposed to steer and communicate with the government and public administration, and not with citizens outside election time. Instead, civil servants feel urged to answer online questions and opinions of citizens using e-mail, websites or social media, questions that should be responded to by politicians and governors because the issues are in fact political. So Chadwick (2006, p. 199) is right in stating that e-government potentially blurs the distinction between executive and legislative functions.

E-participation and Democracy

Communication between governments and citizens is purposely organized in e-participation projects. They have even more affinity with digital democracy than online public services. According to the United Nations, e-participation has three dimensions: information, consultation and decision making. So, it "provides citizens with public information and access to information", it engages "citizens in contributions to and deliberation on public policies and services" and "[empowers] citizens through co-design of policy options and co-production of services" (United Nations, 2014, p. 197). E-participation projects can be initiated by government departments (for example, consulting citizens about government plans) or by citizens themselves (e.g. organizing petitions).

As e-participation deals with government policy, it can be related to the well-known phases of the policy process: agenda setting, policy preparation, decision making, policy execution and policy evaluation. Currently, most experience in e-participation has taken place in the phases of agenda setting, policy preparation and policy evaluation (van Dijk, 2010). Applying e-participation to government decision making and policy execution is contested. The views of democracy that strongly emphasize representation and representative democracy, the legalist and competitive views, have doubts about directly engaging citizens in decision making and policy execution.

Agenda Setting

Governments sometimes not only inform citizens about their policies, but also invite citizens to reply or to have an input with their own ideas, suggestions or complaints (Lee & Kim, 2017). Information provision is the most frequently used application in e-participation. However, information provision on its own is not a sufficient condition for participation. At least an invitation to react to the information supplied should be added.

In many countries, citizens initiate or use e-petitions to put single issues, complaints or requests on the political or government agenda. In Scotland, this has become an official initiative of parliament (citizens are invited to sign petition lists on a website). E-petitions are likely to become very important tools in countries with a legal right to put issues on the agenda of parliament after having collected a particularly large number of signatures. The Internet is a much more powerful tool to reach this goal than traditional means of signature collection. In the UK, at least one petition had an impact on decision making in the UK. In 2007 the Brown government withdrew a plan for road pricing after a petition against it reached a level of mass support.

Policy Preparation

During the years of the Internet hype, many Western governments launched official online consultations of citizens to discuss government plans that had already been prepared. The intention was to engage more citizens in the process of making plans than only those citizens that were known as more or less professional lobbyists gathered in official meetings. In general, the results were disappointing as the same kind of lobbyists showed up as before and because governments did not accept the results as they were deemed to not be representative (Åström & Grönlund, 2012; Bright & Margetts, 2016).

However, on the contemporary Internet both governments and citizens have more technological opportunities for online plan consultations. Governments can use multimedia visualization and simulation for demonstrating plans, for example about urban planning (He, Boas, Mol, & Lu, 2017; Marzouki, Lafrance, Daniel, & Mellouli, 2017, Sivarajah et al., 2016). Citizens are able to play with them (simulation or games). In this way, complex plans can be explained to people with a low level of education and to young people who love games. On their own initiative, citizens can use social media to discuss current government plans and make their own plans.

Decision Making

Except for e-voting in general elections, e-participation projects with a focus on decision making have been organized by governments in several countries. Citizens have solicited and sometimes achieved local referenda with both traditional and online voting options. In some countries such as Germany and Brazil, electronic participatory budgeting projects have been supported by local governments where citizens could discuss and virtually "vote" on public budget options (Barros & Sampaio, 2016; Roeder,

Poppenborg, Michaelis, Märker, & Salz, 2005). However, often the results ("votes") were not adopted by the local administrations.

Outside election time, e-campaign methods are used by citizen organizations and pressure groups trying to change government policy. In election times, e-voting guides or voting advice applications (Kleinnijenhuis & Krouwel, 2008; van Camp, Lefevere, & Walgrave, 2014) are popular in particular countries, such as Stemwijzer and Kieskompas in the Netherlands, Vote Compass in Canada and Questatildeo Puacuteblica in Brazil. They are decision-support systems offered by more or less independent public policy and research institutes, helping voters to choose the best party, candidate or referendum option on the basis of a number of positions and statements.

Policy Execution

Of course, governments use digital media extensively to control for criminality, terrorist plots and normal offenses of rules and regulations. However, governments can use additional eyes to survey what happens in society. This certainly is a kind of participation in policy execution. We are talking about municipal and police sites on which citizens are able to report all kinds of offenses, from child pornography, suspicious behavior (terrorism) to having seen someone driving a car using a mobile phone that is not hands-free. These "snitching sites" are increasingly popular among the population. They can also turn against governments as they can also be used to report offenses by civil servants and to launch complaints against government acts.

Other initiatives by governments are invitations for citizen input in designing and improving online public services in advance. This is called user-centered service design.

Citizens themselves are also able to launch sites for e-complaints against wrong or badly executed government policy. This happens, for instance, in environmental, juridical, mobility and minority or immigration issues and even cases of corruption (Goldsmith, Halsey, & Groves, 2016).

Policy Evaluation

Some governments, mainly at the local level, have installed online quality panels or individual feedback systems in their online public service supply. This enables citizens to rate the level of service provision and to leave suggestions. For governments this gives them the opportunity to continually improve services.

More traditional political outlets for citizen control of the behavior of their representatives in parliament (voting records, expenses, speeches etc.) are special websites for and by citizens such as *TheyWorkForYou.com* in the UK. However, the fastest growing applications of e-participation are all kinds of applications for policy evaluation of governments or political representatives and quality evaluation panels of public services by citizens.

These applications enable citizens to evaluate official policy results on a daily basis and to use them for their own decisions in daily life, such as the choice of a place to live. They have proven to be very attractive to average citizens, including those with no political motivation. Examples of these control sites are sites where local residents are able to report the level of noise around airports and the pollution of particular regions or waters. Extremely popular are social geographical maps of quarters and neighborhoods reporting their statistics of criminality, housing prices and quality of life.

A general evaluation of e-participation projects so far might conclude that the results are mixed. They offer new opportunities for communication between governments and citizens. However, "difficulties and inequalities in terms of facilitating access and provision exist, while results are often disappointing both for policymakers and citizens" (Bright & Margetts, 2016, p. 219). Panapoulou, Tambouris, & Tarabanis (2014, p. 203) have listed the success factors of e-participation and evaluated 230 European projects. The most frequently observed success factors were: (1) value of citizens, user needs or expectations and solving the digital divide (citizens' access and skills); (2) value and support of government managers; and (3) clear plans or objectives and promotion of the project. Citizens often are disappointed about the quality of interaction with government officers or civil servants and about the poor quality of feedback from governments, leading to less instead of more trust in government (Bright & Margetts, 2016; Mossberger, Wu, & Jimenez, 2017; van Dijk, 2010)

The real political results often are disappointing as well. Few decisions of government, political representatives and civil servants have changed on account of the input of individual citizens in e-participation. The most plausible explanation is that governments and public administrations rarely allow entry to the core decision making and policy executing phases. They claim that this does not correspond to our representative political system and the responsibilities of the public administration. Decision makers doubt the representativeness, surplus value and quality of the input offered by the new channels.

Therefore, it is no surprise that governments and public administrations have problems with incorporating the initiatives and results of e-participation into their regular operations and modes of governance. In terms of democracy, the sober conclusion is that "most administrations do not (yet) have mechanisms and capacities in place to cope with a significant increase in participation" (Millard, 2007, p. 76). Coleman (2017, p. 110) suggests that "a new constitutional architecture has to be designed to capture public ideas and experiences in the right moments of the constitutional process".

Conclusions

The use of internal computer networks of the public administration and the external information networks of public administrations and governments for citizens, societal organizations and corporations using the Internet have a decisive influence on democracy in every view of it. These networks can both improve democracy, creating an open, transparent and service-oriented government and reduce democracy by generating a closed, bureaucratic government and a surveillance state.

Forms of network government are not only the political online democracy we have discussed in this book; they are also joined-up government, networked government, global networking and the deployment of local online public services. Joined-up government might lead to a smooth-running, effective and transparent government that is less bureaucratic than before. Networked government enables more interaction between governments and citizens' organizations, public-private organizations and businesses. Global networking might create better public diplomacy and international relationships. Finally, government online public services and e-participation projects are able to forge a better relationship between government and citizens as clients.

In online public services and e-participation applications, government-to-citizen communication increases. Rarely does this lead to new services and changes in the political decisions of the public administration and government. However, it might lead to stronger relationships between citizens and public administrations than between citizens and their political representatives. All citizens use public services, and some engage in e-participation, but only a minority communicate with representatives. In this way, the executive power of government takes the place of the elected legislative power in managing society. What this means for the future of democracy remains to be seen.

References

Åström, J., & Grönlund, Å. (2012). Online consultations in local government: What works, when, and why. In S. Coleman (Ed.), *Connecting democracy: Online consultation and the flow of political communication* (pp. 75–96). Cambridge, MA; London: The MIT Press.

Barros, S.A., & Sampaio, R. C. (2016). Do citizens trust electronic participatory budgeting? Public expression in online forums as an evaluation method in Belo Horizonte. *Policy & Internet*, *8*(3), 292–312.

Bright, J., & Margetts, H. (2016). Big data and public policy: Can it succeed where e-participation has failed?. *Policy & Internet*, *8*(3), 218–224.

Chadwick, A. (2006). *Internet politics: States, citizens, and new communication technologies*. Oxford, UK: Oxford University Press.

Coleman, S. (2017). *Can the Internet strengthen democracy?* Cambridge, UK, Malden, MA: PolityCorn.

Corn, J. (Ed.) (1986). *Imaging tomorrow: History, technology and the American future*. Cambridge, MA: The MIT Press.

Goldsmith, S., & Eggers, W. (2004). *Governing by network: The new shape of the public sector*. Washington, DC: The Brooking Institution.

Goldsmith, A., Halsey, M., & Groves, A. (Eds.) (2016). Uncovering and reporting corruption. In *Tackling Correctional Corruption* (pp. 129–141). London: Palgrave Macmillan UK.

Hacker, K. L., & van Dijk, J. (2000). *Digital democracy: Issues of theory and practice.* London; Thousand Oaks, CA; New Delhi: Sage.

Hagen, L., Kropczynski, J., Dumas, C., Lee, J., Vasquez, F. E., & Rorissa, A. (2015). Emerging trends in the use and adoption of E-participation around the world. *Proceedings of the Association for Information Science and Technology, 52*(1), 1–4.

Hague, B., & Loader, B. (1999). *Digital democracy: Discourse and decision making in the Information Age.* New York: Routledge.

He, G., Boas, I., Mol, A. P., & Lu, Y. (2017). E-participation for environmental sustainability in transitional urban China. *Sustainability Science, 12*(2), 187–202.

Kamarck, E. (2007). *The end of government as we know it: Making public policy work.* Boulder, CO, London: Lynne Riener Publishers.

Kettl, D. F. (2002). *The transformation of governance: Public administration for twenty-first-century America.* Baltimore. MA: John Hopkins University Press.

Kleinnijenhuis, J., & Krouwel, A. (2008). *Simulation of decision rules for party advice websites.* Paper presented at the Annual Meeting of the American Political Science Association, Boston.

Lee, J., & Kim, S. (2017). Citizens' e-participation on agenda setting in local governance: Do individual social capital and e-participation management matter? *Public Management Review, 99*, 1–23.

Macintosh, A. (2004). Characterizing e-participation in policy-making. In *System Sciences, 2004. Proceedings of the 37th Annual Hawaii International Conference on System Sciences* (pp. 1–10). IEEE.

Marzouki, A., Lafrance, F., Daniel, S., & Mellouli, S. (2017, June). The relevance of geovisualization in citizen participation processes. In *Proceedings of the 18th Annual International Conference on Digital Government Research* (pp. 397–406). Staten Island, NY: ACM.

Millard, J. (2007). *European eGovernment 2005–2007: Taking stock and good practice and progress towards implementation of the eGovernment Action Plan* (pp. 219–238). Luxemburg: European Commission. Retrieved from https://joinup.ec.europa.eu

Mossberger, K., Wu, Y., & Jimenez, B. S. (2017). Developments and challenges in e-participation in major US cities. In Y. C. Chen & M. J. Ahn (Eds.), *Routledge handbook on information technology in government* (pp. 219–238). New York; London: Taylor & Francis.

Osborne, S. P. (Ed.) (2010). *The new public governance? Emerging perspectives on the theory and practice of public governance.* London; New York: Routledge.

Panopoulou, E., Tambouris, E., & Tarabanis, K. (2014). Success factors in designing eParticipation initiatives. *Information and Organization, 24*(4), 195–213.

Perri (2004). Joined-up government in the Western world in comparative perspective: A preliminary literature review and exploration. *Journal of Public Administration Research and Theory*: J-PART, *14*, 103–138. doi:10.1093/jopart/muh006.

Pollitt, C., & Bouckaert, G. (2004). *Public management reform: A comparative analysis* (2nd ed.). Oxford, UK: Oxford University Press.

Powell, W. (1990). Neither market nor hierarchy: Network forms of organizations. In B. Slaw (Ed.), *Research in Organizational Behaviour* (Vol. 12; pp. 295–336). Greenich, CI: JAI.

Roeder, S., Poppenborg, A., Michaelis, S., Märker, O., & Salz, S. R. (2005). "Public budget dialogue" – an innovative approach to e-participation. In M. Böhlen, J. Gamper, W.

Polasek, & M. Wimmer (Eds.), *E-government: Towards electronic democracy* (pp. 48–56). Berlin; Heidelberg: Springer.

Shane, P. M. (Ed.) (2004). *Democracy online: The prospects of political renewal through the Internet*. New York; London: Routledge.

Sivarajah, U., Weerakkody, V., Waller, P., Lee, H., Irani, Z., Choi, Y., ... Glikman, Y. (2016). The role of e-participation and open data in evidence-based policy decision making in local government. *Journal of Organizational Computing and Electronic Commerce, 26*(1–2), 64–79.

Slaughter, A.-M. (2004). *A new world order.* Princeton, NJ: Princeton University Press.

Slaughter, A.-M. (2017). *The chessboard and the web: Strategies of connection in a networked world*. New Haven, CT; London: Yale University Press.

United Nations. (2014). *E-Government Survey 2014: E-government for the future we want*. Retrieved from https://publicadministration.un.org/egovkb/portals/egovkb/documents/un/2014-survey/e-gov_complete_survey-2014.pdf

van Camp, K., Lefevere, J., & Walgrave, S. (2014). The content and formulation of statements in voting advice applications: A comparative analysis of 26 VAAs. In D. Garzia & S. Marschall (Eds.), *Matching voters with parties and candidates: Voting advice applications in comparative perspective* (pp. 11–31). Colchester: ECPR Press.

van Dijk, J. (1999). *The network society*. London; New Delhi; Thousand Oaks, CA; Singapore: Sage.

van Dijk, J. A.G.M. (2010). Participation in policy-making: Study on the social impact of ICT. Final report. In *EU-SMART PROJECT: CPP N 55A – SMART N 2007/0068. Study on the social impact of ICT (Topic Report 3)*. Brussels: European Commission.

van Dijk, J., & Winters-van Beek, A. (2009). The perspective of network government: The struggle between hierarchies, markets and networks as modes of governance in contemporary government. In A. Meijer, K. Boersma, & P. Wagenaar (Eds.), *ICT's, citizens and governance: After the hype!* (pp. 235–255). Amsterdam; Berlin; Tokyo; Washington, DC: IOS Press.

van Dijk, J., van de Wijngaert, L., & Ebbers, W. (2015). E-government services. In C. Steinfield (Ed.), *The International encyclopedia of digital communication & society*. doi: 10.1002/9781118767771.wbiedcs109

Wikipedia (2007). Criticism of government response to Hurricane Katrina. Retrieved from https://en.wikipedia.org/wiki/Hurricane_Katrina#Government_response

9 Conclusions

Introduction

To organize the conclusions of this book we will use the same model of structuration theory applied to political action and structures as put forward in the Introduction. The model is repeated again in Figure 9.1. We will start with the basis of the model: political action and its components. Then the axis of this model, the role of digital media as mediators of political action and political structures or systems, will be highlighted. We will summarize the conclusions made in this book about the role of digital media and networking in the two directions of domination and power. The first is the bottom-up direction of political action that might lead to more or less participation and democracy. The second is the top-down direction of political systems or institutions using the same media for the purposes of providing information, persuasion or surveillance of citizens.

Political action or systems and democracy are not only shaped around media and domination or power. They also result from communication or signification of political messages and the legitimation or consent of power. These are pure political dimensions. In this book we have chosen to focus on politics first and media second following a politics-media-politics cycle. We have criticized media and communication scholars focusing on the instrumental role of media and neglecting political context and theory. We have emphasized political trends and contexts. For example, the victory of Donald Trump in the American elections of 2016 might be part of the trend of growing political populism in the Western world, and not primarily caused by smart social media strategies and Internet use.

We will summarize our conclusions about trends in views of democracy, without and within the context of digital media use. These views are changing in the context of a reconstruction of the public sphere on account of networking and a particular framing of politics in terms of images and concepts in this sphere. We will then summarize our conclusions about political norms, such as the digital political culture and ideologies such as populism.

We finish with the final conclusion of the book about the structuration of political systems and democracy. The big question we have tried to answer

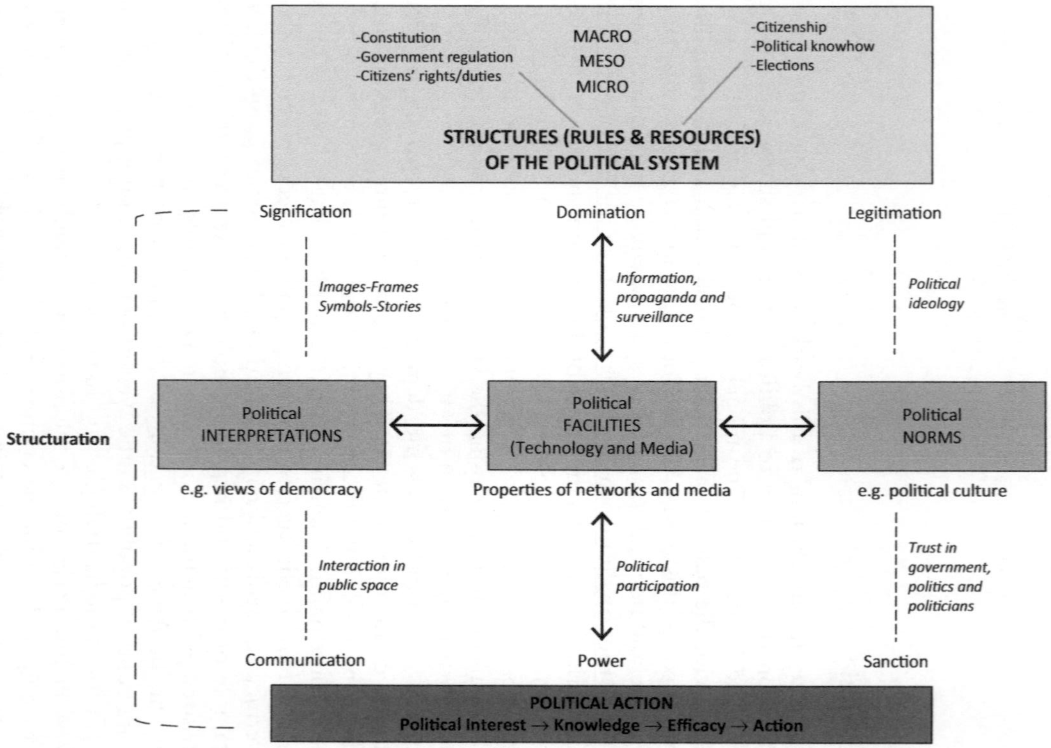

Figure 9.1 A structuration model of political systems and actions.

in this book is whether the use of digital media and networks, together with political views and norms, have changed political systems in the last 25 years. We have seen both continuity and transformation. The context of the network society reveals particular trends in political systems. To limit this big question we will focus on the topic of the book: democracy.

Political Action

Digital democracy entails a shift from offline to online political activity. In this way, the age of Internet democracy begins while the age of television and press democracy comes to an end. This shift is only gradual. For the time being, we will perceive a cross-media period with close interaction between online, television and press channels organizing political communication. After this period, we will witness an age of predominant online political communication with both professionally edited and amateur non-edited content combined with face-to-face meetings and interactions.

When we consider the size of the role of television and the press in current and past politics, we can assume that the role of online communication must be equally important. However, there is no certainty that this role will lead to more democracy. This is the most important problem in this book. The appearance and the forms of political action and communication may change in the digital age but not the substance and the level of democracy attained. We have seen that all views of democracy, from liberal to authoritarian democracy, can benefit from using digital media and networking in ways that suit their preferences. When a particular party or candidate is more or less successful in deploying digital or social media, this only means *that they themselves are winning, not necessarily democracy*. Only in cases where they either abolish democracy or (re)invent it as soon as they are in power might they be able to change democracy as a system of governance.

This does not mean that changing the appearance and forms of democracy and political activity have no influence on the substance of democracy. The online and digital evolution of political action will lead to a quite different culture of daily political activity to the one we knew only recently. In Chapters 1 and 3 we argued that the traditional political practice of speaking, talking, physical action and manual action is changing into a practice of typing and clicking of keyboards, downloading and uploading texts, pictures or videos, designing and adding content to websites or blogs and using apps. Those are more technical and informational acts and this entails that politics becomes a more intellectual practice than it was previously. This also means that information skills become more important and that the 'information elite' in society gains.

Another consequence is that the cognitive effects of digital political content are becoming more important. This leads to the growing importance of images, frames, symbols and stories, either fictive (fake news) or true, as we will discuss below. This means other appearances of visibility and identity frames in politics in which our 'own eyes' are less and less reliable witnesses of what really happened.

A final outcome of the digital culture is the changing political discourse. Online debate and reactions such as in social media are different from those in offline face-to-face discussion in meetings of groups or pairs.

Because of the shift from offline to online political action, it is difficult to estimate whether the addition of the new online channels have led to a greater level of political action overall. This does not seem likely according to the arguments discussed in this book. The rise and decline of political action at a particular time is primarily caused by the current social or political movements, satisfaction about the government and the state of social and political affairs in a country. Increasing use of social and other digital media in the Arab Spring was initiated by the prevailing discontent and uprising, and not the other way round (Chapter 6). In Chapter 3 we have seen that *political interest* was by far the most important background factor in the majority of surveys about political participation, both online and offline.

After political interest, *political knowledge* is the second factor driving people into action. We have found no certainty that using online political applications will lead to more political knowledge than when using traditional applications. The level of political and other knowledge of a population is primarily determined by the quality of the education system and of the availability of public media to all. In this book, we have concluded that better information retrieval and exchange between governments, politicians and citizens is the best achieved claim of digital democracy (Chapter 1). But there is no guarantee that information will lead to more knowledge, nor that it will lead to better decision making. In Chapter 1 it was argued that both the selection and processing of knowledge and decisions are ultimately matters of judgement.

We have a problem with one of the most striking trends of public and media affairs today: the blending of the distinction between fact and opinion, if not fiction (fake news). In the 2016 American presidential election the difference between facts, opinions, untruths and outright lies was very thin. And what's worse, most followers of the main candidates did not even seem to care. They believed and voted what/for whom they wanted. A prime cause is the declining trust in the authority of institutions such as media, science and even courts in many 'advanced' democracies. In the case of the U.S. it was also the complete polarized political climate of the country. Additionally, social media and other autonomous websites and blogs are to blame. Not because they will necessary lead to a merger of fact and opinion, but because they have no, or very weak, editing functions. So, social media have become easy vehicles for distributing fake news (deliberately created false messages) and for disinformation. The potential for disinformation in digital and social media is a threat to democracy in every view. It will also paralyze political action because many citizens no longer believe the information and the call to action suggested online and offline.

The final condition for people to embark on political action is sufficient internal and external *political efficacy*. Internal efficacy is the feeling of citizens that they can make a difference because they are able to act effectively. In using digital media and networks this is not certain. First, citizens need digital skills, in particular strategic skills. Second, they require the capacity to find the platforms in these media for political action. There are so many channels and applications to choose from, some of them brand new and never tested, that they do not know which is the most effective.

The external political efficacy of citizen political action is the belief that political representatives will be responsive to online political action. This belief is often broken by politicians who are not responsive to this type of action and do not act on the findings derived from e-participation projects. They do not trust online political communication as a valid or reliable source of citizen input. Some politicians still prefer the traditional mass media as the most important political channel and find tangible votes at the ballot box more important than opinion and action created via digital media.

The last condition of political action is the *nature of activities* concerned. They can be more emotional or rational, private or public; they can look like entertainment or politics only. The traditional image of political action is that it is a rational and public affair. Over the course of the 20th century, emotional, personal and entertainment aspects characterized politics and election campaigns, especially in the era of television democracy (Hart, 1994). Additionally, a ever-lasting 'politics of scandals' appeared (Castells, 2009). Some observers are even discussing 'emotional or drama democracy' (Elchardus, 2002; Hjarvard, 2008). The rise of the Internet and online politics has increased the emotional, personal and entertainment aspects. Reworking the available footage and images from political television shows by contemporary users of social media and personal websites or blogs, where the distinction between public and private discourse is ever decreasing, has intensified these aspects. In online political discourse, emotion, rumor and entertainment are only one click away. Emotion has always been the main driver of political action, but it depends on one's view of democracy whether it also supports democracy as a process of rational debate and decision making.

Mediation of Networks and Digital Media

The most important contemporary mediator between political action and political systems or democracies in this book is the use of digital media and networks. This is also the main perspective of media and communication scholars. The overarching question for them is whether the use of these media and networks will lead to more or less democracy. We accept the question but we reject the popular frame that is used to answer it: instrumentalism – the idea that these technologies are simply tools and that these tools can be beneficial for democracy or not. In the Introduction we argued that this idea is far too simplistic. The nuance is neatly summarized by Deibert and Rohozinski (2012, p. 19):

> Communications technologies are neither empty vessels to be filled with products of human intent nor forces unto themselves, imbued with some kind of irresistible agency. They are complicated and continuously evolving manifestations of forces at a particular time and place. Once created, technologies in turn shape and limit the prospects of human communication and interaction in a constantly iterative manner.

In this book we have shown, in the case of political communication, that digital media are not tools or 'empty vessels' to be used for any purpose imaginable in particular circumstances.

The second main argument against instrumentalism is that the tool concerned is not neutral. This is another reason why the tool cannot be used for every purpose one likes. Particular characteristics of digital media and networks have consequences for potential use, including democratization. In Chapter 2 we listed a large number of so-called network properties that might not only enable but also *define* use. At the *level of hardware*, networks offer a central exchange with decentralized terminals. So, networks also have centers; they are not 'flat'. This means that fully autonomous decentralized work and networking without a center are impossible. Connectivity, connectedness and physical access of networks are necessary conditions for any use of networks for democracy. The size, density and centralization of networks either support or limit their democratic potential.

At the *level of software*, digital networks are defined by so-called code. Networks have technical standards that make them powerful and inevitable. The TCP/IP protocol simply *is* the Internet. Without this protocol, no peer-to-peer principle on the Web will work, so often seen as the basis of Internet democracy. Network software also enables and defines datification and the use of algorithms. The network property datification allows tracing, quantifiying, interpreting and predicting the behavior of people, among them citizens and voters. For instance, the rise of big data analysis and digital or social media marketing that micro-targets voters has boosted the power of political parties and governments with large staff and money.

However, in using algorithms the big American Web platforms of Google, Microsoft, Apple, Facebook and Amazon have become more powerful than political parties and governments. The secret algorithms driving their search engine and social media products decide what users or citizens actually see on their search result lists and timelines. The network property of selection in networks is initiated by users adding their search questions and demonstrating their preferences. Then they are reinforced by the algorithms of the providers supporting confirmation bias and leaving them in filter bubbles and echo chambers. The five American platform companies are the new gatekeepers of the Internet. They might be more powerful than the gatekeepers of the traditional mass media.

This power is backed by the power law in networks that shows that rich actors on the Web get even richer or that the winner takes all. Simultaneously, an endless number of small actors are appearing on the Web according to 'the long tail' observed by Anderson. This results in both concentration and fragmentation on the Internet. And the number of medium-sized media and communities is decreasing. A consequence is that a majority of users or citizens are using and following the same big platforms mentioned above and the big online content media (online newspapers, political sites or blogs), while a minority follows the trail of a large number of small platforms, online communities and information providers. In fact, the media concentration for political communication is bigger than in the traditional mass media.

At the *level of application* of digital networks, these networks have inbuilt limits of attention and simultaneous input. These properties reduce the democratic effectiveness of user-generated content and online participation by citizens. The popular assumptions that everybody can speak simultaneously and equally on the Internet are partly wrong. One of the main uses of the Internet for citizens is expression, but we have seen that it might be easy to speak on the Internet but not to be heard. Most input of social media, blogs and online forums is read by few people, or even by no one. Simultaneous input, for instance in online forums, also has a limit. Without moderation and other discussion rules, a large number of disadvantages in group dynamics cannot be mitigated. Discussion leadership seems to be even more important in online than in offline settings.

Taking these technological properties into consideration, it is questionable whether online political participation and grassroot influence through using digital media will be effective. We are now looking at the power and domination axis between political action and systems, as portrayed in Figure 9.1. In Chapter 3 we have seen that general claims about the positive or negative effects of digital media use on political participation cannot be made, following Anduiza et al. (2012). In the meantime, digital media use in the political system and participation has become common. For young people it is obvious. It is no longer possible to really compare society or politics with and without digital media. We can only compare online and offline participation in a digitized network society. Another reason is that digital media such as the Internet are continually changing. And finally, we have to take into account the fact that the context of every political system is also different and continually changing. Who would have expected, only five years ago, that the phenomenon of 'fake news' would become so important in political discourse and that political leaders and even some presidents would no longer make a distinction between fact, opinion or fiction? Who could have imagined at that time that foreign governments would go to the lengths of interfering in the democratic elections of another country?

The main claim of political research in terms of digital media use and networking is that they have a significant effect on political engagement, involvement or participation. Most often the claims are that positive effects have been found. However, we have doubts about these claims. Online political participation research has several pitfalls and caveats (see Chapter 3). Only very modest positive effects can be shown at this stage of Internet use for political action. Comparing the mobilization and reinforcement theses, we argued that the latter was stronger. This means that those who already have a high level of political interest and digital skills are benefiting more from digital media for political participation (reinforcement) than the supposed new groups entering the arena of political communication because the use and entry costs of accessing the Internet are low (mobilization). The only exception is the online participation of young people. Evidently, they use the Internet for everything. However, it is not obvious at all whether they are now participating more in political action than before the emergence of the Internet.

This conclusion about political participation might be qualified by stating that we are not only looking for institutional but also for non-institutional or informal political participation. Digital media and networks have strong capacities for mobilization and collective action. They have become main instruments for recruitment, protest, petitioning and campaigning. Here again, the *forms* of collective action are changing: we have found no convincing evidence that the *substance*, that is, the quantity and quality of collective action and non-institutional political action, have increased overall and worldwide over the last three decades on account of using digital media and networks.

Of course, the pivotal questions are whether online political action leads to political system change and the improvement or decline of democracy. These questions will be discussed in the final section of this chapter.

Bottom-up political action changing political systems and democracies is the utopian perspective of the power and domination axis of Figure 9.1. The other direction, the top-down action of representatives of the political system manipulating the same digital media and networks, is the dystopian perspective. This is a less popular area in the literature about digital democracy but it is just as legitimate. Governments, security and police organizations, public administrations and political representatives in parliaments and councils can also use digital media for domination. Information, propaganda, surveillance and cyber-intervention are the goals of every political and government institution.

In the Introduction of this book we concluded that information supply by governments or political institutions and information retrieval options for citizens are the biggest achievements of digital democracy so far. Potentially, both governments or political representatives and citizens can be better informed about public and political affairs than ever before. Whether this is in fact the case for citizens remains an open question. It is certainly the case for governments and political organizations with many resources. With the rise of continual online polling and big data analysis of citizen behavior, these institutions can be informed in much detail about the needs, moods, opinions and acts of the citizenry. If they were to truly respond or act to this information, this would be the greatest achievement of digital democracy. It might be better than continually organizing referenda and other polls. However, this same information can also be used to manipulate citizens in order to maintain the goals of the government and other political interests.

In particular political systems this could lead to *networked authoritarianism*, where more or less democratic governments use the same digital media for surveillance, censorship, manipulation of opposing views and in counter-information campaigns (Deibert & Rohozinski, 2012; MacKinnon, 2012). In Chapter 7 we have seen that the Chinese government has developed networked authoritarianism to a very high level of sophistication. Considering the case of China, we have asked ourselves whether the use of digital media and networks supports network authoritarianism more than the fight for democratization (see Chapter 7). The old totalitarianism system of completely controlling every information source for citizens is giving way to a smart new totalitarianism with a very sophisticated system of surveillance and information management of alleged free Internet use by Chinese citizens.

Views of Democracy

There are other mediators between political action and political systems than media. The substance of politics consists of political conceptions and norms. Conceptions are created and changed in communicative political action affecting political systems with more or less democracy. This involves continual interaction in public space and the signification of political conceptions by the daily practices of using resources in political systems. Of course, communication and signification are enacted by media. The discourse of political conceptions and the contagion of political messages have shown typical expression in digital media and networks. Typical manifestations are the multi- and cross-media visibility of political viewpoints and candidates in the digital media and the contagion of political conceptions in networks.

Currently, interaction in public space is created in a networked public sphere. In Chapter 4 we defined this sphere as an infrastructure of online and offline public spaces linked to each other. In the network society the public sphere is both extended and more intensive compared to the mass society. The networked public sphere consists of a multitude and mosaic of online and offline public spaces at a local, national and global level. It is also more intensive, completely penetrating society because the sharp public-private distinctions of the mass society are blurring in the network society as a result of the individualization and commercialization of public spaces which are still social and open. This goes beyond Habermas's conception of the public sphere because the presumed independence of the public sphere and the media system from administrative power, the business world and special interest groups is falling apart. Instead, the networked public sphere is marked by *self-organization* with a combination of public and private or commercial interests. For instance, the editing function of professional journalists in the mass media is giving way to editing by online media users themselves and by their providers filtering content using algorithms. This is a problem in many views of democracy where autonomously and professionally working public media are important as reliable mediators between citizens and the political system.

In Chapter 4 we saw that the opportunities of the *selection* of sources, messages or receivers and of *expression* have multiplied in networked public space. However, *reception* has limits as most of these sources, messages and receivers have no audience. And in online discussion, some people have a strong voice while others are silent. This means that consensus and conclusions are difficult to find in the networked public space. This brings us to the general assumption that so far the views of democracy with the goal of opinion making have benefited more from digital media and network use than the views of democracy focusing on decision making. Clearly, the Internet is first of all an expressive medium for citizens.

As the Internet is used so frequently for expression of political communication, signification in political discourse is also becoming more and more important. This is especially when we were talking about emotion or drama democracy a few pages earlier. Images, frames, symbols and stories on the Internet might even be more consequential for political efficacy than on television. Internet users, not only journalists, are creating, reshaping and forwarding political imaginary on the Web. Particular YouTube videos and pictures can make or break political candidates. Powerful metaphors such as building a wall between the U.S. and Mexico are portrayed in all kinds of Web artifacts and affect the minds of citizens. Potent frames such as the gap between the people and the elite, found in many expressions on the Internet, support populism. Symbols such as likes, dislikes or shares and being or becoming a follower are becoming more and more important. Finally, stories such as scandals about candidates are going viral on the Web and might be more influential than in the television era because Internet users can magnify the content and change it in all kinds of directions.

Images, symbols, frames and stories are part of the substance of political communication. Their mental impact on citizens and voters might be bigger than the structural transformations we have discussed in this book. We regret that we have not paid more attention to these issues.

In this book we have distinguished several views of democracy, both substantial (ideological) and formal (strategic). A first conclusion of this book about these views is that none of them appears to be stronger or weaker on account of the use of digital media and networks such as the Internet. All of them have some affinity with a particular use of these media and networks, as we have argued in this book. The second conclusion is that the rise of digital media and networking has not increased or decreased the support for democracy as a type of governance in the world overall. The ups and downs of support for democracy are political, driven by hopes and disappointments occurring in the political situation concerned, and not by the prospects of new media use. This must be frustrating for all of the people who in the last 25 years have hailed the democratic potential of digital media and the Internet.

According to the last World Value Surveys, democracy is supported by very big majorities of people worldwide (Shin, 2015; Welzel, 2013). The world population sees democracy in very general terms of freedom and empowerment. However, more than three out of five supporters of democracy in the global population appear to be poorly informed about the characteristics of democracy, in any view of it. They have problem listing more than one characteristic in a survey. They see no difference between particular autocratic and democratic governments and they do not see that generally accepted basic features such as free elections and civil liberties are essential for democracy (Shin, 2015). People in the non-Western world tend to understand democracy more as government *for* the people than as government *by* the people (Shin, 2015, p. 18). They value democracy more for its real outcomes (freedom and rights) than for its means, the procedures that are foregrounded in the definitions of political scientists (Dalton et al., 2007).

In Chapter 1 we introduced the definitions of political scientists: the basic or substantial and the strategic or formal definitions. At the end of this book we have to conclude that all these definitions have some affinity with particular uses of digital media and networks, and that none of them is now becoming more popular on account of the use of digital technology. In the *basic definitions* we have differentiated between views of liberal democracy (social, market and conservative), populism (left- and right-wing) and authoritarian democracy (emphasis on a strong state/military, religious leadership or one-party dominance). Authoritarian democracy is always on the brink of not being democratic at all. It has a clear affinity with using digital media for surveillance and control, not only for maintaining the power of autocrats but also for the needs of security or safety of the people. In this book, we have called this use networked authoritarianism. It is very popular in China, Russia, Turkey, Iran, the Arab world and many other countries (see Chapters 6 and 7). Some of these countries have a so-called 'formal democracy' because they have elections, albeit not free elections.

The counterpart is liberal democracy in all its versions. Almost every publication about the prospects of digital democracy in fact supports this view, only the strategy used is different (see below). In general, it supports freedom on the Internet, while authoritarian democracy wants to curtail it. However, there is a wide variety of uses of digital media and networks to achieve particular goals in the strategies of liberal democracy.

The variety is even bigger in populist views of democracy. The affinity of using digital media and networks in left-wing populism is bottom-up or autonomous participation against the elite or the ruling class. They are looking for a kind of direct and Internet democracy from below. Some European left-wing populist parties such as the Five Star Movement in Italy, Podemos in Spain and the Pirates in Iceland and Germany have mainly been built online.

Right-wing populism is using digital media and the Internet in two ways. The self-proclaimed 'people' are using every online outlet from social media to blogs, forums and letters to online newspapers to express their views from the bottom up, blaming the so-called 'elite'. However, in right-wing populism 'the people' are putting their voice, trust and power in the hands of alternative leaders. Those leaders are using the same online outlets to certainly not discuss issues with 'the people' but to give them directions in rhetorical ways. Remember how Donald Trump is using Twitter as a megaphone.

In the *formal and strategic views* of democracy where the first goal is either opinion or decision making and the means are representative or direct democracy, particular digital media and network use is preferred (see Chapter 1). We have seen that legalist democracy, which is often backed by liberal democracy, favors applications of information exchange between governments or political representatives and citizens. Information exchange is seen as the glue of the political system. The backbone of this view is the constitutional state with the separation of the three powers (executive, legislative, and judiciary). In competitive democracy, digital media and networks are used to find and elect the best leaders. Here, digital technology is primarily used for election campaigns and as tools for leaders to address their grassroots support. This view is backed by liberal democracy and right-wing populism.

The third formal or strategic view is pluralist or deliberative democracy. Evidently, the numerous outlets of online discussion or forums are the favorite applications. Opinion making is the prime goal and support comes from both liberal and populist democracy. The fourth view is participatory democracy. This supports all digital applications that build citizenship and political participation for all citizens. The main problem of using them is the digital divide. This view is backed by liberal democracy, especially in the social version, and by left-wing populism.

The fifth view is plebiscitary democracy, a view that was already popular when the Internet first emerged in the age of 'tele-democracy' (Arterton, 1987; Becker, 1981). This involves the use of continual online polls, petitions and referenda. These instruments are versions of direct democracy. This view is backed by populism, first of all left-wing populism.

The last view is libertarian democracy, which conceives of digital media and networks as the instruments of collective action of autonomously working citizens in online communities and social movements. The basic support comes from left-wing populism, anarchism and liberal democracy in the market version, sometimes called the 'Californian ideology' (Barbrook & Cameron, 1996).

In this book, we have refrained from explicitly giving our own views of democracy. Our intention was to provide descriptions and explanations of the many views available and how their supporters think they benefit from digital media and networking. Steven Coleman (2017, p. vii) wants "to move the debate away from what the Internet *does to* democracy and open a discussion about the kind of democracy we want to *make for ourselves*". Subsequently, he develops his own views and solutions that come close to the participatory and pluralist (deliberative) views of democracy described in this book. These views are not the only ones offered to solve the problems of democracy today.

Views of Politics

The third mediator between political action and political systems are the political norms of the citizenry (see the right-hand side of Figure 9.1). This consists of the political culture and the views of politics in a country. The questions to be asked are whether current political systems are legitimate for citizens, whether citizens sanction by consent existing political practices in political action and whether they accept the culture of digital politics. The first question is whether citizens trust governments, politicians, politics 'as usual' and the representative political system.

In Chapter 3 we saw that the trust in government, politicians and common political routines is declining, even in 'advanced democracies'. However, the trust in the representative system of democracy is still alive, if only because no viable alternative has been presented or realized. It is questionable whether this can go on much longer. In this time of e-commerce, digital networking and fast media politics everywhere, only voting every four or five years and then committing your vote to people you barely trust, the current political system of representation seems to be outmoded. Many observers are looking for a democracy of the 21st century. The most cited alternatives are searching for forms of direct democracy such as referenda or for citizen assemblies other than parliaments. In Chapter 3 we discussed the opportunities and risks of online referenda, polls, petitions and forums. Other alternatives are the unofficial Citizen Assemblies in Ireland and the G 1000 citizen forum in Belgium. They are samples of 100 to 1,000 citizens invited by lot (not by voting) and which discuss the same items as parliaments. Those online and offline alternatives are still at an experimental stage. They have a number of advantages and disadvantages in terms of democracy, depending on the view endorsed. However, so far they have not restored trust in politics for many citizens.

It is also questionable whether digital political culture in general will restore trust in politics. We have seen that this culture is quite different from traditional political culture. It contains so many technical and informational acts that it is most appropriate for people with strong digital skills, that is, the 'information elite' of society. Contemporary politicians who still prefer traditional political culture often doubt the representativeness of online expression and action. Partly they are right because digital tool use might not have an easy entry point, but represents a barrier for participation in politics for people who have a lower level of education and are of older age. The digital divide is still the biggest hazard to digital democracy. However, partly they are wrong because these politicians often are not responsive to the real and legitimate input and participation of citizens online.

The representativeness of online and offline participation touches the most important problem of democracy and the representative political system today. This is the widening gap between people with a low level of education and low social class as voters and people with a high level of education and higher social class as representatives. It is our estimation that representative bodies such as parliaments are more than 95% inhabited by people with at least university or college education. In some parliaments, such as the U.S. Congress, the same percentage seem to be millionaires. This is one of the main social causes of the lack of trust in government, politics and politicians.

This is also the most important background factor behind the rise of populism in large parts of the world. The core of populism is the conceptual frame of the gap between the people and the elite. In the Introduction of this book we argued that populism is both a corrective of and a threat to democracy (Mudde & Rovira Kaltwasser, 2012). It is a corrective because it gives a voice to people that usually is not heard. It is a threat because it questions the legitimacy of the constitutional state with the separation of powers and it leans toward a limitation of freedom and protection of minority rights. Oppositional views and minorities divide the unity of the sovereign people in expressing their general will.

Populism can be defined as a political ideology that considers society to be separated into two homogeneous and antagonistic groups, 'the pure people' and 'the corrupt elite'. It argues that politics should be an expression of the general will of the people (Mudde & Rovira Kaltwasser, 2012, p. 8). Mudde and Rovira Kaltwasser (2012, pp. 16–18) provide lists of positive and negative effects of populism for democracy. Some of them are linked with digital media and network use. The first positive effect is that populism gives a voice to groups that are part of the 'silent majority' and that do not feel represented by the elites. For these groups, social media, online forums and reactions to online newspaper articles are outlets that are frequently used. In this way, excluded sections of society can be more or less integrated into the political system. In the same manner, these outlets introduce or emphasize issues in the political realm that are often ignored, such as problems of immigration. Finally, the virulent expression and polarization of online debate at least revitalize both public opinion and social movements.

The first negative effect of using digital media and networks for populism is that this virulent and polarizing expressions often call for majority rule and a denial of minority rights. This might promote a shrinkage of 'the political' and confines an effective democratic space to one focusing on real and plural discussion. This again leads to a political cleavage between us and others and makes it difficult to reach compromises or stable political coalitions. Here the network property of computer-mediated communication shows problems in reaching consensus and conclusions in online debates (Chapters 2, 4 and 5) and is supported by a substantial political drive to polarize. A second negative effect is the frequent call of populists not yet in power for direct Internet democracy (polls, referenda, petitions) in a way that undermines the legitimacy and power of political institutions such as parliaments. They want to elect and give the power to the leader of the people (right-wing populism) or power to grassroots communities and councils of the people (left-wing populism).

Political Systems: Continuity and Transformation

Now we reach the final and pivotal conclusions of this book. What is the structuration of political systems or democracies by political action via digital media and network use, via political conceptions such as views of democracy and via political norms defining views and cultures of politics? Our general answer is that in the short run we see more continuity than transformation of political systems via these modalities. In the long run we might expect some transformations in the context of the nascent network society.

The first realistic conclusion is that the use of digital media and networks have so far scarcely transformed political systems in political action or participation (Chapter 3). No *rules* of the constitutions, no government laws or regulations, no electoral systems and no citizen rights or duties have been changed on account of digital media and networks. Governments have passed changes of Internet regulation, for instance, but not in the political domain. In terms of *resources*, the use of digital media and networks has barely increased or decreased citizenship such as political participation and voter turnout in elections. It is doubtful whether the political knowledge and know-how of citizens has been changed via digital media use.

The only transformation we observe is with the means adopted: a shift from offline to online political participation. This has consequences for the practice and culture of politics in the future as we have seen, but so far has not results in any structural changes in the political system. For example, neither Obama nor Trump won the presidency through their presumed superior strategy of using social and digital media in 2008, 2012 and 2016. They won due to their popularity, their image and their promises at that particular time and the sentiment among voters. Of course, *particular* parties and candidates can win an election by using digital media and networks more frequently, better and smarter than their competitors, but this has no consequences for *democracy overall*.

Again, our perspective is to see politics first and media second. This means that the modalities of political views and norms might be more important for political system and democracy transformation than the modality of digital media and technology use, which in any case works in two directions (bottom-up and top-down). The influence that Donald Trump might have on the American political system and democracy will be made far more important by his right-wing populist views, norms and decrees hitting the constitutional state, not accepting judges and questioning the legitimacy of election results, than by his use of Twitter and other digital media in trying to both bypass and to manipulate the traditional media. Victorious populism can change political systems, not social or digital media use on its own.

Adopting a realistic view of political power and digital communication does not ask binary or dichotomous questions such as whether or not democracy increases with more digital media use. It rather seeks qualified observations about where and when democracy is facilitated, when it is not affected at all, and when it is hindered or blocked. As Larry Diamond and Marc Plattner (2012) argue, "There is an ongoing analytic debate about whether the digital age is improving or diminishing the quality of democratic politics. Probably it is doing some of both." (p. x).

The Network Society and Democracy

The structuration of political systems through political action is partly occurring via the mediation of digital and social networks. Not for nothing have we called the book *Internet and Democracy in a Network Society*. In every chapter we have shown the network perspective on political action, structures, systems and democracy. Networks are mediating individual citizens and political systems. They have both social and technological characteristics, such as the social network and network properties discussed. The so-called 'laws of the Web', for instance the power law, are relevant for political communication. What are the general conclusions of this book about the structuration of democracy with the characteristics of the network society?

First, a *new mode of organization* of our society is inserted in between the modes we knew before: the hierarchy ruling the bureaucracies of the government, big corporations or political parties, and the market (van Dijk, 1999, adapted from Powell, 1990). This is the network mode of organization characterized by both centralized and decentralized control and coordination. This mode has a clear democratic appeal when it works in communities, cooperatives, peer-to-peer working, social networking, sharing and crowdsourcing or collective intelligence in between the state and the market. States tend toward central control and markets to decentralize control. In different ways historically both states and markets often behave in an unequal manner and in this way are undemocratic.

Whether networks can realize their democratic potential depends on their relationship with the modes of the hierarchy (governments and other bureaucracies) and the market. These old modes are staying and the future of the network society will be a tense synthesis of networks, hierarchies and markets. The Internet as the most important network in this book was invented by a government initiative and by organizations such as the American ministries of Defense and Commerce. In the 1980s it was inhabited by the first users shaping Internet user groups and imagining that they had a perfect tool for democracy. However, in the 1990s with the advent of the World Wide Web, the market took over. They largely designed the commercialized Web as we know it now.

So the future of democracy of the network society will be decided by who will *design* the Internet and other digital networks, such as private and closed networks. At the time of writing we see that a few American commercial social media platforms and other Internet businesses largely control the Web. Governments are desperately trying to roll back the growing influence of hostile hackers, foreign enemies and cybercriminals. All of these actors, commercial platforms, governments and cybercriminals can become a threat to democracy when they harm the privacy of users, interfere in election campaigns and try to manipulate any free information and communication on the Web. For instance, we have seen that the rise of 'fake news' and the vanishing distinctions between opinion, facts and fiction on the Internet might be caused by basic social, cultural and educational trends in society. However, the current technical and business properties of social media platforms and other outline applications are very much reinforcing them. The rise of 'fake news', covert election manipulation and the merging of opinion, facts and fiction are lethal trends for democracy in every view.

Networks will chiefly have systemic influences on politics and democracy. The properties of digital media and especially networks will first of all *speed-up* or accelerate every process in political systems. This will put representative democracy, governments and parliaments under pressure. This is why people are looking for alternatives which are faster and immediately respond to the needs and voices of citizens. But is, for instance, direct democracy a viable option?

So far, the solutions offered have not been particularly successful. In this respect, Morozov (2013, pp. 5–7) talks about 'solutionism' and defines is as an ideology of easily fixing complex problems that are presumed instead of investigated and offers answers before the questions have been fully asked. In fact, solutionism is a case of instrumentalism. Morozov gives the examples of the European Pirates Parties and other Internet-based parties that offer permanent Internet polls and referenda as solutions to problems of democracy. The politics of these 'parties' is empty. They have no program and expect the solution to come from Internet users and their views. We see this as a case of what we call the *paradox of solutionism*. While the complexity of society and social or public (inter)national affairs grows by the day, the means offered are simple means such as referenda (yes/no) and voting for a single leader who will solve everything. The complexity of the problems concerned is not analyzed and the straightforward solutions will only cause more problems.

There is a good reason for the fact that the politics of the representative democracy are slow. Deliberation among both citizens and their representatives and between them simply needs time (Saward, 2015). Solutions are not easy to find because the problems of our technologically and organizationally advanced societies are increasingly complex. The high speed of network communication helps in collecting data and information, even in big data analysis, but interferes in the drawing of well-considered conclusions or decisions.

A related problem of political communication in the network society is the growing *instability of political systems* on account of network messaging. Network communication is not only fast but also viral or contagious. Views, opinions, facts and fiction, including rumors and scandals, are also multiplied. They urge governors, representatives and other politicians to respond immediately. Not only can a career be destroyed in a day after a wrong Tweet, but also the support of a particular party, candidate or legislation can collapse within a few days.

The final 'law' of the Web working toward the structuration of political systems we want to discuss here is the *law of trend amplification*. "Networks are relational structures that tend to amplify existing social and structural trends" (van Dijk, 2012, p. 42). Some of these structures are power relationships. This law also applies to digital media and networks. In the domain of this book, this means that when in a particular political system a trend of growing democratization occurs, digital networks can reinforce this trend. When the opposite trend happens, when democracy is weakened or even falls apart, digital networks will reinforce this too. For example, it is no wonder that the use of social media multiplied in the assumed wave of democratization of the Arab Spring and no miracle either that a practice of networked authoritarianism stepped up when the regimes managed to control the situation in what we called an Arab Winter. This observation is not a case of instrumentalism because it is not the tool of digital media that causes this shift but the changing structural relation of power between Arab citizens and Arab regimes in a particular political context. This is a final case of politics first and media second, one of the mottos of this book.

Final Conclusions and Further Research

A second main theme of this book is the question of whether or not the use of digital media and networking strengthens democracy. This is a question about causes and effects. We have seen that general claims about the positive or negative effects of digital media use on political participation cannot be made (Anduiza et al., 2012). We have also argued that asking whether generally the Internet strengthens or weakens democracy it is not a binary question of yes or no. In this book we have qualified the question with *where and how* Internet use strengthens democracy and where and how it does not.

We can also frame this question in the terminology of *first, second and third-level effects of technology* sometimes used in the literature (Berkhout & Hertin, 2001; Dowling, 2005; Holmström & Romme, 2012; Kelly, 2010). In this way we will finish this book with a number of very general conclusions.

First-order effects are the intended and direct affordances of a technology that is supposed to work to achieve a particular goal. Examples are finding political documents, posting political views on social media and in general using new opportunities for online participation. In our case these goals are mostly positive. However, some scholars and ordinary citizens suggest a positive first-order effect, claiming that Internet use for political expression and participation is democratic in itself, ignoring the goal of the activity. For critics they could just as well be negative, for example, when surveillance and political manipulation prevail. In first-order effects, the technical characteristics of the application are decisive. This more-or-less technological determinist argument easily leads to the pitfalls of a technical fix and instrumentalism often discussed in this book.

Second-order effects are the unintended, often unexpected, indirect effects of a technology as a kind of rebound. These effects frequently overrule the first effects or affordances after some time. This often happens when the actual human and social behavior of users and social or political contexts comes into play. For example, the affordances of digital media for political participation are not realized because many people lack political interest and digital skills. Another example is easily finding relevant political information on the Internet. We have seen that this claim of digital democracy has been achieved the best (Chapter 1). However, currently even this achievement is at risk when second-order effects produce information overload, disinformation and even "fake news". In this book, many other of these second-order effects have been discussed. However, this more-or-less social constructivist argument easily leads to the pitfalls of social continuity (no structural changes occur and there is no disruption from technology at all) and an extreme version of technical fix (anything users want can be achieved).

Third-order effects are the overall social and political effects after some time when the technology has matured. These are non-linear, neither simple direct nor indirect effects of technology use in the long run. These effects cannot be predicted when the use of a technology in a particular system is new and immature. Contemporary systems such as societies and advanced technologies are extremely complex. The same goes for the political systems we have investigated in this book. For this reason, we have elaborated a model of structuration of political system and action, with many factors inspired by the work of Anthony Giddens.

Even taking all these factors in account we have not found a conclusive answer to whether the use of the Internet strengthens or harms democracy in the long term. We think we have found the answer that *so far* Internet use has caused no substantial changes in the political systems of both democracies and autocracies such as China and most Arab countries. The era of traditional television politics is now approaching its end and a historical evaluation can be made. Increasingly, TV as we know it is integrated with the Internet. However, we cannot yet make an evaluation for the beginning Internet age. Even after about 30 years the Internet is still an immature technology in terms of political opportunities and applications.

The most interesting and important effects of Internet use for politics and democracy are the third-level, long-term effects. In this book, we have searched for them in the context of the nascent network society. In the long term the practices of network politics, of a digital political culture with substantial mental or cognitive effects in terms of good and bad information and of artificial intelligence or micro-targeting political marketing on the basis of datafication might be more important than the first-level instrumental effects of digital media use for democracy that people assume to be in operation today. The use of big data and micro-targeting by governments or political organizations might be more effective and informative for democracy, positively or negatively, than online or offline political petitions, discussion, action and even voting. Using daily online opinion polling, ubiquitous algorithms and big data, governments and political representatives actually and precisely know what citizens want. The question is whether they use this information as a responsive government or for shameless manipulation. We do not expect that using big data and artificial intelligence for e-participation is a solution for a failing democracy (see the suggestion of Bright & Margetts, 2016). See our views in Chapter 2. Decision making with these analytic tools ultimately is a matter of judgement. Currently, judgement after using these tools is the privilege of governors, political parties and business people. Often they do not even reveal the algorithms they use. Citizens do not have to act, participate or vote; they only have to leave data traces. For most people this is poor democracy.

So, the story of the relation between Internet and democracy is continuing. Further research has to be conducted with more of a network perspective and less with individual characteristics or demographics only. We have to investigate the effects of a digitally networked political culture compared to the traditional political culture of speaking, meeting and organizing people face to face. A political psychology of the mental, cognitive and emotional effects of using digital channels and their political content of (dis)information has to become an important part of the research program too. Finally, the advantages and disadvantages of datification, artificial intelligence and micro-targeting political marketing for democracy have to be put on the agenda.

References

Anduiza, E., Jensen, M. J., & Jorba, L. (2012). *Digital media and political engagement worldwide*. Cambridge, UK; New York: Cambridge University Press.

Arterton, C. F. (1987). *Teledemocracy: Can technology protect democracy?* Newbury Park, CA: Sage.

Barbrook, R., & Cameron, A. (1996). The Californian ideology. *Science as Culture*, *6*(1), 44–72.

Becker, T. L. (1981). Teledemocracy: Bringing power back to the people. *Futurist*, *15*(6), 6–9.

Berkhout, F., & Hertin, J. (2001). Socio-economic scenarios for climate impact assessment. *Global Environmental Change*, *10*(3), 165–168.

Bright, J., & Margetts, H. (2016). Big data and public policy: Can it succeed where e-participation has failed? *Policy & Internet*, *8*(3), 218–224.

Castells, M. (2009). *Communication power*. Oxford, UK: Oxford University Press.

Coleman, S. (2017). *Can the Internet strengthen democracy?* Cambridge. UK; Malden, MA: Polity Press.

Dalton, R. J., Sin, T. C., & Jou, W. (2007). Understanding democracy: Data from unlikely places. *Journal of Democracy*, *18*(4), 142–156.

Deibert, R., & Rohozinski, R. (2012). Liberation vs. control: The future of cyberspace. In L. Diamond & M. Plattner (Eds.), *Liberation technology: Social media and the struggle for democracy* (pp. 18–32). Baltimore, MD: The Johns Hopkins University Press.

Diamond, L., & Plattner, M. F.(2012). *Liberation technology: Social media and the struggle for democracy.* Baltimore, MD: Johns Hopkins University Press.

Dowling, R. G. (2005). *Predicting air quality effects of traffic-flow improvements: Final report and user's guide* (Vol. 535). Hapeville, GA: Transportation Research Board.

Elchardus, M. (2002). *Dramademocratie (drama-democracy)*. Tielt, Belgium: Lannoo.

Hart, R. P. (1994). *Seducing America: How the television charms the modern voter.* Oxford, UK; New York: Oxford University Press.

Hjarvard, S. (2008). The mediatization of society. *Nordicom Review*, *29*(2), 102–131.

Holmström, J., & Romme, A. G. L. (2012). Guest editorial: Five steps towards exploring the future of operations management. *Operations Management Research*, *5*(1–2), 37–42.

Kelly, K. (2010). *What technology wants*. New York: Viking.

MacKinnon, R. (2012). *Consent of the networked: The worldwide struggle for Internet freedom*. New York: Basic Books.

Morozov, E. (2013). *To save everything, click here: The folly of technological solutionism*. New York: PublicAffairs.

Mudde, C., & Rovira Kaltwasser, C. (2012). *Populism in Europe and the Americas: Threat or corrective for democracy?* New York: Cambridge University Press.

Powell, W. (1990). Neither market nor hierarchy: Network forms of organizations. In B. Slaw (Ed.), Research in organizational behavior (Vol. 12; pp. 295–336). Greenwich, CT: JAI Press.

Saward, M. (2015). Agency, design and 'slow democracy'. *Time & Society*, *26*(3), 362–383.

Shin, D. C. (2015). *Assessing citizen responses to democracy: A review and synthesis of recent public opinion research*. CSD working paper. Center for the Study of Democracy, University of California-Irvine, Irvine, CA.

van Dijk, J. (1999). *The network society*. London; New Delhi; Thousand Oaks, CA; Singapore: Sage.

van Dijk, J. (2012). *The network society* (3rd ed.). London; New Delhi; Thousand Oaks, CA; Singapore: Sage.

Welzel, C. (2013). *Freedom rising: Human empowerment and the quest for emancipation* (*World Values Surveys*). New York: Cambridge University Press.

Index